www.ingramcontent.com/pod-product-compliance
Lightning Source LLC
Chambersburg PA
CBHW082113230426
43671CB00015B/2690

Haggadah Yehi Ohr
Let There Be Light!

Avraham (Avi) Weiss

Teaneck, New Jersey

HAGGADAH YEHI OHR ©2025 Avraham Weiss. All rights reserved. No part of this book may be used or reproduced in any manner whatsoever without written permission except in the case of brief quotations embodied in critical articles and reviews or for copying individual pages for classroom or other educational use.

The font of this work is somewhat larger than average to make it easier for seniors and those who are visually impaired to read the text. A cornerstone of Rav Avi's understanding of Torah is that it be accessible to all.

Published by Ben Yehuda Press
122 Ayers Court #1B
Teaneck, NJ 07666
http://www.BenYehudaPress.com

To subscribe to our monthly book club and support independent Jewish publishing, visit
https://www.patreon.com/BenYehudaPress

Ben Yehuda Press books may be purchased at a discount by synagogues, book clubs, and other institutions buying in bulk. For information, please email markets@BenYehudaPress.com.

ISBN13 978-1-963475-43-2 pb
ISBN13 978-1-963475-67-8 hc

Cover illustration by Shifra Scheinman

25 26 27 / 10 9 8 7 6 5 4 3   20250303

Contents

In Solidarity..vi
Foreword...viii
Passover Ritual Symbols..xi

THE CHILDREN'S HAGGADAH — 1

KADESH...2
URCHATZ...12
KARPAS..14
YACHATZ...16

PAST — 19

MAGGID...20
    Storytelling...25
    Learning..55
    Reenacting..95
    Thanksgiving..103

PRESENT — 115

RACHTZAH..116
MOTZI MATZA..118
MAROR...120
KORECH...122
SHULCHAN ORECH...124
TZAFUN..126
BARECH...128

FUTURE — 149

HALLEL...154
    National Redemption...155
    Universal Redemption...178

BIDDING FAREWELL — 197

NIRTZAH..198
    Hatikvah..244
    Go and Come in Peace..249

DEDICATION

My deep gratitude, blessings and love
to my dear friend and mentor,

Tova Bulow,

for the indispensable role she played in the creation of this work.

Tova is the epitome of *yehi ohr*, let there be light –
the light of God, the light of Torah,
the light of Israel and Tzion,
the light of the world.

To you, dear Tova, and your beloved Norman, of blessed memory,
our blessings for continued teaching of the message of light,
the light of love, reaching higher and higher – *ohr ahavah*.

IN SOLIDARITY

As we turn to the pages of the Haggadah to recall our oppression in and liberation from Egypt, our prayers and conversations around the Seder table will be under the acute and painful shadow of the trauma of Shabbat Simchat Torah October 7, 2023.

On that day of barbaric savagery, we began reading the Torah again. The opening sentences contain a description of a world of utter darkness – much like the darkness of 10/7. To that darkness, God commands, *Yehi Ohr* – "Let there be light" – the title of this Haggadah.

Indeed, this Haggadah is written in solidarity with the soldiers of Israel who came forth on that day and on all the days, weeks and months that followed, to defend our people and our land. While that was a dark time, it was and continues to be a remarkable time, as Israelis, Jews throughout the world and people of moral conscience enlisted, some wearing the green IDF uniform, and others giving, giving, giving any way they could.

May each of us in our own way strive to do the same, inspired and uplifted by God's first call in the Torah –

Yehi Ohr: Let There Be Light.

FOREWORD

Perhaps the sweetest moment of family togetherness is the Passover Seder. How I will forever remember – as so many of us do – the Sedarim of my youth. Led by my parents, Miriam & Rabbi Moshe Weiss, surrounded by my siblings, Tova, Mordy, Suri and Dovie – the experience was spiritually nurturing, enhancing our love for each other, a love that continues to this day.

But not everyone has family. And so, our responsibility to open our homes to the poor, the lonely, the forgotten. For this reason, at the Bayit, the Hebrew Institute of Riverdale, we developed the idea of the Free Seder. Over the decades, thousands joined us. Together, as a larger family, we read, sang, danced, learned and joined in uplifting camaraderie.

In no small measure, the Passover Haggadah is a microcosm of Jewish history, of Jewish theology, of a God who loves and cares, and of our people's commitment to lovingly partner with God to overcome all challenges, to better ourselves and the world. The title of this Haggadah, "Yehi Ohr: Let There Be Light," reflects this history and theology. No matter the darkness, with God's help, light triumphs.

In this work, emphasis is placed on the structure of the Haggadah: The first half, before the Seder meal, deals with the past redemption from Egypt. The second half, after the meal, is critical too, as it deals with the hope of future redemption, national and universal, and of course, the unique place that Israel, the Jewish State, has in the redemptive process. The latter half is given as much attention as the first, as its theme reflects our hopes and aspirations for what it yet to come. Between these halves is the Seder meal and its surrounding rituals, focusing on the present.

The commentary gleans from the many Shabbat Hagadol discourses I was blessed to give at the Bayit. Comments are purposefully concise, attempting to compress lengthy multi-layered teachings into pithy, accessible ideas. While many of these teachings were inspired by Midrashic texts, I try to offer new creative approaches focusing not only on the black fire Torah of the mind, but the white fire Torah of the heart – in sum, a Loving Torah, a *Torat Ahavah*.

The English translation of the Haggadah is the Sefaria Edition, with some of my own emendations. Sefaria deserves endless credit and thanks for giving Torah texts "new life" and generously releasing their editions freely for the benefit of the public. At times I have turned to the Passover Haggadah edited by Nahum N. Glatzer and the JPS translation. In the Hallel and Hallel HaGadol I've relied upon the poetic translation of Rabbi Jonathan Sacks in the Koren Siddur.

I am deeply grateful to Shuli Boxer Rieser, my outstanding assistant, who not only typed every word (as I do not type), but offered, as she's done for virtually all my writings, critical insights and language suggestions to help make my thoughts more accessible to the reader.

I am *maleh hoda'ah* as well to my dear friend and colleague Rabbi Aaron Frank, who encouraged me to pen this commentary, masterfully reviewing the manuscript while, together with Tzvi Richter, pinpointing and suggesting some relevant passages from my other writings for this Haggadah.

My gratitude to Rabbi Dr. Zvi Ron, a talmid chacham of rare brilliance and humility, for reviewing the text and offering his insightful critique.

My gratitude, as well, to Dr. Gillian Steinberg for her brilliant, incisive editing.

To Rabbi Nati Helfgot, Rabbi Jeffrey Fox and Gabriella de Beer for reviewing parts of this Haggadah commentary and for their invaluable input.

To Shifra Scheinman for her beautiful artistic cover, and to *yedidi* Larry Yudelson and the entire Ben Yehuda Press team – thank you, thank you, thank you.

As I wrote this commentary, I often thought of Rabbi Shlomo Kahn, to my knowledge the first rabbi to write an English commentary to the Haggadah. His idea birthed a plethora of English Haggadot, each unique, each of significant value. He was the spark and deserves much credit. May his soulful teachings be forever remembered.

This humble work is written with endless love for my inner family, my children, Dena & Mark, Elana & Michael, Dov & Shayndi, and my Toby. How I remember our Sedarim in our home in the early years, and how I remember your graciously stepping back, making room, embracing our expanded Free Seder family.

As Mommy and Abba embrace our older years, we offer the prayer that God grant you and your children, our grandchildren, and your children's children, our great-grandchildren, health and life – always, always loving each other, unconditionally, endlessly, declaring – *Yehi Ohr*.

Passover Ritual Symbols

Ke'arah

The Seder Plate is circular, shaped much like a wheel. My Abba, who was a great storyteller, told the tale of a man, once destitute, now quite wealthy, marrying off his daughter. In the midst of the ceremony he began to call out, "*Gib mir a nahgel!*" (Yiddish for "Give me a nail!"). His guests thought he had gone crazy and tried to calm him. Still, he called out, "*Gib mir a nahgel, gib mir a nahgel!*" Finally, he explained.

Life, he said, is like a wheel, a *galgal hachozer*, a wheel that forever turns. Sometimes you're up, sometimes you're down. When I came from Europe, I was at rock bottom. But now, as I marry off my youngest child, I am at the top of the world. As much as I'm enjoying the moment, I recognize the inevitability that the wheel will not remain at the top – it will one day descend. So I call out, "*Gib mir a nahgel*," and let me take it and drive it into the wheel, so that it never moves – so that it remains at its greatest height.

Of course, this is not the way of life. Most often, the wheel moves at its pace, turning and turning and turning, much like life's ups and downs, much like the exhilarations and disappointments we've experienced as a people, much like the Haggadah's theme – from Egypt to Israel, from exile to redemption.

There are times, however, against the norm, when we fancifully wish that the wheel stop moving, stop turning, thus letting the good times prevail forever.

Beitzah

On the top left of the ke'arah is an egg, commemorating the holiday sacrifice (*korban chagigah*). More deeply, an egg cooks the way Jews in Egypt responded to their enslavement: Virtually all foods become soft when boiled; the egg, in contrast, becomes harder. So, too, the Torah tells us, the more Jews were afflicted, the more they increased, multiplied and grew stronger.

Zeroa

On the top right is the roasted shankbone, symbol of the Passover sacrifice (*korban Pesach*). That sacrifice was not cooked in the "comforts," if you will, of boiling water. Instead, it was roasted, suspended on a spit, exposed to fire on all sides, reflecting the plight of Jews betwixt and between, suffering from the "slave fire" of Egypt.

Karpas

On the bottom left is a vegetable, commonly celery or a potato, that represents the cheap foods consumed by Jewish slaves. The eating of this vegetable in the early karpas ritual of the Seder is especially child-friendly. The vegetable is edible, comfortably teaching youngsters how Jewish slaves in Egypt endured.

Maror

In the middle of the plate is the maror – bitter herbs. Not coincidentally, the very term maror not only comes from the word *mar*, bitter, but recalls myrrh, a spice used to sweeten Temple sacrifices. This double entendre teaches that within bitterness there can be sparks of sweetness; within slavery, freedom is born.

Charoset

On the lower right is the charoset – a mixture of nuts, wine, cinnamon, and apples in the Ashkenazic tradition and dates, cinnamon, and other dried fruits in the Sephardic tradition, symbolizing the mortar Jews used to build Egyptian pyramids. More deeply, the maror is dipped in the charoset, softening its sting.

Chazeret

In the center bottom is the chazeret, the horseradish used in Hillel's sandwich, as explicated in our Haggadah commentary.

Kittel

Some at the Seder wear a white robe called a kittel. White is the symbol of purity and humility. As we celebrate the exodus from Egypt, we remember that we emerged as a collective newborn. We were innocent and pure. And as we celebrate our freedom, the kittel reminds us to remain humble, inspiring us to etch in our minds and souls the horrors of slavery so that we in contrast always be there for the most destitute, the most in need, the most vulnerable.

Arba Kosot - The Four Cups

Why four cups? The simple

understanding (as I grow older, I like simple) follows the outline of the Haggadah. The first, the kiddush, is in sync with what we do at every Shabbat or festival meal. The second completes the half of the Haggadah before the meal, celebrating our past redemption (after Maggid). The third completes the ritual celebration of present redemptions (after Shulchan Orech; indeed, it doesn't stand out, as Grace After Meals on Shabbat and festivals is said over a cup of wine). The fourth completes the half of the Haggadah after the meal, celebrating the hope for our future redemption (after Hallel).

The Fifth Cup

Some have the custom of drinking a fifth cup, representative of a fifth word of redemption, *v'heiveiti* – "I (God) will bring you into Israel." A dream our generation has miraculously realized; a dream we should never take for granted.

Kos Eliyahu

On the table is Elijah's cup, reserved for Elijah, harbinger of the messianic era.

Kos Miriam

Some add Miriam's cup prominently. After all, Miriam played a critical role in the exodus story – standing a short distance from Moses' basket when he was placed in the water to protect him; singing out in celebration with Moses after the Sea was split; and inspiring the well of water which miraculously provided for the Jews wandering in the desert.

Pillow

A pillow is placed on Seder chairs so that participants can lean like queens and kings when drinking the ritual wine, symbolic of our freedom.

Three Matzot

Traditionally, the three matzot represent the three major groupings in Judaism – Cohen, Levi, and Yisrael. My sense is that it represents as well the three broad sections of the Seder relating to our past, present and future redemption.

The Children's Haggadah

The Seder follows a formula of "double ritual." What we normally do once before the Shabbat or Festive meal, we do twice before the Seder meal – adding other "double rituals." And so, before eating, we drink wine twice, we wash hands twice, we dip twice, we break matza twice, and we even review the history of the exodus twice.

The Talmud records that the rituals performed at the outset of the Seder are meant to inspire children to ask questions. Recognizing that youngsters may not be able to stay awake into the night and also may not be able to follow the intricacies of the Haggadah narrative, "child friendly" rituals and the Mah Nishtanah questions were developed. Every step is repeated for adult consumption – in more depth and length – as the Seder moves along.

Children's Haggadah	Adult Haggadah
Kadesh (kiddush over wine)	Second cup (at the closing of Maggid)
Urchatz (washing hands)	Rochtzah (washing hands before the meal)
Karpas (dipping a vegetable)	Maror-Korech (dipping bitter herbs)
Yachatz (splitting the middle matza)	Motzi Matza (breaking the matza before eating)
Maggid (*Ha Lachma Anya, Mah Nishtanah*)	Maggid (telling of the exodus in its entirety)

Educational lessons for children can have deep meaning for adults. Hence, after presenting how the early rituals especially stir a child's imagination, we will attempt deeper explanations of each.

קַדֵּשׁ

מוזגים כוס ראשון. המצות מכוסות.

Kadesh

Shabbat and festival meals begin with kiddush, from the word kadosh, to make holy. Similarly, most happy lifecycle events – e.g. circumcision (*brit*), baby naming (*zeved habat*), redemption of the first born (*pidyon haben*), marriage ceremony (*kiddushin, nisuin*) include a blessing over wine, symbol of joy. So, too, we begin Passover night with kiddush, framing the Seder as a joyous and sacred experience.

The kiddush also marks the first of the four Seder cups, corresponding to the biblical four languages of *ge'ulah* – "I will bring you out" (*v'hotzeiti*), "I will deliver you" (*v'hitzalti*), "I will redeem you" (*v'ga'alti*), and "I will take you" (*v'lakachti*). Each term relates to a stage in the redemption process. The stages indicate that redemption is gradual.

Yet, throughout Jewish history, when faced with brutal oppression, Jews believed that the only hope was an immediate coming of the Messiah. Note that after the destruction of the Second Temple, the great Rabbi Akiva thought that the second-century military leader Bar Kochba was the Messiah (Jerusalem Talmud, Ta'anit 4:6).

Similarly, the belief that Shabtai Tzvi was the Messiah occurred in the seventeenth century as the decrees of the notorious Ukrainian Jew killer Bogdan Chmielnicki took hold. And during the Holocaust, Jews prayed, sang, and hoped for the immediate arrival of the Messiah.

Beginning with *ve'hotzeiti* of kiddush, the four "languages" remind us that redemption comes slowly. The rabbis point out that just as the *ohr* (light) of day ascends gradually, so too, redemption (Shir HaShirim Rabbah 6:1). They even describe the process of redemption as "a poor person riding on a donkey" (Zechariah 9:9; Sanhedrin 98a). A donkey moves slowly, sometimes forward, sometimes bucking and lurching – but ultimately it reaches its destination. No matter the obstacles, we must never give up hope, for gradually redemption will be upon us. This is the miracle of the establishment of the State of Israel, which marks the beginning of the dawn of our redemption (*reishit semichat ge'ulateinu*).

KADESH

We pour the first cup. The matzot are covered.

בשבת, מתחילים מכאן:

וַיְהִי-עֶרֶב וַיְהִי-בֹקֶר יוֹם הַשִּׁשִּׁי. וַיְכֻלּוּ הַשָּׁמַיִם וְהָאָרֶץ וְכָל-צְבָאָם. וַיְכַל אֱלֹהִים בַּיּוֹם הַשְּׁבִיעִי מְלַאכְתּוֹ אֲשֶׁר עָשָׂה וַיִּשְׁבֹּת בַּיּוֹם הַשְּׁבִיעִי מִכָּל-מְלַאכְתּוֹ אֲשֶׁר עָשָׂה. וַיְבָרֶךְ אֱלֹהִים אֶת-יוֹם הַשְּׁבִיעִי וַיְקַדֵּשׁ אוֹתוֹ כִּי בוֹ שָׁבַת מִכָּל-מְלַאכְתּוֹ אֲשֶׁר בָּרָא אֱלֹהִים לַעֲשׂוֹת. [בראשית א:לא-ב:א]

וַיְכַל אֱלֹהִים בַּיּוֹם הַשְּׁבִיעִי - And on the seventh day God finished His work: Shabbat is first mentioned in the Genesis narrative (Genesis 2:3). There, we are told that God finished His work on the seventh day, implying that God was engaged in work on Shabbat; it follows in the spirit of *imitatio Dei* that humans should also work on Shabbat.

But Shabbat work differs dramatically from weekday work. During the week, we are involved in the external world, asking how we can achieve ultimate success. On Shabbat, we consider the harder question of why one works in the first place. On Shabbat, creativity is refocused from one's environment to one's self. Shabbat is a celebration of inner work, of inner creativity. It is not a day "of rest" but rather a day of being "at rest," at peace with oneself.

A classic story tells of the rebbe Reb Bunim who was absentminded, even forgetting where he put his clothes when going to sleep. Once, his wife jotted down exactly where he placed his clothes at night. The next morning, the rebbe was able to

On Shabbat, begin here:

> And there was evening and there was morning, the sixth day.
> And the heaven and the earth were finished, and all their host.
> And on the seventh day God finished His work which He had done; and He rested on the seventh day from all His work which He had done.
> And God blessed the seventh day, and sanctified it; because He rested on it from all of His work which God created to do (Genesis 1:31-2:3).

dress quickly. Pleased with himself, he looked in the mirror and realized that while he found his clothes, he couldn't find himself. The story goes that, for the rest of his life, he engaged in that search. Shabbat helps facilitate that journey for each of us.

אֲשֶׁר בָּרָא אֱלֹהִים לַעֲשׂוֹת - **Which God created to do:** God created the world imperfectly for the benefit of humankind. After all, in a society that is totally good, there essentially is no good, as *good* is a relative term. In a society that is perfect, there are no challenges – there would be nothing to overcome. In a society without evil, we would be bereft of freedom of choice, as we could not make a wrong decision. Choice is foundational to being human. And in this society, we would not be physical or have physical desires, as built into physicality is the reality that sometimes our needs are satisfied and sometimes not.

Thus, the last word of the creation story is *la'asot*, "to do." God in effect tells us that creating the world incompletely, imperfectly, "I leave it to you to finish what I started." In partnership, we will redeem the world.

בימי חול, מתחילים מכאן, ומשמיטים את הפסקאות שבסוגריים למטה:

סַבְרִי מָרָנָן וְרַבָּנָן וְרַבּוֹתַי:

בָּרוּךְ אַתָּה יהוה, אֱלֹהֵינוּ מֶלֶךְ הָעוֹלָם, בּוֹרֵא פְּרִי הַגָּפֶן.

בָּרוּךְ אַתָּה יהוה, אֱלֹהֵינוּ מֶלֶךְ הָעוֹלָם
אֲשֶׁר בָּחַר בָּנוּ מִכָּל-עָם וְרוֹמְמָנוּ מִכָּל-לָשׁוֹן
וְקִדְּשָׁנוּ בְּמִצְוֹתָיו.

וַתִּתֶּן-לָנוּ יהוה אֱלֹהֵינוּ בְּאַהֲבָה
(שַׁבָּתוֹת לִמְנוּחָה וּ) מוֹעֲדִים לְשִׂמְחָה,
חַגִּים וּזְמַנִּים לְשָׂשׂוֹן,
(אֶת יוֹם הַשַׁבָּת הַזֶּה וְ) אֶת יוֹם חַג הַמַּצּוֹת הַזֶּה

וַתִּתֶּן-לָנוּ - **And You have given us:** Holidays reflect Israel's particular and universal concerns. When the Torah lists only the three holidays of Passover, Shavuot and Sukkot, it reflects the cornerstone of what makes up our nationhood. On Passover, as we left Egypt, we were birthed as a people – Am Yisrael. On Shavuot, we received the law – Torat Yisrael. On Sukkot, the festival that marks our marching through the desert to Israel, we commemorate the gift of the Land of Israel – Eretz Yisrael. From this perspective, the holidays send a very nationalistic message, which became the foundation of the Religious Zionist movement – Am Yisrael (the people of Israel) according to Torat Yisrael (the Torah of Israel) in Eretz Yisrael (the Land of Israel).

There are other times in the Torah when the holiday list is expanded to include Rosh Hashana and Yom Kippur. One could argue that the actual order presented – Passover, Shavuot, Rosh Hashanah, Yom Kippur, Sukkot – highlights another aspect of Judaism: the *universal* vision of our religion. Through the exodus from Egypt, we physically came into being; we emerged as a people. But a people without a purpose, like a body without a soul, has no meaning. Hence, Shavuot

On weekdays, begin here, and omit the passages in parentheses below:

With the permission of all present:

Blessed are You, Lord our God, Ruler of the universe,
who creates the fruit of the vine.

Blessed are You, Lord our God, Ruler of the universe,
who has chosen us from all the nations and has raised us above all tongues
and has sanctified us with His commandments.

And You have given us, Lord our God, with love,
(Sabbaths for rest,) appointed times for happiness,
holidays and special times for joy,
(this Santisth day, and) this Festival of Matzot,
our season of freedom (in love) a holy convocation
in memory of the Exodus from Egypt.

commemorates the day we received the Torah, the infusion of spirituality into the physicality of Am Yisrael. The holidays now become more expansive as the list moves forward to Rosh Hashanah and Yom Kippur. Rosh Hashanah marks the anniversary of God creating all of humankind. This theme reaches its crescendo on Yom Kippur with the reading of Jonah, the Jewish prophet who was told by God to take the message of repentance to Nineveh, a heathen city. Note Ninveh is a composite of *nin* and *kah* – even the wicked are children (*nin* - literally, grandchildren or great-grandchildren) of God (*Kah*). And Sukkot is the most universal of festivals; during the week of the festival, we offer seventy sacrifices symbolic of the nations of the world and dwell for all to see in outdoor booths.

There has been long debate whether Judaism is fundamentally nationalistic or universalistic. Some express their Judaism by separating themselves from the larger world while others feel that their mission to perfect the world is so predominant that they forget their roots. The two archetypal Torah listings of the holidays indicate that we are both. As Natan Sharansky wrote in *Defending Identity*, "Identity

זְמַן חֵרוּתֵנוּ, (בְּאַהֲבָה) מִקְרָא קֹדֶשׁ זֵכֶר לִיצִיאַת מִצְרָיִם.
כִּי בָנוּ בָחַרְתָּ וְאוֹתָנוּ קִדַּשְׁתָּ מִכָּל הָעַמִּים,
(וְשַׁבָּת) וּמוֹעֲדֵי קָדְשֶׁךָ (בְּאַהֲבָה וּבְרָצוֹן) בְּשִׂמְחָה וּבְשָׂשׂוֹן הִנְחַלְתָּנוּ.

בָּרוּךְ אַתָּה יהוה, מְקַדֵּשׁ (הַשַּׁבָּת וְ) יִשְׂרָאֵל וְהַזְּמַנִּים.

במוצאי שבת מוסיפים:

בָּרוּךְ אַתָּה יהוה, אֱלֹהֵינוּ מֶלֶךְ הָעוֹלָם, בּוֹרֵא מְאוֹרֵי הָאֵשׁ.

בָּרוּךְ אַתָּה יהוה, אֱלֹהֵינוּ מֶלֶךְ הָעוֹלָם, הַמַּבְדִּיל בֵּין קֹדֶשׁ לְחֹל,
בֵּין אוֹר לְחֹשֶׁךְ, בֵּין יִשְׂרָאֵל לָעַמִּים, בֵּין יוֹם הַשְּׁבִיעִי לְשֵׁשֶׁת יְמֵי הַמַּעֲשֶׂה.
בֵּין קְדֻשַּׁת שַׁבָּת לִקְדֻשַּׁת יוֹם טוֹב הִבְדַּלְתָּ, וְאֶת־יוֹם הַשְּׁבִיעִי מִשֵּׁשֶׁת יְמֵי
הַמַּעֲשֶׂה קִדַּשְׁתָּ. הִבְדַּלְתָּ וְקִדַּשְׁתָּ אֶת־עַמְּךָ יִשְׂרָאֵל בִּקְדֻשָּׁתֶךָ.

בָּרוּךְ אַתָּה יהוה, הַמַּבְדִּיל בֵּין קֹדֶשׁ לְקֹדֶשׁ.

without democracy can become fundamentalist and totalitarian. Democracy without identity can become superficial and meaningless." From my perspective, loving all people begins by loving one's own people. An enlightened sense of national identity, rather than being a contradiction to a universal consciousness, is a prerequisite for it.

כִּי בָנוּ בָחַרְתָּ וְאוֹתָנוּ קִדַּשְׁתָּ - **For You have chosen us and sanctified us:** It has been suggested that the status of Jerusalem as the chosen place does not necessarily mean that it is a holy place. God can declare a place chosen, and that designation remains forever. But whether it is holy in real life depends on us.

What is true of a place is also true of a nation. Because we are the "chosen people" doesn't mean we are a "holy people." That status must be earned by the nation as a whole.

מְקַדֵּשׁ - **Who sanctifies (the Sabbath and) Israel and the appointed times of festivals:** Hence, our text posits that God alone sanctified the Sabbath, but the holidays receive their sanctity from Israel as well. God declares the holidays we are to observe, but the

For You have chosen us and sanctified us above all nations.
(In Your gracious love,) You granted us Your (holy Sabbath, and) special times for happiness and joy.

Blessed are You, Lord, who sanctifies (the Sabbath and) Israel and the appointed times of festivals.

On Saturday night we add the following:
> Blessed are You, Lord our God, Ruler of the universe, who creates the light of the fire.
>
> Blessed are You, Lord our God, Ruler of the universe, who distinguishes between the holy and the profane, between light and darkness, between Israel and the nations, between the seventh day and the six working days. You have distinguished between the holiness of the Sabbath and the holiness of the Festival, and You have sanctified the seventh day above the six working days. You have distinguished and sanctified Your people Israel with Your holiness.
>
> Blessed are You, Lord, who distinguishes between the holy and the holy.

---

dates on which they fall depends upon humans – specifically, the *beit din*, the Jewish courts.

While covenant is generally understood as the partnership between God and humans to redeem the world, the partnership extends to the evolution of Jewish law. As God creates the world incompletely, asking that we partner with Him in its redemption, so, too, does God give the law, the *halacha*, incompletely, leaving it to us to immerse ourselves in partnership with Him, to make the law more whole.

בּוֹרֵא מְאוֹרֵי הָאֵשׁ - **Who creates the light of the fire:** Shabbat commences and concludes with the kindling of fire. While beginning with the lighting of two independent candles, it concludes with the intertwining of two wicks, symbolic of the intensified unity that Shabbat attempts to foster.

הַמַּבְדִּיל בֵּין קֹדֶשׁ לְחֹל - **Who distinguishes between the holy and the profane:** Although the *havdalah* paragraph distinguishes between the holy (Shabbat) and the profane (weekdays), there is an overlap. This idea especially resonates when considering an interesting phenomenon: The Shabbat

בכל הלילות מברכים שהחיינו:

בָּרוּךְ אַתָּה יהוה, אֱלֹהֵינוּ מֶלֶךְ הָעוֹלָם, שֶׁהֶחֱיָנוּ וְקִיְּמָנוּ וְהִגִּיעָנוּ לַזְּמַן הַזֶּה.

שותה בהסיבת שמאל.

commences and concludes in similar ways.

Shabbat begins by welcoming angels in and concludes with inviting Elijah the Prophet as a guest.

Shabbat begins with wine (kiddush) and ends with wine (havdalah).

Shabbat begins with the sweet aroma of the Shabbat meal and ends with smelling the spices (*besamim*).

As noted, Shabbat begins and ends with the kindling of fire.

Why so?

Perhaps these similarities exist to remind us that, even as Shabbat ends, it begins again, in the hope that its message permeates the entire week. In this way, the division between Shabbat as *kodesh* and the weekdays as *chol* is a soft division – as by integrating the Shabbat into the week, we may be drawn closer to achieving the ideal era of messianic peace, the time when "the Merciful One [will let us inherit 'the day' when 'every day' will be Shabbat."

More generally, the categories of holy and profane relate to the way one deals with disciplines outside the Torah. Here, the Orthodox Right and the Modern Orthodox differ: For the Orthodox Right, disciplines that are not pure Torah, are *chol* (profane). *Chol* is studied to better understand *kodesh* (the holy) – through chemistry, for example, one can better evaluate the *kashrut* of food products. Or *chol*-like language is studied so one will be viewed as a cultured member of Western civilization, and Torah

On all nights, recite this:

Blessed are You, Lord our God, Ruler of the universe,
who has granted us life and sustenance and permitted us to reach this season.

We drink while reclining on our left side.

will be more respected. Or the *chol* of medicine is studied to be able to provide for one's family or one's charity. But *chol*, in this view, is intrinsically not *kodesh* and can never become *kodesh*.

We Modern Orthodox Jews disagree. Chemistry, language, medicine and all disciplines are potentially aspects of Torah. Study Torah and it will give new meaning, new direction, new purpose and, in the end, it will sanctify *chol*. *Chol* is not intrinsically and permanently *chol*; it can become *kodesh*. In a word, there is nothing in the world devoid of God's imprint. The way one loves, the way one conducts oneself in business, the way one eats – all are no less holy than praying and fasting.

שֶׁהֶחֱיָנוּ - **Who has granted us life:** In general terms, the *Shehecheyanu* helps us appreciate this moment on many levels:

Shehecheyanu – for giving us life.

V'kiyemanu – for allowing us the opportunity to give meaning (*kiyum*) to life.

V'higiyanu – for encouraging us to reach for and succeed at our mission of impacting our people and inspiring the world.

If participants wish, they can now take a moment to express why they are most grateful this Passover.

וּרְחַץ

נוטלים את הידים ואין מברכים "עַל נְטִילַת יָדַיִם."

Urchatz

The Children's Haggadah: Urchatz may inspire children to ask, "Why no blessing?"

Urchatz is the only title of a Seder section that begins with a conjunctive. Perhaps the connection to Kadesh points to the contrast between Kadesh and Urchatz. Note that the kiddush runs parallel to the normative festival kiddush. Urchatz, on the other hand, takes us in a different direction – the washing differs from the norm, as no blessing is recited. The sudden shift may inspire children to ask – why the deflection?

Vegetables dipped into water are susceptible to *tum'ah* (impurity), and so we wash our hands, making sure they are *tahor* (pure).

Conceptually, water is the symbol of life. We are born when the amniotic fluid breaks. Humans cannot live without water. When we search for life on other planets, we first ask, "is there water?" In a similar vein, we were born as a people when walking through the split sea. We passed through the Jordan when entering Israel. And, when one converts, beginning life anew as a Jew, immersion takes place in the *mikvah*. Hence, as we begin the Seder narrative, remembering when our people were redeemed from Egypt, we wash our hands, symbolic of celebrating our national birth.

URCHATZ

We wash our hands without reciting a blessing.

כַּרְפַּס

לוקחים מן הכרפס, טובלים במי מלח, מברכים "בורא פרי האדמה" ואוכלים.

בָּרוּךְ אַתָּה יהוה, אֱלֹהֵינוּ מֶלֶךְ הָעוֹלָם, בּוֹרֵא פְּרִי הָאֲדָמָה.

Karpas

The Children's Haggadah: Karpas can be seen as a light maror.

In Egypt, Jewish slaves were fed cheap food – often vegetables. Karpas therefore evokes memories of the Egyptian bondage. Dipped into salt water symbolic of human tears, it ritually represents our subjugation in Egypt. The karpas does not have the sting of the sharp maror eaten at the beginning of the Seder meal, as it is meant to be more suitable for children, who may not be able to tolerate the regular maror but can tolerate karpas.

Note that the term *karpas* can be an anagram of the word "ke-pras" – like a *pras*, a term denoting in the *halacha* the recitation of partial prayers before saying the morning Shema. At the Seder too, *karpas* relates to *pras* as it is kind of a child's half-*maror* – bitter but not too bitter.

Pras could also mean "prize." The prize here could relate to the miracle of the exodus, the journey from oppression to freedom.

The word *karpas* also sounds similar to *kapores*, the covering on the ark. Our exodus from Egypt took on meaning when we stood at Sinai to receive the Ten Declarations placed into the Ark that stood in the Temple Holy of Holies.

KARPAS

*We take from the greens, dip them into salt water,
recite the following blessing and eat.*

Blessed are you, Lord our God, Ruler of the universe,
who creates the fruit of the earth.

יַחַץ

חוצים את המצה האמצעית לשני חלקים, ומצפינים את הנתח הגדול עבור האפיקומן.

Yachatz

The Children's Haggadah: Setting aside a half-matzah for children to find is an incentive for youngsters to remain involved, searching for the afikoman.

Virtually all Seder symbols represent either slavery or freedom. Bitter herbs, for example, remind us of the bitterness of servitude; wine and reclining on a pillow, on the other hand, remind us of the joy and comforts of freedom.

Matza is unique amongst the Seder symbols in that it represents both. It was the flat, cheap bread we ate in Egypt as slaves; and it was the food we ate when taking leave of Egypt. Thus, the matza is a microcosm of the Passover story – from slavery to freedom.

In truth, that story has been repeated throughout history. Persecution after persecution pointed to our inevitable demise, but somehow we prevailed.

And so, we break the middle matza. One half remains on the table

YACHATZ

We split the middle matzah and conceal the larger half for the afikoman.

as we tell the story of our past victory in Egypt – doing so before the Seder meal. The other is set aside to be the last food we eat at the meal, which sets the stage for our expressing the hope for future ultimate redemption, the subject matter of the Haggadah after the Seder meal. Note that the Hebrew term for Egypt, *Mitzrayim*, comes from the word *meitzar*, distress, and is in the plural form, alluding to the many "Egypts" we would face throughout history as a nation (as well as in our personal lives).

Not surprisingly, the larger piece (no matza can be perfectly split) is the one designated for later (*afikoman*), as the future redemption will be greater, more significant, than any of our past redemptions, even the exodus from Egypt.

Within the Yachatz, we spell out the structure of the Haggadah. Before the meal, we immerse ourselves in the past. After the meal, we immerse ourselves in the future. The meal, as explicated later, may symbolize the present.

Maggid

The history of our past redemption makes up the core of the Maggid. It is divided into four sections.

STORYTELLING
LEARNING
REENACTING
THANKSGIVING

In sum, Maggid is an historical review. As noted, before the Passover meal, the Seder deals with the past.

The term Maggid can be associated with the word *gid*, literally sinews that connect body parts. Similarly, participants at the Seder are encouraged to feel an interdependence. There is no one dominating figure; rather, each participant chimes in, creating a collective whole.

מַגִּיד

מגלים את המצות, מגביהים את הקערה ואומרים בקול רם:

הָא לַחְמָא עַנְיָא דִּי אֲכָלוּ אַבְהָתָנָא בְּאַרְעָא דְמִצְרָיִם.

כָּל דִּכְפִין יֵיתֵי וְיֵיכֹל, כָּל דִּצְרִיךְ יֵיתֵי וְיִפְסַח.

הָשַׁתָּא הָכָא, לְשָׁנָה הַבָּאָה בְּאַרְעָא דְיִשְׂרָאֵל. הָשַׁתָּא עַבְדֵי, לְשָׁנָה הַבָּאָה בְּנֵי חוֹרִין.

Ha Lachma Anya

The Children's Haggadah: We continue with the *Ha Lachma Anya*, a summary of the story. Written in Aramaic, it is meant to be shared in any language children understand.

הָא לַחְמָא עַנְיָא - **This is the bread of affliction:** Maggid opens with a summary paragraph. The first sentence recalls the past bondage in Egypt. The second focuses on the present reality – the hungry and needy seeking relief. The third sentence centers on the hope for future redemption.

כָּל דִּכְפִין - **Anyone who is famished… anyone who is in need:** Hunger and need refer to two different conditions. The former deals with a physical shortcoming while the latter speaks of those with meta-physical needs — the lonely, the sick, the grieving — those who may have everything but have nothing.

Homiletically, the sentence also suggests that even the poor should be asked to contribute to the Seder experience, giving those who feel lowly a taste of the self-dignity they may have lost. In fact, freedom, as Dr. Viktor Frankl posits, is the readiness – no matter one's state of being – to share with another.

הָשַׁתָּא הָכָא - **Now we are here, next year we will hopefully be in the Land of Israel; this year we are**

MAGGID

The matzot are uncovered; the Seder plate raised; we sing aloud:

This is the bread of affliction that our ancestors ate in the land of Egypt.

Anyone who is famished should come and eat,
anyone who is in need should come and share the Pesach meal.

Now we are here, next year we will hopefully be in the land of Israel;
this year we are slaves, next year we will hopefully be free people.

slaves, next year we will hopefully be free people: These two "hopes" may be understood as one; that is, next year may we be living in the sovereign Land of Israel, free, in control of our own destiny. In contemporary times, this dream has become reality. Today, Israel – the Jewish state – is important not only as the place that guarantees political refuge for Jews; not only as the place where more *mitzvot* can be performed; not only as the place where, given the high rate of assimilation and intermarriage in the exile, our continuation as a Jewish People is assured. It is rather the place where we have the means to achieve our mandate. Only in a Jewish state do we have the political sovereignty and judicial autonomy to potentially establish a just and ethical society from which others can learn.

Of course, Jews living in the diaspora can also make significant individual contributions to the betterment of the world. And there are model diaspora communities that impact powerfully on *Am Yisrael* and humanity. But I would insist that the national destiny of the Jewish People can only be realized in the Land of Israel as it is the central place from where the core values of Judaism emanate. Only there, as a nation, in *Medinat Yisrael*, do we have the potential to contribute to repairing the larger world.

מסירים את הקערה מעל השולחן. מוזגים כוס שני.
הילדים\ות שואלים:

מַה נִּשְׁתַּנָּה הַלַּיְלָה הַזֶּה מִכָּל הַלֵּילוֹת?

שֶׁבְּכָל הַלֵּילוֹת אָנוּ אוֹכְלִין חָמֵץ וּמַצָּה,
הַלַּיְלָה הַזֶּה – כֻּלּוֹ מַצָּה.

שֶׁבְּכָל הַלֵּילוֹת אָנוּ אוֹכְלִין שְׁאָר יְרָקוֹת –
הַלַּיְלָה הַזֶּה כֻּלּוֹ מָרוֹר.

שֶׁבְּכָל הַלֵּילוֹת אֵין אָנוּ מַטְבִּילִין אֲפִילוּ פַּעַם אֶחָת –
הַלַּיְלָה הַזֶּה שְׁתֵּי פְעָמִים.

שֶׁבְּכָל הַלֵּילוֹת אָנוּ אוֹכְלִין בֵּין יוֹשְׁבִין וּבֵין מְסֻבִּין –
הַלַּיְלָה הַזֶּה כֻּלָּנוּ מְסֻבִּין.

Mah Nishtanah

The Children's Haggadah: The Children's Haggadah concludes with the Mah Nishtanah as the Four Questions are asked by the youngest present, or by every child present.

מַה - **Why?** The Haggadah instructs: Here a child asks his or her parents. One wonders, who is the child and who is the parent? In the end, we are all children. Never will I forget my father's words to me as he was dying (I was already beyond 70). "Just remember," Abba said, "You'll always be my little boy. My child."

And who is the parent? Especially in times of challenge, the parent may be God, the Parent of Parents, Av Harachaman (*av*, father; *rachaman*, mother from *rechem* – womb). We ask, *mah* – why, how? And more expansively, when, when will all these attacks end? No one, even great faith leaders is immune from asking such questions as they see fit. This reminds me of the funeral for the five members of the Dutch Schijveschuurder family murdered in the Sbarro terror attack of 2001. Rabbi Yisrael Meir Lau, speaking

The plate is removed from the table. We pour a second cup of wine. Here, the children ask:

Why is this night different from all other nights?

On all other nights we eat chametz and matza; this night, only matza.

On all other nights we eat other vegetables; tonight only maror.

On all other nights, we don't dip our food even once; tonight we dip it twice.

On all other nights, we eat either sitting or reclining; tonight we all recline.

---

in front of the coffins looked heavenward and asked, "Dear Beloved God, I do not ask why, but I do ask *ad matai* (until when)."

מה - **Why?** *Mah* can be interpreted "why" or "how" is this night different from other nights. More broadly, how and why are two sides of the same coin, asking not only how one follows halachah, but why. What are the deeper reasons that give meaning to observing Jewish law?

מַה נִּשְׁתַּנָּה - **Why is this night different?** Right at the outset, we are reminded that the key to understanding the exodus is to ask questions. There is a Yiddish expression – *foon a kasha ken mir nit shtarben*, no one has died from a question. When learning Talmud as a youngster, I learned from my rebbi that 98% of the answer is the question. So, too, built into the *mah nishtanah* questions are the answers. The first two relate to slavery – the eating of the poor person's matza and bitter herbs. The last two relate to our freedom – eating while dipping and reclining. Yes, we've experienced difficult times, but from bitterness, sweetness can come.

STORYTELLING

Stories distinguish Passover from the everyday mention of the exodus in our prayer services. The pathway to soulfully connect may not only be through intellectual somersaults or endless footnotes…but through the story. What is the magic of storytelling?

One can receive a message on an intellectual level just as one can receive a message on an experiential level. If one were teaching the exodus story, she or he might teach texts that describe the servitude. On the experiential level, on the other hand, one might ask the listener to try to experience the pain of an offended person.

A story, however, can bridge these two approaches. Even if it is impossible to subject the listener to the actual experience, to the real pain of the insult, the listener can, through the story, feel the experience, enhancing its understanding.

Thus, stories can enrich and enhance because they can arouse powerful emotions. They can make bitter pills palatable. They can teach softly and sensitively. In a particularly Jewish framework, stories can help us grow in Torah: they can even show us the way to redemption.

The Stories of Shmuel and Rav

The Talmud records two ways to tell the exodus story. While they differ, they have commonality, "beginning with disgrace and conclud[ing] with freedom" (Pesachim 116a).

מחזירים את הקערה אל השולחן. המצות תהיינה מגלות בשעת אמירת ההגדה.

עבדים היינו לפרעה במצרים

עֲבָדִים הָיִינוּ לְפַרְעֹה בְּמִצְרָיִם,
וַיּוֹצִיאֵנוּ יהוה אֱלֹהֵינוּ מִשָּׁם בְּיָד חֲזָקָה וּבִזְרֹעַ נְטוּיָה.

וְאִלּוּ לֹא הוֹצִיא הַקָּדוֹשׁ בָּרוּךְ הוּא אֶת אֲבוֹתֵינוּ מִמִּצְרַיִם, הֲרֵי אָנוּ וּבָנֵינוּ וּבְנֵי בָנֵינוּ מְשֻׁעְבָּדִים הָיִינוּ לְפַרְעֹה בְּמִצְרָיִם.

וַאֲפִילוּ כֻּלָּנוּ חֲכָמִים כֻּלָּנוּ נְבוֹנִים כֻּלָּנוּ זְקֵנִים
כֻּלָּנוּ יוֹדְעִים אֶת הַתּוֹרָה
מִצְוָה עָלֵינוּ לְסַפֵּר בִּיצִיאַת מִצְרָיִם.
וְכָל הַמַּרְבֶּה לְסַפֵּר בִּיצִיאַת מִצְרַיִם הֲרֵי זֶה מְשֻׁבָּח.

Shmuel's Story

Avadim Ha'yinu

עֲבָדִים הָיִינוּ - **We were slaves to Pharaoh in the land of Egypt:** Here we begin to tell the physical story of the exodus in accordance with the Talmudic sage Shmuel: We were slaves and then we were freed.

וַיּוֹצִיאֵנוּ - **And the Lord, our God, took us out:** Much like a child just born is unilaterally cared for by mother and father, so, too, when we were born as a people, God was the sole redeemer.

בְּיָד חֲזָקָה וּבִזְרֹעַ נְטוּיָה - **With a mighty hand and an outstretched arm:** God carried us to freedom with a "mighty hand" that dealt

We put the Seder plate back on the table.
The matzot are uncovered as we begin reciting the Haggadah.

עֲבָדִים הָיִינוּ We were slaves to Pharaoh in the land of Egypt. And the Lord, our God, took us out from there with a mighty hand and outstretched arm.

And if the Holy One, blessed be He, had not taken our ancestors from Egypt, then we and our children and our children's children would all] be enslaved to Pharaoh in Egypt.

And even if we were all sages, all discerning, all elders,
all knowledgeable about the Torah,
we would still be commanded to tell the story of the exodus from Egypt.
And anyone who spends extra time in telling the story of the exodus from Egypt is praiseworthy.

harshly with our enslavers, but concomitantly with an "outstretched arm," perhaps symbolic of a godly hug, embracing us, ensuring that all will be well.

וְאִלּוּ לֹא הוֹצִיא הַקָּדוֹשׁ בָּרוּךְ הוּא אֶת אֲבוֹתֵינוּ מִמִּצְרָיִם - **If the Holy One, blessed be He, had not taken our ancestors from Egypt:** Sometimes opportunity arises but once; we were given but one chance, no more. This was our moment – if not then, who knows when?

וַאֲפִילוּ כֻּלָּנוּ חֲכָמִים - **And even if we were all sages…we would still be commanded to tell the story:** Even the rabbinic scholars, women and men, need stories.

מעשה ברבי אליעזר

מַעֲשֶׂה בְּרַבִּי אֱלִיעֶזֶר וְרַבִּי יְהוֹשֻׁעַ וְרַבִּי אֶלְעָזָר בֶּן־עֲזַרְיָה וְרַבִּי עֲקִיבָא וְרַבִּי טַרְפוֹן שֶׁהָיוּ מְסֻבִּין בִּבְנֵי־בְרַק וְהָיוּ מְסַפְּרִים בִּיצִיאַת מִצְרַיִם כָּל־אוֹתוֹ הַלַּיְלָה, עַד שֶׁבָּאוּ תַלְמִידֵיהֶם וְאָמְרוּ לָהֶם רַבּוֹתֵינוּ הִגִּיעַ זְמַן קְרִיאַת שְׁמַע שֶׁל שַׁחֲרִית.

אמר רבי אלעזר בן־עזריה

אָמַר רַבִּי אֶלְעָזָר בֶּן־עֲזַרְיָה הֲרֵי אֲנִי כְּבֶן שִׁבְעִים שָׁנָה וְלֹא זָכִיתִי שֶׁתֵּאָמֵר יְצִיאַת מִצְרַיִם בַּלֵּילוֹת עַד שֶׁדְּרָשָׁהּ בֶּן זוֹמָא, שֶׁנֶּאֱמַר (דברים טז:ג), לְמַעַן תִּזְכֹּר אֶת יוֹם צֵאתְךָ מֵאֶרֶץ מִצְרַיִם כֹּל יְמֵי חַיֶּיךָ. יְמֵי חַיֶּיךָ הַיָּמִים. כֹּל יְמֵי חַיֶּיךָ הַלֵּילוֹת. וַחֲכָמִים אוֹמְרִים יְמֵי חַיֶּיךָ הָעוֹלָם הַזֶּה. כֹּל יְמֵי חַיֶּיךָ לְהָבִיא לִימוֹת הַמָּשִׁיחַ:

Ma'aseh Be'Rabbi Eliezer

מַעֲשֶׂה בְּרַבִּי אֱלִיעֶזֶר - **A happening with Rabbi Eliezer:** But stories have their limitations. As the rabbis living under Roman siege were caught up in recounting the tales, the morning dawn was approaching. Full of youthful exuberance, their students charged in, declaring the time had come to turn storytelling into action, doing our share to bring about redemption.

Amar Rabbi Elazar Ben Azaryah

אָמַר רַבִּי אֶלְעָזָר בֶּן־עֲזַרְיָה - **Rabbi Elazar ben Azaria said "Although I am like a man of seventy years":** Storytelling most often takes place in homogeneous groups, older with older, younger with younger. Here the Haggadah teaches that it is best to tell stories intergenerationally – the younger Rabbi Elazar Ben Azaria with his much older colleagues. Youthful exuberance and mature deliberation are both needed for redemption. As Moses tells Pharaoh, "with our younger and older we will go out."

לֹא זָכִיתִי שֶׁתֵּאָמֵר - **I did not merit [to understand why] the exodus from Egypt should be retold at night:** Night is the symbol of exile. It's one matter to share stories of

מַעֲשֶׂה בְּרַבִּי אֱלִיעֶזֶר A happening with Rabbi Eliezer, Rabbi Yehoshua, Rabbi Elazar ben Azariah, Rabbi Akiva and Rabbi Tarfon, who were reclining in Bnei Brak and were telling the story of the exodus from Egypt that whole night, until their students came and said to them, "Our teachers, [the time of reciting] the morning Shema has arrived."

אָמַר רַבִּי אֶלְעָזָר בֶּן־עֲזַרְיָה Rabbi Elazar ben Azariah said, "Although I am like a man of seventy years, [I did not merit to understand why] the exodus from Egypt should be retold at night until Ben Zoma explicated it, as it is stated (Deuteronomy 16:3), 'In order that you remember the day of your going out from the land of Egypt all the days of your life.' 'The days of your life' refers to the day, 'all the days of your life' includes even the night. But the Sages say, 'the days of your life' refers to this world, 'all the days of your life' includes even the days of the Messiah."

redemption when all is well, but recounting the story at night, in a state of peril, is much more difficult. And yet, throughout Jewish history, we believed even in the darkest times that redemption will come. We told the story.

יְמֵי חַיֶּיךָ - **"The days of your life" refers to the day; "all the days of your life" includes even the night:** One wonders whether, according to Ben Zoma, the ultimate redemption story will be so powerful that it will eclipse, yes push away (or relegate to a lower status) the mention of any prior redemption, even the exodus from Egypt. After all, the sentence "all the days of your life" refers to the telling of the story by day and night, leaving no room to mention the Egyptian exodus in future redemptive times.

Here, if we are blessed to have grandparents at the table, is a wonderful opportunity to ask them to share their childhood Seder memories; alternatively, to have grandchildren tell stories about their grandparents.

ארבעה בנים

ברוך המקום

בָּרוּךְ הַמָּקוֹם, בָּרוּךְ הוּא,
בָּרוּךְ שֶׁנָּתַן תּוֹרָה לְעַמּוֹ יִשְׂרָאֵל, בָּרוּךְ הוּא.

Four Children

Baruch HaMakom

בָּרוּךְ הַמָּקוֹם - **Blessed be the Omnipresent (*HaMakom*), Blessed be He (*Hu*):** As the source for each of the Four Sons is found in the Torah, Baruch Hamakom, as noted by others, resembles the blessings said over the Torah. Perhaps, too, the paragraph is descriptive of characteristics of God, characteristics which we in turn should emulate – in part, because they offer good parental advice.

HaMakom is a term that refers to our closeness to God. Rabbi Levi Yitzchak of Berdichev said it well:

"Wherever I walk, whenever I talk… In my head and heart… there is only You. In good and bad times, to the East, West, North and South, only You." You, You, You. This is the I-thou relationship.

In fact, Rabbi Yosef Dov Soloveitchik suggests that the term *HaMakom* is used to indicate the presence of God in places where one would least expect Him to be: e.g., the condolence phrase of *HaMakom* at a shiva (*HaMakom yenachem etchem*) and in the prayer for those in distress

Four Children

בָּרוּךְ הַמָּקוֹם - Blessed be the Omnipresent, Blessed be He;
Blessed be the One who Gave the Torah to His people Israel, Blessed be He.

(*Acheinu…HaMakom yerachem aleihem*).

In contrast, Baruch Hu, Blessed be He, is third person – God is more distant. Such is the story of our people: Sometimes we feel the closeness of God (*HaMakom*); at other times, we feel the distance (*Baruch Hu*). In dialectic, our relationship to God – on a personal level as well – can vacillate, move to and fro, what mystics call "*ratzo vashov.*"

In the spirit of *imitatio Dei*, depending on their child's needs, parents must decide when to intervene and when to step back, when to be loving and when to be firm (the same may be true in a teacher-student relationship). From this perspective, Baruch Hamakom serves as a meaningful preamble to the Arba'ah Banim. Using Haggadah terminology – as there are Four Children, so are there Four Parents – all needing guidance.

כנגד ארבעה בנים

כְּנֶגֶד אַרְבָּעָה בָנִים דִּבְּרָה תוֹרָה:
אֶחָד חָכָם, וְאֶחָד רָשָׁע, וְאֶחָד תָּם, וְאֶחָד שֶׁאֵינוֹ יוֹדֵעַ לִשְׁאוֹל.

K'neged Arba'ah Banim

כְּנֶגֶד אַרְבָּעָה בָנִים - **Corresponding to four sons:** Sons should be understood expansively, referring to daughters as well. Also, as already noted, bearing in mind that no matter our age we are all children, the four could refer to adults. They are listed separately, reminding us that each has a unique story, traveling their individual journeys, needing to be reached in their own particular way.

Notwithstanding these differences, they sit at the same table, conversing with one another. Of course, this does not mean that they cannot disagree. It means that when we disagree, we do so agreeably. Suggestions for what can be called the "ethics of dissent" can be elicited from participants. Here are some ideas:

- Language must be used with care. While a word is a word and a deed is a deed, words lead to deeds.
- Dissent is acceptable; delegitimization is not. No purpose is served in invalidating the other.
- Right and left should recognize that neither has a monopoly on loving the land, Torah and people of Israel. When disagreeing, we should not malign the motives of the other, instead asking questions in a spirit of curiosity and generosity.
- As difficult as it is to imagine, even when confident in our position, we have – as beit Hillel and beit Shammai modeled – much to learn from those who are equally sure their opinion is correct. The key is to listen to the other, cull from their thinking, and assess how their perspectives can inform our own views.

It is possible, too, that one could imagine all four individuals cohering into one persona. Sometimes, individuals have aspects of all four. Perhaps, too, they cohere in that they deal with four distinct stages in life working in reverse: As infants we do not know how to ask; as children we speak in simple terms; as teenagers we are more rebellious; ultimately, when maturing, we are wiser.

My Abba suggested that the

כְּנֶגֶד אַרְבָּעָה בָנִים - Corresponding to four children did the Torah speak; one wise, one rebellious, one simple, one who does not know how to ask.

children represent four generations. The first is the pious, observant and knowledgeable *chacham*, who emigrated from Europe in the early 1900s. His child – exposed to the American way of life – rebelled, becoming the ignorant *rasha*. The *rasha*'s child only experiences a taste of Judaism when visiting his grandparents' home. Thus, he knows something but not much – he is the simpleton *tam*. The *tam*'s child has no Jewish role model to emulate. His father lacks knowledge (*tam*), his grandfather is totally alienated (*rasha*) and his great-grandfather (*chacham*) has passed away. This child doesn't even know how to ask the question. I often shared with my holy father, that, with the *ba'alei teshuva* movement gaining traction, the fourth child may yield a next generation who, souls ignited, yearn to return.

Participants may consider reading the poem – prayer "A Pintele Yid," that follows this brief introduction as a kavvanah *for ahavat Yisrael, loving other Jews.*

The poem begins with the phrase "*a pintele yid*," normally understood to refer to the spark (*nitzotz*) in every Jew. No matter how distant, every Yid, deep, deep down, has a Jewish inner soul, with the potential to grow. Here, we take a different approach, understanding *pintele* as a small, lonely Jew. And yet, two Jews beside each other, no matter how vulnerable, can find relief.

I first heard this thought many decades ago during the first International Conference for Soviet Jewry, held in Brussels. At its close, a tall, young man was given the floor. Sharing that he came from Buenos Aires, where, as a Jew, he felt particularly isolated and alone, like a *pintele Yid*, he looked out at the thousands in attendance. Through tears he shared, "and now, standing with you in unity, in common cause, I feel like a yud near another yud, together spelling the name of God."

A Pintele Yid

A pintele Yid	אַ פִּינְטֶעלֶע יִיד
A lonely Jew	יְהוּדִי בּוֹדֵד
A vulnerable Jew	יְהוּדִי שַׁבְרִירִי
A pintele yud	א פינטעלע יו״ד
A lone mark	סִימָן בּוֹדֵד
A tiny Hebrew letter	אוֹת עִבְרִית זְעִירָה
A yud aside another	נִצֶּבֶת יו״ד בְּצַד יו״ד
A Jew beside an other	עוֹמֵד יְהוּדִי בְּצַד אָחִיו
Evokes the Name of God	וּפוֹרֵץ שֵׁם הָאֱלֹהִים
In unity, God sees	בְּאַחְדוּת, וַיַּרְא אֱלֹהִים
It is good	כִּי טוֹב
Unity is never uniformity	אַחְדוּת לְעוֹלָם אֵינֶנָּה אֲחִידוּת
Uniformity is uni form	כִּי הָאֲחִידוּת הִיא
Crushing other views	רִסּוּק שֶׁל דֵּעוֹת אֲחֵרוֹת
Unity is uni tied, united	אַךְ אַחְדוּת הִיא חַיֵּי יַחַד
Despite differences	לַמְרוֹת כָּל הַהֶבְדֵּלִים
Dear dear God	הוֹ, אֱלֹהִים הַיָּקָר
Help us to know that	סַיַּע לָנוּ לְהַכִּיר
Am Yisrael is more than	שֶׁעַם יִשְׂרָאֵל
The Nation of Israel	הוּא יוֹתֵר מֵעַם,
We are Family	שֶׁכֻּלָּנוּ בְּנֵי מִשְׁפָּחָה אַחַת
And the test of family	וּמִשְׁפָּחָה נִבְחֶנֶת
Is not how we love	לֹא רַק בְּאַהֲבָתָהּ
When we agree	כְּשֶׁכֻּלָּהּ בְּדֵעָה אַחַת
But how we love	אֶלָּא כֵּיצַד הִיא אוֹהֶבֶת
When we disagree	כְּשֶׁאֵין בְּקִרְבָּהּ הַסְכָּמָה
May we be careful with our words	נַקְפִּיד עַל מוֹצָא שְׂפָתֵינוּ
For while a word is a word	כִּי בְּעוֹד מִלָּה הִיא מִלָּה
And a deed is a deed	וּמַעֲשֶׂה הוּא מַעֲשֶׂה
Words we say	דְּבָרִים הַיּוֹצְאִים מִן הַפֶּה
Can lead to harmful, fatal deeds	עֲלוּלִים לְהָבִיא לְתוֹצָאוֹת נוֹרָאוֹת, אֲיֻמּוֹת

May we not question	לֹא נְעַרְעֵר עַל
The motives of the other –	מְנִיעָיו שֶׁל הָאַחֵר
But instead	אַדְרַבָּא –
Listen to the other	נַאֲזִין אֶל הָאַחֵר
Learn from the other	נִלְמַד מִן הָאַחֵר
Sing and dance	נִרְקֹד וְנָשִׁיר
The Psalmist's dream	אֶת חֲזוֹנוֹ שֶׁל הַמְּשׁוֹרֵר
"Behold how beautiful how sweet	"הִנֵּה מַה טּוֹב וּמַה נָּעִים
Sisters and brothers	שֶׁבֶת אַחִים
Together."	גַּם יַחַד"
Illuminate the Chassidic vision:	הָאֵר אֶת חֲזוֹנָהּ שֶׁל הַחֲסִידוּת:
Every Yid has a single light	לְכָל יְהוּדִי אוֹר מְיֻחָד מִשֶּׁלּוֹ
That begins and ends	הַנִּדְלָק וְדוֹעֵךְ
But together, our lights fuse	אַךְ יַחְדָּיו, מִתְמַזְגִים אוֹרוֹתֵינוּ
Endless, eternal	בְּלֹא קֵץ, לְעוֹלָמִים
With You	עִמְּךָ
In unity	בְּאַחְדוּת
As family	כְּמִשְׁפָּחָה
In togetherness	יַחְדָּיו
With light forever	בְּאוֹר נִצְחִי
Help us, help us declare:	עֲזֹר לָנוּ, עֲזֹר לָנוּ לְהַכְרִיז
I am a *kitzoni* — an extremist Jew.	כִּי "יְהוּדִי קִיצוֹנִי" אֲנִי
Not on the right, not on the left,	לֹא לְיָמִין אוֹ לִשְׂמֹאל
But an extremist in	אֶלָּא קִיצוֹנִי,
Loving Other Jews.	קִיצוֹנִי בְּאַהֲבַת אַחַי הַיְּהוּדִים
Ahavat Yisrael	אַהֲבַת יִשְׂרָאֵל

(Translation to Hebrew by Dr. Avigdor Shinan.)

חָכָם מָה הוּא אוֹמֵר? מָה הָעֵדוֹת וְהַחֻקִּים וְהַמִּשְׁפָּטִים אֲשֶׁר צִוָּה יהוה אֱלֹהֵינוּ אֶתְכֶם (דברים ו:ז). וְאַף אַתָּה אֱמוֹר לוֹ כְּהִלְכוֹת הַפֶּסַח: אֵין מַפְטִירִין אַחַר הַפֶּסַח אֲפִיקוֹמָן.

רָשָׁע מָה הוּא אוֹמֵר? מָה הָעֲבוֹדָה הַזֹּאת לָכֶם (שמות יא:כב). לָכֶם – וְלֹא לוֹ. וּלְפִי שֶׁהוֹצִיא אֶת עַצְמוֹ מִן הַכְּלָל כָּפַר בְּעִקָּר. וְאַף אַתָּה הַקְהֵה אֶת שִׁנָּיו וֶאֱמוֹר לוֹ: "בַּעֲבוּר זֶה עָשָׂה יהוה לִי בְּצֵאתִי מִמִּצְרָיִם (שמות יג:ח)". לִי וְלֹא-לוֹ. אִלּוּ הָיָה שָׁם, לֹא הָיָה נִגְאָל.

Chacham - The Wise Child

חָכָם - **What does the wise child say… We may not eat after consuming the Pesach afikoman:** The wise child has the sophistication to ask about the Passover statutes and testimonies. Accordingly, our response deals with the minutiae of Jewish law. Our final instruction, however, is to focus on the eating of the *afikoman*, the hidden matza, reminding us that sometimes the message that resonates most, even for the *chacham*, is experiential, dealing with religious ritual, inspiring spiritual striving.

Rasha - The Wicked Child

רָשָׁע … הַקְהֵה אֶת שִׁנָּיו - **What does the rebellious child say… Blunt his/her teeth (*hak'heh et shinav*).** Normatively, the response to the wicked child is understood to be stern, *hak'heh et shinav*, meaning "blunt his/her teeth;" after all, the wicked child separates from the community.

Hak'heh, however, can be seen

חָכָם - **What does the wise child say?** "'What are these testimonies, statutes and judgments that the Lord our God commanded you?' (Deuteronomy 6:20)" And accordingly you will say to the child, as per the laws of the Pesach sacrifice, "We may not eat after consuming the Pesach afikoman" (cf. Pesachim 10:8).

רָשָׁע - **What does the rebellious child say?** "'What is this worship to you?' (Exodus 12:26)" 'To you' and not 'to him or her.' And since the child excluded him or herself from the collective, s/he denied a principle of the Jewish faith . And accortdingly, you will blunt his/her teeth and say, "For the sake of this, did the Lord do this for me in my going out of Egypt' (Exodus 13:8)." 'For me' and not 'for him or her.' If s/he had been there, s/he would not have been saved.

as the name of God, as each of its letters refers to God (*hey, kuf*). In the same breath, *shinav* may be related to the word "*veshinantam*" – and you shall teach, teach your children Torah. From this perspective, the response to the rebellious child should be to offer teachings that are suffused with God's love. The pathway to the soul is not harsh words but words reflecting unconditional love.

Here, the noun *rasha* may be a composite of *rash-yeshua*, literally, "paucity of salvation." Thus, the *rasha* is not a wicked child but one whose desire to do good is somehow limited. Our goal is to lovingly light the fire within his or her soul, turning the *rasha* around.

And if we do not succeed and the *rasha*, as the Haggadah tells us, is not redeemed, our sacred task – as pointed out to me by my dear friend and mentor, Tova Bulow, in a comment in sync with my theology – is to love the *rasha* no matter what. As a member of the family – even if opting out – our love for the *rasha* is infinite and unconditional.

תָּם מָה הוּא אוֹמֵר? מַה זֹּאת (שמות יג:יד). וְאָמַרְתָּ אֵלָיו "בְּחֹזֶק יָד הוֹצִיאָנוּ יהוה מִמִּצְרַיִם מִבֵּית עֲבָדִים (שמות יג:יד)".

וְשֶׁאֵינוֹ יוֹדֵעַ לִשְׁאוֹל – אַתְּ פְּתַח לוֹ, שֶׁנֶּאֱמַר (שמות יג:ח), וְהִגַּדְתָּ לְבִנְךָ בַּיּוֹם הַהוּא לֵאמֹר, בַּעֲבוּר זֶה עָשָׂה יהוה לִי בְּצֵאתִי מִמִּצְרָיִם.

Tam - The Simple Child

תָּם - **What does the simple child say… What is this (Mah zot)?** Actually, this is not such a simple question. The word *zot* most often refers to something complex; when lifting the Torah, for example, we sing out "*Vezot HaTorah* – and this is the Torah," referring to the sacred of sacred books that requires careful analysis. Notable also is the Psalmist's question, "Who understands this (*zot*)?" Here, *zot* deals with the ever-complicated question of why the righteous suffer. Sometimes we hear a question and assume it is shallow, but beneath the surface it is the deepest of the deep.

She'eino Yodeah Lishol - The One Who Doesn't Know How to Ask

וְשֶׁאֵינוֹ יוֹדֵעַ לִשְׁאוֹל – אַתְּ פְּתַח לוֹ - **And [regarding] the one who doesn't know how to ask, you will open [the conversation] for him or her, as it says "and you will speak (*higadta*) to your children":** Counterintuitively, we should do the reverse; rather than speaking frontally to this child, we should offer a comment that elicits his or her thinking. Note that the term *higadta* sounds similar to *gud aseik*, a halachic concept that literally

תָּם - **What does the simple child say?** "'What is this?' (Exodus 13:14)" And you will say to that child, "'With the strength of His hand did the Lord take us out from Egypt, from the house of slaves' (Exodus 13:14).'"

וְשֶׁאֵינוֹ יוֹדֵעַ לִשְׁאוֹל - **And regarding the one who doesn't know how** to ask, you will open the conversation for him or her, as it says (Exodus 13:8), "and you will speak to your children on that day saying, for the sake of this, did the Lord do this for me in my going out of Egypt."

means extend the wall – imagining it continues upward. This association brings to mind the idea that, we speak to the child who does not know how to ask in a way that takes the child to a particular height, leaving space for the child to actively participate – reaching higher and higher.

My dear Eitan Ashman, who suffered a debilitating stroke and now lives with aphasia, has inspired me to look at the *she'eino yode'ah li'shol* as one who faces serious speech challenges. In his beautiful Haggadah, *Empowering Seder Conversations*, he writes: "When Moshe was commanded by God to take the Jewish people out of Egypt, he said: 'I am not a man of many words.' However, tonight we read how Moshe led the Jewish People from slavery to freedom, which shows us that even with limited words, we can achieve great things."

A Fifth Child

As has been noted by many, beyond the four children is the fifth who is not present – our task is to go out of our comfort zone into the streets, warmly inviting the unaffiliated in.

יכול מראש חודש

יָכוֹל מֵרֹאשׁ חֹדֶשׁ? תַּלְמוּד לוֹמַר בַּיּוֹם הַהוּא. אִי בַּיּוֹם הַהוּא יָכוֹל מִבְּעוֹד יוֹם? תַּלְמוּד לוֹמַר בַּעֲבוּר זֶה – בַּעֲבוּר זֶה לֹא אָמַרְתִּי, אֶלָּא בְּשָׁעָה שֶׁיֵּשׁ מַצָּה וּמָרוֹר מֻנָּחִים לְפָנֶיךָ.

Yachol Me'Rosh Chodesh

יָכוֹל מֵרֹאשׁ חֹדֶשׁ - **Could it be from Rosh Chodesh (the New Moon) [that one would have to discuss the exodus]?** Why would one so think? Perhaps it is because on the first day of Nissan we were given the laws of the Pascal lamb. In the end, however, more than a verbal sharing is necessary. Hence, the story is told at the Passover Seder when we reenact the exodus by eating bitter herbs and drinking wine, symbolic of our transitioning from slavery to freedom. "Doing" ritual is one of the best ways to transmit tradition and values to the next generation.

Note as well that this paragraph could be connected to the preceding one, offering suggestions on how the reticent, quiet child who doesn't inquire can be engaged and inspired to converse. For that reason, the sentence explicated is the same recorded in the previous paragraph ("For the sake of this"). The best way to reach the child who does not know how to ask may not be through verbal communication, but pointing to the ritual objects on the Seder table, which may spur this child to become involved.

יָכוֹל מֵראֹשׁ חֹדֶשׁ - Could it be that we must begin on the first of Nissan? The Torah teaches, "on that day." Could it be that "on that day" requires us to begin while it is still day? The Torah teaches, "for the sake of this"—I could not have said "this," except with matzah and maror resting before you.

מתחילה עובדי עבודה זרה היו אבותינו

מִתְּחִלָּה עוֹבְדֵי עֲבוֹדָה זָרָה הָיוּ אֲבוֹתֵינוּ,
וְעַכְשָׁיו קֵרְבָנוּ הַמָּקוֹם לַעֲבוֹדָתוֹ, שֶׁנֶּאֱמַר (יהושע כד:ב-ד):
וַיֹּאמֶר יְהוֹשֻׁעַ אֶל־כָּל־הָעָם,
כֹּה אָמַר יהוה אֱלֹהֵי יִשְׂרָאֵל,
בְּעֵבֶר הַנָּהָר יָשְׁבוּ אֲבוֹתֵיכֶם מֵעוֹלָם.

Rav's Story

Rav's story expands on Shmuel's, stressing other values:
- SPIRITUALITY
- ISRAEL
- LEADERSHIP
- ROOTS
- FAMILY
- MATRIARCHS
- COVENANTAL CONTINUITY

Mitchilah

Spirituality

מִתְּחִלָּה - **In the Beginning:** Here begins the second account of the storytelling, as presented by the Talmudic rabbi Rav. While the story of Shmuel, *avadim hayinu*, we were slaves, offers a physical recounting from slavery to redemption, Rav's story is spiritual: We once worshipped idols but were brought to Sinai where we received the Torah. For Rav, redemption is not only freedom *from*, but freedom *to*, to proactively carve out a new mission, receiving and then sharing the Torah's message of ethical monotheism with Israel and the world.

Israel

וַיֹּאמֶר יְהוֹשֻׁעַ - **Joshua said:** This storytelling is taken from the Book of Joshua, not the Pentateuch. Why so? Unlike the Book of Exodus, Joshua's speech is given after the settling of the

מִתְּחִלָּה - In the beginning, our ancestors were idol worshippers, but now the Omnipresence has brought us close to His worship, as it is said (Joshua 24:2-4), "Joshua said to the whole people, so said the Lord, God of Israel: Your ancestors formerly dwelt beyond the river.

Land of Israel. Here, Rav makes clear that built into the story of the exodus is the centrality of Israel. It is not necessarily, as some claim, that Israel is apart from the Passover story; it is built in – hence, the words of Joshua.

Leadership

בְּעֵבֶר הַנָּהָר יָשְׁבוּ אֲבוֹתֵיכֶם - Your ancestors formerly dwelt beyond the river: At its core, leadership involves identifying a need and doing something about it – demanding change. It is standing up for a cause not because it is popular but because it is right. The founder of Judaism, Abraham our patriarch, showed the way as he introduced one of the most novel ideas in the annals of human history – belief in one God. But Abraham was alone in this belief. He is therefore called *ivri*, a person from "beyond [the river]." The whole world, say the Rabbis, was on one side of the river, and Abraham stood by himself on the other.

Resistance to change is inevitable, primarily because people are naturally comfortable with the status quo. Sometimes the resistance is extreme. And so, Abraham's belief in one God was challenged. He comes from Ur Kasdim – literally, the fire of Kasdim, because, say the Rabbis, his detractors attempted to murder him by burning him alive.

So, too, today: Neither the American civil rights movement nor the anti–Vietnam War movement began in the mainstream; the struggle to free Ethiopian Jewry was, for years, the lonely cause of the heroic Graenum Berger and a small number of activists; the Soviet Jewry movement was pioneered by visionaries like Jacob Birnbaum and Glenn Richter, who, by and large, stood alone. For years, these

תֶּרַח אֲבִי אַבְרָהָם וַאֲבִי נָחוֹר, וַיַּעַבְדוּ אֱלֹהִים אֲחֵרִים. וָאֶקַּח אֶת־אֲבִיכֶם אֶת־אַבְרָהָם מֵעֵבֶר הַנָּהָר וָאוֹלֵךְ אוֹתוֹ בְּכָל־אֶרֶץ כְּנָעַן.

courageous leaders were subjected to an avalanche of criticism.

The establishment is rarely the first to introduce change. This is because change involves taking risks, and the establishment cannot afford to fail. Furthermore, the establishment is slow moving, mired in red tape and bureaucracy, weighted down by process and committee meetings – often losing touch with the *am'cha*, the very people it is serving. This is why change most often begins from those who are not encumbered by establishment constraints — leaders who are outsiders.

While those who introduce new ideas often begin alone, they cannot remain alone. Leadership is navigating the resistance and inspiring everyone to climb on board – no easy feat, but a critical step to achieve victory.

Roots

תֶּרַח - **Terach:** Terach, for the Midrash, is an idol worshipper, accentuating the greatness of his son Abraham, who broke from him. The reverse is also true, as the literal text portrays Terach positively. He adopts his grandson Lot after Lot's father, Haran (Terach's son, Abraham's brother) dies. On his own initiative, Terach, without being commanded by God, begins to journey to Canaan, intrinsically recognizing its spiritual loftiness. And, of course, all of the patriarchs and matriarchs descend from Terach. He is the foundation of the Abrahamitic family. While roots of trees are often not seen, they are essential to the

Terach, the father of Abraham and Nachor—
and they worshipped other gods.
But I took Abraham from beyond the river
and led him through the whole land of Canaan,

tree's health, much like Terach — unseen, unnoticed, but critical to our birth – deserves acclaim.

Family

אֲבִי אַבְרָהָם - **The father of Abraham:** Herein lies yet another difference between the Shmuel and Rav stories. For Shmuel, the exodus story begins with our servitude in Egypt (*avadim hayinu*). For Rav, the starting point is Avraham our forefather and his descendants – the primary story of the Book of Genesis. Indeed, Genesis is laden with the travails of fractured families. There is, however, magic in its finale. A reconciliation occurs. The family is reunited. All of Jacob's sons are blessed. It is only then, when the family is whole at last, that Bereishit ends and Shemot, the Book of Exodus, which centers on the birth of the nation, begins, teaching that the best model of nation is family. Hence, my practice: When considering the needs of the nation of Israel, I substitute the word "family" for "nation" and try to act accordingly.

Matriarchs

וַאֲבִי נָחוֹר - **And the father of Nachor:** Why does Nachor, usually unmentioned, appear here? While Abraham is the father and grandfather of the patriarchs Isaac and Jacob, Nachor is the grandfather and great-grandfather of the matriarchs Rebecca, Rachel and Leah. The matriarchs are of equal importance; hence the critical recognition of their direct ancestor Nachor.

וָאַרְבֶּה אֶת־זַרְעוֹ וָאֶתֵּן־לוֹ אֶת־יִצְחָק.
וָאֶתֵּן לְיִצְחָק אֶת־יַעֲקֹב וְאֶת־עֵשָׂו,
וָאֶתֵּן לְעֵשָׂו אֶת־הַר שֵׂעִיר לָרֶשֶׁת אוֹתוֹ,
וְיַעֲקֹב וּבָנָיו יָרְדוּ מִצְרָיִם.

Covenantal Continuity
וָאֶתֵּן־לוֹ אֶת־יִצְחָק. וָאֶתֵּן לְיִצְחָק אֶת־יַעֲקֹב וְאֶת־עֵשָׂו - **And gave him Isaac, and I gave Jacob and Esau to Isaac:** Why is there no mention of Ishmael, Isaac's brother? Truth be told, the question of who would be the covenantal heir of Abraham – Isaac or Ishmael – is more a question of who would be the first matriarch, Sarah or Hagar, as Sarah birthed Isaac and Hagar birthed Ishmael. While Abraham loved Ishmael, he was never a real candidate to be Abraham's spiritual inheritor, as Sarah was always destined to be the first matriarch. Thus, Ishmael is not in the running. This contrasts with the twins Jacob and Esau, both children of Isaac and Rebecca, who had equal claim to the spiritual heirship. And so, the Haggadah makes clear that Jacob not Esau is the third patriarch. Esau inherits Mount Seir, while Jacob and his family go down to Egypt from where his descendants will be enslaved and then freed – ultimately becoming the nation of Israel.

The relationship between Abraham and Ishmael needs further clarification, as for a time Abraham believed that Hagar would be the bearer of his covenantal seed. He may have felt this way as Hagar came on the scene just after the Covenant of the Pieces. There, God tells Abraham redemption will come only after his children become *gerim* (strangers) and *avadim* (slaves) who

And I increased his seed and gave him Isaac,
and I gave Jacob and Esau to Isaac.
And I gave Mount Seir to Esau to inherit,
while Jacob and his children went down to Egypt."

will be *inuim* (afflicted) by others (Genesis 15:13).

In the very next chapter, the Torah tells us of Hagar's relationship with Abraham. She is called Hagar, which may be a play on the word *ger* (stranger). She was also a maidservant, the female counterpart of a slave. And the Torah declares she was afflicted by Sarah – *va'te'aneha* (16:6). These three factors reflect the necessary conditions built into the Covenant of the Pieces.

Thus, in chapter 17, when God reaffirms the *brit* (covenant) with Abraham, Abraham assumes it will be through Ishmael – the son born to him and Hagar (17:1–8). It is here that God tells Abraham that a child will be born to Sarah (17:16).

Abraham, understandably confused, cries out, isn't Ishmael that child? It is here that God definitively declares that while Ishmael will become a great nation, the covenantal continuity will be through Isaac (17:19–21).

There are great similarities between Isaac and Ishmael. Both are given names by God. Both are involved with the number twelve, as from Ishmael twelve princes will come, and from Isaac the twelve tribes will emerge.

While Ishmael, like Isaac, is beloved by Abraham, covenantal continuity will be the exclusive domain of Isaac, whose descendants will liberate and settle the Land of Israel.

ברוך שומר הבטחתו לישראל

בָּרוּךְ שׁוֹמֵר הַבְטָחָתוֹ לְיִשְׂרָאֵל, בָּרוּךְ הוּא.
שֶׁהַקָּדוֹשׁ בָּרוּךְ הוּא חִשַּׁב אֶת־הַקֵּץ,
לַעֲשׂוֹת כְּמוֹ שֶׁאָמַר לְאַבְרָהָם אָבִינוּ בִּבְרִית בֵּין הַבְּתָרִים,

Baruch Shomer Havtachato l'Yisrael

בָּרוּךְ - **Blessed be the One:** The just outlined origins of our peoplehood is but the genesis of the overwhelming challenges we've faced over the millennia. One wonders, how have we, against all odds endured. After all, as some historians have noted, a rational assessment of the forces of history would conclude that Judaism today should be a fossil. We would respond that Jewish history is not logical or rational; the improbability and vast breadth of Jewish history points to the covenant established between God and Am Yisrael.

בָּרוּךְ שׁוֹמֵר הַבְטָחָתוֹ לְיִשְׂרָאֵל - **Blessed be the One who keeps His promise to Israel:** God first promises Abraham children. Although quite elderly and already living with his wife Sarah for decades, Abraham believes, he just knows, that God's promise will be fulfilled. God then promises Abraham the Land of Israel, a far more believable commitment. And yet Abraham doesn't immediately believe God's words but wonders, what must he do to be deserving of the land? Why the difference in Abraham's reactions?

Covenant always includes two elements: "children" and "land" – with a notable distinction. The promise of children, that is, the eternality of the Jewish people, is a unilateral commitment from God. No matter what Abraham or his descendants do, God assures there will always be a Jewish people. Hence, Abraham believes, knowing God will be faithful to his promise. The promise of land, however, is a bilateral contract; that is, we will be sovereign in the land *if we are worthy*. "Being" is not enough. "Doing" is necessary. Hence, Abraham asks, what must he do to be deserving of the land?

This distinction has played out in history as we were bereft of sovereignty for two thousand years before the modern State of Israel was

בָּרוּךְ שׁוֹמֵר הַבְטָחָתוֹ לְיִשְׂרָאֵל - Blessed be the One who keeps His promise to Israel, blessed be He; since the Holy One, blessed be He, calculated the end of the exile, to do as He said to Abraham, our father, in the Covenant between the Pieces,

established. But our existence as a people continued without pause. This is still an important message today: To remain sovereign in Israel, we must be worthy.

בְּרִית בֵּין הַבְּתָרִים - **Covenant between the Pieces:** While there is unanimity among Jewish religious thinkers that the primary covenant, *brit Sinai*, took place at Sinai, there is disagreement about its precursor.

In his *Kol Dodi Dofek*, Rabbi Yosef Dov Soloveitchik argues that the foundational covenant is *brit Mitzrayim*, the covenant formed through the Egyptian bondage, first alluded to in the Covenant of the Pieces. There, God tells Abraham that his seed will be slaves in Egypt for hundreds of years.

Rabbi Soloveitchik identifies this covenant as the covenant of fate forged through the Jewish People's shared suffering. "Fate signifies in the life of the nation…an existence of compulsion." In simple terms, even if a Jew doesn't wish to identify as a Jew, he or she will be so labeled by the enemy. For the antisemite, there is no distinction between the observant and the less observant. Such divisions are irrelevant. What counts is that you're a Jew. If so, you're the enemy. This commonality equalizes and unites all Jews.

Rav Kook sees the precursor to *brit Sinai* differently. In his view, the foundational covenant stems from an inner, soulful superiority intrinsic to Jews – what he calls *brit Avot* (the covenant of the patriarchs), established in the Covenant of the Pieces. *Brit Avot*, says Rabbi Kook, is "the higher soulfulness that Jews possess."

These two brilliant, saintly rabbis are my revered teachers. And yet, I struggle with both their positions. Rooting covenant in suffering poses the danger that Judaism will be misunderstood as primarily reactive, focused on victimhood, fighting forces wishing to annihilate us. At the same time, anchoring covenant in the theory

שֶׁנֶּאֱמַר (בראשית טו:יג-יד): וַיֹּאמֶר לְאַבְרָם, יָדֹעַ תֵּדַע כִּי-גֵר יִהְיֶה זַרְעֲךָ בְּאֶרֶץ לֹא לָהֶם, וַעֲבָדוּם וְעִנּוּ אֹתָם אַרְבַּע מֵאוֹת שָׁנָה. וְגַם אֶת-הַגּוֹי אֲשֶׁר יַעֲבֹדוּ דָּן אָנֹכִי וְאַחֲרֵי-כֵן יֵצְאוּ בִּרְכֻשׁ גָּדוֹל.

of soul superiority flies in the face of the Torah's primary teaching that all human beings are of equal value – all created in the image of God.

My humble sense is that the foundational covenant is that of family, found as well in the Covenant of the Pieces, which is bracketed by God's promise that Abraham and Sarah will be the first patriarch and matriarch of the Jewish People. Covenantal heirship will come from them (Genesis 15:4; 17:19).

It is from the family of Abraham and Sarah that the nation of Israel is born at Sinai. There – at the covenant established at Sinai – we are given the mandate to bring ethical monotheism into the world.

From this perspective, the nation of Israel is also the family of Israel, as *brit Sinai* emerges from and remains forever linked to what can be called *brit mishpachah* (the covenant of family). As a loving family, the nation becomes closer than ever, consisting of brothers and sisters caring unconditionally for each other and ultimately for the larger family of humankind – *mishpechot amim*.

וַעֲבָדוּם וְעִנּוּ אֹתָם - And they will enslave them and afflict them… and afterwards they will go free: Built into redemption is suffering. The paradigm of this phenomenon is the exodus from Egypt – where we were enslaved, afflicted – and then freed.

The Midrash offers this generic parable. A father and son were walking in the forest. The son asks: "Father, dear father – where is the city?" "Son, oh dear son," the father responds: "When you see the cemetery, you'll know you're on its outskirts." In Israel today, this image has become the reality. Virtually every city has its cemetery, often on the outskirts, including graves of soldiers, heroes who gave their lives so Israel could live.

וְאַחֲרֵי-כֵן יֵצְאוּ בִּרְכֻשׁ גָּדוֹל - And they will enslave them and afflict them… and afterwards they will go free: How could it be that as the Jews left Egypt, at Moses' behest, they despoiled the Egyptians (*vayenatz'lu*) and took their goods (Exodus 12:36)?

Based on this verse, many

as it is stated (Genesis 15:13-14), "And He said to Abram,
'You should surely know that your seed will be strangers
in a land that is not theirs,
and they will enslave them and afflict them four hundred years.
And also that nation for which they shall toil will I judge,
and afterwards they will go free with much wealth.'"

antisemites have claimed that Jews are thieves, stealing from others. The mainstream response to this accusation is that the taking of Egyptian possessions was, in fact, a small repayment for all the years of Jewish enslavement.

But a different approach to the text has far-reaching consequences in contemporary times. Perhaps the Jews did not take from the Egyptians after all. Possibly the Egyptians, upon request of the Jews, willingly gave their property as a way of atoning for their misdeeds. This approach would read the word *vayenatz'lu* not as meaning "despoil" but "to save" (from the word *l'hatzil*). In giving money to the Jews, the Egyptians' souls repented and, in some small way, were saved.

To paraphrase Benno Jacob, an amicable parting from Egypt would banish the Jews' bitter memories of the Egyptians. Jews would come to understand that the oppressors were Pharaoh and other Egyptian leaders as opposed to the entire Egyptian people. The gifts ensure "a parting [of] friendship and goodwill with its consequent clearing of the name and vindication of the honor of the Egyptian people."

All this has much in common with a burning issue that surfaced in the early 1950s. Should Jews accept reparation money from Germany? Some argued for accepting such money, feeling that Germany should at least pay monetarily for their villainy.

Others argued the reverse. Payment would be viewed as blood money, an atonement to wash away German sins – and, of course, nothing could ever obviate the evil of the Third Reich.

The contemporary debate concerning recouping monies and plundered assets from the Germans and Swiss and others for their misdeeds during the Holocaust has its roots in the exodus from Egypt. Was *vayenatz'lu*, mandated as it was by God, a unique event never to be repeated, or did it set a precedent to be emulated later in history?

והיא שעמדה

מכסים את המצות מגביהים את הכוס, ואומרים:

וְהִיא שֶׁעָמְדָה לַאֲבוֹתֵינוּ וְלָנוּ. שֶׁלֹּא אֶחָד בִּלְבַד עָמַד עָלֵינוּ לְכַלּוֹתֵנוּ, אֶלָּא שֶׁבְּכָל דּוֹר וָדוֹר עוֹמְדִים עָלֵינוּ לְכַלּוֹתֵנוּ, וְהַקָּדוֹשׁ בָּרוּךְ הוּא מַצִּילֵנוּ מִיָּדָם.

Vehi She'am'da

וְהִיא - **And this (*vehi*) is what has sustained our ancestors:** Some understand the numerical value of each of the letters of "*vehi*" as hinting to a foundational Jewish idea which has sustained us. "*Vav*," the numerical value of six, is the six orders of the Mishna (*Shas*). "*Hey*," five, is the five Books of Moses. "*Yud*," ten, refers to the Ten Declarations. "*Alef*," one, is the foundation of all foundations, the One God.

While a sweet teaching, this paragraph, with its conjunctive "*vav*," literally refers to what has just been discussed, the Covenant of the Pieces. Notwithstanding the price we've paid, the losses we've incurred, the crusades, pogroms, expulsions and Holocaust – against all odds, we are, with God's help, still here, proving the efficacy of the *brit* – covenant.

שֶׁעָמְדָה - **And this is what sustained (*amdah*) our ancestors:** Amdah reflects varying types of protection. It is a term of prayer associated with the Shmoneh Esreh, the Amidah. It also may refer to the *amud anan*, the pillars of cloud accompanying Israel through the desert. And it also stirs images of commanders ordering Israeli troops, *amod dom*, attention – be on the alert to defend the Homeland.

לַאֲבוֹתֵינוּ וְלָנוּ- **Our ancestors and us:** For many decades after the Shoah, antisemitism was not rampant. In the shadow of Six Million murdered, Jew haters understood their repugnant biases would not resonate for the masses. Eighty years after the Holocaust, as memory fades, antisemites are coming out of the woodwork. What

We cover the matzot. Lifting up the cup we say:

וְהִיא שֶׁעָמְדָה - And this is what has sustained our ancestors and us; since it is not only one person or nation that has stood against us to destroy us, but rather in each generation, they stand against us to destroy us, but the Holy One, blessed be He, rescues us from their hands.

was experienced in the past by our ancestors (*avoteinu*), is tragically spiraling exponentially against us (*lanu*) today.

שֶׁלֹּא אֶחָד בִּלְבָד - **Not only one:** Not just one person (*she'lo echad bilvad*), but many in every generation have tried to destroy us. And yet, God, the Echad, the One who is described in the Torah as *ein od milvado*, "there is none beside Him," protects us (Deuteronomy 6:4; 4:35). While *echad bilvad* refers to the enemy, *Echad… ein od Milvado* will always prevail.

Courageous singular heroes have also, with God's help, joined in. One such hero is the great Yosef Mendelevich who, beginning in 1970, spent eleven years in the Soviet Gulag. Upon his release, Yosef continued to raise a voice of moral conscience on behalf of millions of Jews still trapped in the Soviet Union. Protesting for Soviet Jewry at the 1985 Geneva Reagan-Gorbachev summit I saw Yosef's heroism firsthand. After we were brutally arrested for sitting in the Geneva Soviet Aeroflot office, we were taken to the police station, interrogated for hours, and ordered to strip. When they demanded that Yosef take off his tzitzit (the four-cornered garment with fringes that observant Jews wear), he shouted "I protest!" Yosef repeated "I protest" again and again as they asked him to take off his shirt, undershirt, and finally his kippa, at which time he ripped his undershirt in two and placed half of it on his head. Enraged, the Swiss guard roughly went through Yosef's bag and confiscated his tefillin. Yosef's courage filled me with awe – he is a paragon hero of heroes.

LEARNING

Having completed the stories, the Haggadah now proceeds to present an in-depth study section: *Tzei U'lemad* – Go Out and Learn. It does so by quoting four sentences from Deuteronomy which are to be recited when a farmer brings his first fruits to Jerusalem. These sentences summarize the exodus story. The Haggadah analyzes them phrase by phrase, using support texts cited by the rabbis of the Midrash.

Before commenting on each phrase, a general question needs to be addressed. Why quote the history of the exodus from the Book of Deuteronomy? Why not find salient sentences from the Book of Exodus where the narrative of the enslavement and its ending unfolds? Several answers come to mind.

The portion of the first fruits instructs the native Israeli to thank God for his bounty. Although not personally enslaved in Egypt, he recalls what occurred in the first person, as if he himself experienced the historical exodus. We, too, millennia later, descendants who were not there, tell the story in first person as if we were there.

There is another approach to memory – to recounting a past event. While nothing can substitute for an eyewitness account, history as told by ensuing generations has its advantages. Not having been there, the exodus story is told from a distance; with the passage of time, the telling could be more objective and therefore more precise.

Also, focusing on the farmer in Israel bringing the first fruits to the Temple once again accentuates the centrality of Israel in the Haggadah.

More expansively, the Deuteronomy text iterates the verb *"natan"* (to give), recalling the Egyptians *giving* us over to bondage in contrast to God who *gave* us the land with the proviso that we *give* to the needy and vulnerable.

צא ולמד

מניחים את הכוס ומגלים את המצות.

צֵא וּלְמַד מַה בִּקֵּשׁ לָבָן הָאֲרַמִּי לַעֲשׂוֹת לְיַעֲקֹב אָבִינוּ: שֶׁפַּרְעֹה לֹא גָזַר אֶלָּא עַל הַזְּכָרִים, וְלָבָן בִּקֵּשׁ לַעֲקֹר אֶת־הַכֹּל.

שֶׁנֶּאֱמַר (דברים כו:ה): **אֲרַמִּי אֹבֵד אָבִי, וַיֵּרֶד מִצְרַיְמָה וַיָּגָר שָׁם בִּמְתֵי מְעָט, וַיְהִי־שָׁם לְגוֹי גָּדוֹל עָצוּם וָרָב.**

וַיֵּרֶד מִצְרַיְמָה – אָנוּס עַל פִּי הַדִּבּוּר.

Arami Oved Avi: Exile

אֲרַמִּי אֹבֵד אָבִי - An Aramean sought to destroy my father: The meaning of *Arami oved avi* is "my father (*avi*), Abraham or Jacob, was a wandering (*oved*) Aramean (*Arami*)." In Abraham's case, he journeyed from Aram to Israel and, escaping a famine, to Egypt, and then returned to Israel. In Jacob's case, he wandered from Israel to Aram, back to Israel, and finally to Egypt.

Still, the Haggadah refuses to refer to the patriarchs as *Arami*, as the term implies "deceiver," and the patriarchs were the righteous of the righteous. The deceiver was Laban: on the outside – as his literal name connotes – white, pure, goodly; but on the inside, through chicanery, doing all he could to convince Jacob and his family to forget their roots, assimilate, and cast off their Jewish identity. Thus the phrase *Arami oved avi* is understood by the Haggadah differently: the Aramean (Laban, who was a deceiver) sought to destroy my father (Jacob).

The Haggadah takes this interpretation a step further by comparing Laban and Pharaoh. Indeed, the biblical narrative dealing with Laban and Pharaoh are similar. Jacob testifies that in his father-in-law's home, he felt as a *stranger*, *enslaved* and *afflicted*. In Pharaoh's Egypt, we experienced a similar fate and were described as having been *strangers*, *enslaved*, and *afflicted*. Both are fulfillments of God's decree in the Covenant of the Pieces that we would

Arami Oved Avi: Exile

The cup is put down; the matza uncovered as we begin the "learning" section.

צֵא וּלְמַד - Go out and learn what terrible plan Laban the Aramean sought to do to Jacob, our father; since Pharaoh only decreed death for the males, but Laban sought to uproot the whole people. As it is stated (Deuteronomy 26:5):

אֲרַמִּי אֹבֵד אָבִי - "**An Aramean sought to destroy my father and he went down to Egypt, and he sojourned there with a small number, and he became there a nation, great, powerful and numerous.**"

וַיֵּרֶד מִצְרַיְמָה - "And he (Jacob) went down to Egypt" – helpless on account of the word in which God told Abraham that his descendants would have to go into exile.

be *strangers*, *slaves* and *afflicted*… before liberation (Genesis 31:41,42; 32:5. Exodus 1:11-14; 2:22. Genesis 15:13).

It's fascinating, too, that Israel's exodus from Pharaoh's Egypt parallels Jacob's escape from Laban. Both the people of Israel and Jacob leave in the dead of the night. Both are pursued by their adversary (Pharaoh and Laban); both are caught and a confrontation ensues. Remarkably, the language of both escapes is parallel (Genesis 31:22-25. Exodus 14:5-9).

In fact, the Haggadah concludes that Laban was a greater threat than Pharaoh. Pharaoh tried to kill the boys so we'd lack an army to defend ourselves. Laban's threat was more spiritual: to uproot all that Jacob stood for. In some ways, the challenge to the soul of Israel can wreak greater havoc and destruction than any physical threat.

וַיֵּרֶד מִצְרַיְמָה - **And he [Jacob] went down to Egypt:** Our three forefathers were precursors of three types of modern Israelis. Abraham and Sarah were *olim*, emigrating to Israel from the diaspora. Isaac and Rebecca were *sabras*; born in Israel, they never left. Jacob, born in Israel, left at the behest of his parents to escape his brother Esau and to find a wife in Aram, only to return years later. He was a *toshav chozer* – the Jew who leaves Israel (*yored*) only to make his way back. It was after his final return that the Joseph story played out. Once Jacob finds out that Joseph is alive, he hesitates to leave Israel even to see his beloved son;

וַיָּגָר שָׁם. מְלַמֵּד שֶׁלֹּא יָרַד יַעֲקֹב אָבִינוּ לְהִשְׁתַּקֵּעַ בְּמִצְרַיִם אֶלָּא לָגוּר שָׁם, שֶׁנֶּאֱמַר (בראשית מז:ד): וַיֹּאמְרוּ אֶל־פַּרְעֹה, לָגוּר בָּאָרֶץ בָּאנוּ, כִּי אֵין מִרְעֶה לַצֹּאן אֲשֶׁר לַעֲבָדֶיךָ, כִּי כָבֵד הָרָעָב בְּאֶרֶץ כְּנָעַן, וְעַתָּה יֵשְׁבוּ־נָא עֲבָדֶיךָ בְּאֶרֶץ גֹּשֶׁן.

בִּמְתֵי מְעָט. כְּמָה שֶׁנֶּאֱמַר (דברים י:כב): בְּשִׁבְעִים נֶפֶשׁ יָרְדוּ אֲבֹתֶיךָ מִצְרָיְמָה, וְעַתָּה שָׂמְךָ יְהוָה אֱלֹהֶיךָ כְּכוֹכְבֵי הַשָּׁמַיִם לָרֹב.

וַיְהִי שָׁם לְגוֹי. מְלַמֵּד שֶׁהָיוּ יִשְׂרָאֵל מְצֻיָּנִים שָׁם.

גָּדוֹל עָצוּם – כְּמָה שֶׁנֶּאֱמַר (שמות א:ז): וּבְנֵי יִשְׂרָאֵל פָּרוּ וַיִּשְׁרְצוּ וַיִּרְבּוּ וַיַּעַצְמוּ בִּמְאֹד מְאֹד, וַתִּמָּלֵא הָאָרֶץ אֹתָם.

having left once, he's reluctant to leave again. He does so only at the behest of God. In that sense – as the Haggadah indicates – he was an *anoos*, compelled by God.

וַיָּגָר שָׁם - **And he sojourned there:** This teaches – as presented in the support text – that Jacob's intent was not to remain in Egypt but to live there temporarily. Many have left Israel planning to remain in the diaspora for a short period of time – perhaps to earn more money or for a teaching sabbatical or to rendezvous with family. But the sincerest of plans can sometimes go awry. A short stay can extend a year, another year – who knows, maybe for a lifetime. So, too, for Jacob. He thought he'd remain in Egypt for a short while, but once he sees Joseph, he never returns. In the end, he spends his last seventeen years in Egypt.

Jacob's intention to remain for just a short while is reinforced in the supporting text that the family settled in Goshen. Why Goshen? He may choose this locale to dwell far from the Egyptian capital and remain unaffected by its dangerous political intrigues or, more proactively, to use the time to create a kind of

וַיָּגָר שָׁם - **"And he sojourned there"** - this teaches that Jacob, our father, didn't go down to settle in Egypt, but rather only to reside there, as it is said (Genesis 47:4), "And they said to Pharaoh, 'We have come to reside in the land, since there is no pasture for your servant's flocks, as the famine is heavy in the land of Canaan. And now, please grant that your servants should dwell in the Land of Goshen.'"

בִּמְתֵי מְעָט - **"With a small number"** - as it is said (Deuteronomy 10:22), "With seventy souls did your ancestors go down to Egypt, and now the Lord your God has made you as numerous as the stars of the sky."

וַיְהִי שָׁם לְגוֹי - **"And he became there a nation"** - this teaches that Israel became distinguishable there.

גָּדוֹל עָצוּם - **"Great, powerful"** - as it is said (Exodus 1:7), "And the Children of Israel multiplied and swarmed and increased and grew exceedingly mighty, and the land became full of them."

"state within a state" as Jacob's family prepared to return home, to establish themselves as sovereign rulers of Israel.

בִּמְתֵי מְעָט - **With a small number:** While they were few in quantity, in quality they were quite impressive. This offers a glimpse of future times when Jews, few in number in the exile, powerfully inspire the world – like the stars, says the support text, each glowing, each impactful.

וַיְהִי שָׁם לְגוֹי - **And he became there a nation:** Note the similarity between the term *metzuyanim* (excelled) – as found in the Haggadah's interpretation – and *Tzion* (Zion). The term *Tzion* may come from the word *tziyun* (mark) or *metzuyan* (excellent), as Israel is the place where we are sovereign, where we have the best potential to be a "light to the world." Declaring that in Egypt the Jews were *metzuyanim* is a perversion of the dream of Tzion. No longer is the place of excellence Israel, but Egypt; for the children of Jacob, Egypt – as the spies would later declare – was the land of milk and honey.

גָּדוֹל עָצוּם - **Great, powerful:** The Jews in Egypt grew in reputation (*gadol*) and political power (*atzum*).

וָרָב. כְּמָה שֶׁנֶּאֱמַר (יחזקאל טז:ז):
רְבָבָה כְּצֶמַח הַשָּׂדֶה נְתַתִּיךְ, וַתִּרְבִּי וַתִּגְדְּלִי וַתָּבֹאִי בַּעֲדִי עֲדָיִים, שָׁדַיִם נָכֹנוּ וּשְׂעָרֵךְ צִמֵּחַ, וְאַתְּ עֵרֹם וְעֶרְיָה. וָאֶעֱבֹר עָלַיִךְ וָאֶרְאֵךְ מִתְבּוֹסֶסֶת בְּדָמָיִךְ, וָאֹמַר לָךְ בְּדָמַיִךְ חֲיִי, וָאֹמַר לָךְ בְּדָמַיִךְ חֲיִי (יחזקאל טז:ו).

וָרָב - And materially successful: Metaphorically – as the support text illustrates, growing "to excellent beauty…breasts fashioned… hair groomed…" describing the pleasurable, alluring comforts Jews enjoyed in Egypt. And yet, we were body without soul, mighty, beautiful and plentiful, luxuriating in our physicality, but "naked and bare," empty vessels. We were physically successful but spiritually lost, without a sense of mission, meaning and purpose – ripe for a great fall.

Perhaps for this reason, another support text from Ezekiel is included in some *haggadot*: "And when I passed by you, and I saw you weltering in your blood (*dam*), I said to you…'in your bloods you will live… in your bloods you will live.'" Throughout history, we often reached the highest heights only to assimilate, forget our spiritual and ideological mission, and when our contributions were forgotten by our host country, we plummeted from the loftiest realms. For those who survived, it was at a great price: "By our bloods, by our bloods."

וָרָב - **"And materially successful"** - as it is said (Ezekiel 16:7), "I have allowed you to become numerous like the vegetation of the field, and you increased and grew and became highly ornamented, your breasts were firm and your hair grew, but you were naked and bare." "And when I passed by you, and saw you wallowing in your blood, I said to you, by your blood you will live! Yea, I said to you, by your blood you will live!" (Ezekiel 16:6).

The Klausenberger rebbe, who lost his entire family – his wife and eleven children – during the Holocaust, had a rare interpretation of "by our bloods." While presiding over a circumcision, during the *k'riyat shem*, when the name of the child is given, our sentence from Ezekiel is read. As the Klausenberger came to the words "by your bloods you shall live," he paused. Tears flowed from his eyes. Absolute silence extended interminably. Finally, he called out with deep emotion, *"B'damayich chayi, b'damayich chayi."*

His disciples surrounded him and asked for an explanation. "When I approached these words," the rabbi said, "I thought of my family and was overcome. In my heart I asked God, how could You have allowed the bloods of the innocent to be spilled? All at once, I realized that the word *b'damayich* may not come from *dam* [blood], but *domem* [silence], in the spirit of Aaron the high priest, who remained silent when informed that his sons had died serving in the Temple. Trembling, I was able to cry out those words."

וַיָּרֵעוּ אֹתָנוּ הַמִּצְרִים וַיְעַנּוּנוּ, וַיִּתְּנוּ עָלֵינוּ עֲבֹדָה קָשָׁה (דברים כו:ו).

וַיָּרֵעוּ אֹתָנוּ הַמִּצְרִים – כְּמָה שֶׁנֶּאֱמַר (שמות א:י):
הָבָה נִתְחַכְּמָה לוֹ פֶּן יִרְבֶּה,
וְהָיָה כִּי־תִקְרֶאנָה מִלְחָמָה
וְנוֹסַף גַּם־הוּא עַל שֹׂנְאֵינוּ
וְנִלְחַם־בָּנוּ, וְעָלָה מִן־הָאָרֶץ.

Vayarei'u: Antisemitism

וַיָּרֵעוּ - **And the Egyptians did evil to us**: Why was there a need to deal wisely, as the support text indicates? After all, Pharaoh was the most powerful man in the world. If he feared the Jews, why not immediately clamp down, enslaving them with one swift decree, making clear the Jews would be subjugated?

Nachmanides explains that even tyrants need time to carry out their evil intentions. After all, the Egyptian people had to be convinced to follow Pharaoh's despicable plan. And the Jews, too, initially living the good and free life in Egypt, may have been strong enough at the outset – physically and mentally – to respond by fighting back.

Pharaoh, therefore, acted wisely, beginning with more subtle antisemitism, in time, ordering harsher decrees, leading to attempts at infanticide and other horrors. With time, the Egyptian citizenry would acclimate, becoming convinced of the righteousness of Pharaoh's orders, and the Jews would be broken, void of spirit to fight back.

This is what occurred in Nazi Germany. From 1933-1941, the evil leader of the Third Reich did not carry out his genocidal plans against the Jews. He moved forward more gradually. As the historian Raul Hilberg argues, first he expropriated Jewish lands, forcing Jews who lived in the country to move to the city; from there they were forced into ghettos, from where they could more easily be transported in cattle cars to death

Vayarei'u: Antisemitism

"And the Egyptians did evil to us, and afflicted us, and put upon us hard work" (Deuteronomy 26:6)

וַיָּרֵעוּ אֹתָנוּ הַמִּצְרִים - "And the Egyptians did evil to us" - as it is said (Exodus 1:10), "Let us deal wisely with them, so they not multiply. Otherwise, if war breaks out, they will join with our enemies and fight against us and displace us from our land."

camps in Germany and Poland. Thus, the antisemitism grew gradually – yellow stars, boycotts of Jewish stores, outlawing medical treatment from Jewish doctors, declaring German universities off limits to Jews, Kristallnacht.

Antisemitism is most dangerous when subtle, slowly, slowly becoming acceptable, not only to the enemy but to Jews themselves.

וַיָּרֵעוּ אֹתָנוּ הַמִּצְרִים וַיְעַנּוּנוּ, וַיִּתְּנוּ עָלֵינוּ עֲבֹדָה קָשָׁה - **And the Egyptians did evil to us (*vayarei'u*), and afflicted us (*vaye'anunu*), and put upon us hard work (*avodah kashah*):** Notice, as indicated in the support texts, the gradual uptick of antisemitism: from "did evil" to "afflicted" – forcing Jews to pay the equivalent of taxes by building store cities – to "hard work."

~~~~~

More generally, each step of oppression hints at the different faces of antisemitism that have surfaced over the millennia:

וַיָּרֵעוּ - **And they did evil to us (*vayarei'u*):** *Vayarei'u* comes from the word *re'ah*, a close friend, speaking to the sisterhood and brotherhood of the Jewish people as in *ve'ahavta lerei'acha kamocha*, "Love your neighbor (referring to Israelites) as yourself." This brings to mind Amalek in biblical times or the Nazis in the modern era, and too many others, who focused their venom on *re'ah*, the Jewish people. Their goal was to annihilate us because we were Jews.

וַיְעַנּוּנוּ. כְּמָה שֶׁנֶּאֱמַר (שמות א:יא): וַיָּשִׂימוּ עָלָיו שָׂרֵי מִסִּים לְמַעַן עַנֹּתוֹ בְּסִבְלֹתָם, וַיִּבֶן עָרֵי מִסְכְּנוֹת לְפַרְעֹה אֶת־פִּתֹם וְאֶת־רַעַמְסֵס.

וַיִּתְּנוּ עָלֵינוּ עֲבֹדָה קָשָׁה. כְּמָה שֶׁנֶּאֱמַר (שמות א:יא): וַיַּעֲבִדוּ מִצְרַיִם אֶת־בְּנֵי יִשְׂרָאֵל בְּפָרֶךְ.

וַיְעַנּוּנוּ - **And they afflicted us (vaye'anunu):** *Vaye'anunu* comes from the word *anan*, cloud, or *anah*, to respond, terms found in the revelation narrative, as clouds covered Sinai, and the Jews responded "We will do and hear" God's will and follow His commandments. This brings to mind others who have directed their hatred against our Torah. A prime example is Christian persecution of Jews over the millennia. Their claim was that they had no intention to murder Jews. Rather, they aimed to kill those who rejected their primary belief. Basically, they stated, we accept Jews, but only if they embrace Jesus. In the end, however, it became clear that their goal of destroying our fundamental Torah beliefs was the equivalent of destroying the Jewish People.

עֲבֹדָה קָשָׁה - **Hard work (avodah kashah):** *Avodah kashah* means hard work, the kind of heavy lifting needed to establish and settle the Land of Israel. Indeed, in halachic literature, the term *avodah* is associated with working the Land of Israel or involvement in any effort that contributes to *yishuv ha'aretz* (settling the land). This brings to mind another type of Jewish hatred, anti-Zionism. Truth be told, in the post-Holocaust era, it is most often not considered politically correct to directly target Jews or even their Torah. Hence, the attack is focused instead against the Jewish land. In the end, however, a Jewish land is so fundamental to Judaism that any attempt to deny Jews their homeland is nothing less than an attempted destruction of the Jewish People. While there are anti-Zionists who are not antisemites, anti-Zionists who deny our right to Israel are are antisemites as they actively delegitimize our right to a Jewish homeland.

Not coincidentally, these three pillars form the basis of the three

וַיְעַנּוּנוּ - **"And afflicted us"** - as it is said (Exodus 1:11), "And they placed taskmasters over Israel in order to afflict them with their burdens; and they built storage cities for Pharaoh, Pithom and Ra'amses."

וַיִּתְּנוּ עָלֵינוּ עֲבֹדָה קָשָׁה - **"And put upon us hard work"** - as it is said (Exodus 1:11), "And they enslaved the children of Israel with back-breaking work."

foundational biblical covenants: the Genesis Covenant of the Pieces (People), the Exodus Covenant of Sinai (Torah), and the Deuteronomy Covenant of Mount Grizim and Eval (Land).

When challenged, we must raise a strong voice of Jewish conscience and fight antisemitism in all its forms – whether directed at our peoplehood, ideology, or homeland. To be silent is to be complicit.

~~~~~

And yet, in my decades as a rabbi-spiritual activist, I have found that Jews by and large are afraid to stand up to antisemitism. Wherever we traveled, raising a voice of Jewish moral conscience, the Jewish community urged us to go home, claiming our protests would inspire greater antisemitism. Our response? Antisemitism is inspired by antisemites, not by those fighting antisemitism.

Still, there is a deep-seated feeling in our community that speaking out against antisemites attracts too much attention, compromising the safety of our community. In fact, the opposite is true: the more we speak out against antisemites, the more we are protected, rather than rendered vulnerable.

A fundamental principle of my Spiritual Activism is that while there is an imperative to speak out for the larger universal community, we should demand no less for ourselves than we demand for others. Speaking out for others carries relatively little risk and, moreover, brings the acclaim and approval of the larger community. But speaking out with equal intensity on behalf of our own interests touches upon our insecurities and heightened sensitivity to what others may think of us – insecurities and sensitivities that we, as diaspora Jews, have acquired and absorbed over the years.

וַנִּצְעַק אֶל־יהוה אֱלֹהֵי אֲבֹתֵינוּ, וַיִּשְׁמַע יהוה אֶת־קֹלֵנוּ, וַיַּרְא אֶת־עָנְיֵנוּ וְאֶת עֲמָלֵנוּ וְאֶת לַחֲצֵנוּ (דברים כו:ז).

וַנִּצְעַק אֶל יהוה אֱלֹהֵי אֲבֹתֵינוּ. כְּמָה שֶׁנֶּאֱמַר (שמות ב:כג): וַיְהִי בַיָּמִים הָרַבִּים הָהֵם וַיָּמָת מֶלֶךְ מִצְרַיִם, וַיֵּאָנְחוּ בְנֵי־יִשְׂרָאֵל מִן־הָעֲבוֹדָה וַיִּזְעָקוּ, וַתַּעַל שַׁוְעָתָם אֶל־הָאֱלֹהִים מִן הָעֲבֹדָה.

וַיִּשְׁמַע יהוה אֶת קֹלֵנוּ. כְּמָה שֶׁנֶּאֱמַר (שמות ב:כב): וַיִּשְׁמַע אֱלֹהִים אֶת־נַאֲקָתָם, וַיִּזְכֹּר אֱלֹהִים אֶת־בְּרִיתוֹ אֶת־אַבְרָהָם, אֶת־יִצְחָק וְאֶת־יַעֲקֹב.

וַיַּרְא אֶת עָנְיֵנוּ. זוֹ פְּרִישׁוּת דֶּרֶךְ אֶרֶץ, כְּמָה שֶׁנֶּאֱמַר (שמות ב:כה): וַיַּרְא אֱלֹהִים אֶת בְּנֵי־יִשְׂרָאֵל וַיֵּדַע אֱלֹהִים.

Vanitzak: Relief

Relief begins in earnest when Moses encounters the *s'neh* (burning bush). Why, out of all places, did God reveal himself to Moses through this medium? One possibility is that the experience seems to be a microcosm of revelation. Note the similarity in sound between *s'neh* and Sinai, the mountain where God speaks to the Jewish People. Indeed, the revelation at the *s'neh* and Sinai occurred in the same place: the desert of Horev. Both unfolded through the medium of fire. At the *s'neh*, the fire did not consume the bush. At Sinai, smoke and fire engulfed the entire mountain.

But the meaning of *s'neh* that resonates most powerfully sees the *s'neh* as symbolic not of Sinai but of God Himself. As long as Jews were enslaved, God could only reveal Himself in a lowly burning bush, suggesting that "I am with My people in their pain." God cannot be in a state of comfort, if you will, as long as His people are in distress. Revelation through the *s'neh* teaches that God is with us in the darkest moments and places.

Vanitzak: Relief

"And we cried out to the Lord, the God of our ancestors, and the Lord listened to our voice, and He saw our affliction, and our toil and our duress" (Deuteronomy 26:7).

וַנִּצְעַק - "**And we cried out to the Lord, the God of our ancestors**" - as it is said (Exodus 2:23), "And it was in those great days that the king of Egypt died and the Children of Israel sighed from the work and cried out, and their supplication went up to God from the work."

וַיִּשְׁמַע - "**And the Lord listened to our voice**" - as it is said (Exodus 2:24); "And God heard their groans and God remembered His covenant with Abraham and with Isaac and with Jacob."

וַיַּרְא אֶת עָנְיֵנוּ - "**And He saw our affliction**" - this refers to abstaining from intimate relations, as it is said (Exodus 2:25), "And God saw the Children of Israel and God knew."

וַנִּצְעַק אֶל ה' אֱלֹהֵי אֲבֹתֵינוּ - **And we cried out to the Lord, the God of our ancestors**: A person can only be helped if she or he is ready to help themselves. The first step to redemption is crying out, declaring we are ready to be free.

וַיִּשְׁמַע ה' אֶת קֹלֵנוּ - **And the Lord listened to our voice:** Hearing is external, listening internal. When counseling others, we should see the word WAIT in our minds. WAIT stands for "Why Am I Talking." In other words, the goal is to let the person in need show the way as the parent, sibling or counselor leans over, listening to what is being said and to what is not being said – to the verbal and non-verbal communication. Only then should one react. Here, the support text tells us that God shows the way. He is the ultimate listener.

וַיַּרְא אֶת עָנְיֵנוּ - **And He saw our affliction**: Seeing is not only ocular, but heartfelt; it is an exercise of empathy. Empathy is not sympathy. Sympathy is feeling distraught at the suffering of an other. Empathy is feeling the pain of the other as if it's ours.

וְאֶת עֲמָלֵנוּ. אֵלּוּ הַבָּנִים. כְּמָה שֶׁנֶּאֱמַר (שמות א:כב): כָּל־הַבֵּן הַיִּלּוֹד הַיְאֹרָה תַּשְׁלִיכֻהוּ וְכָל־הַבַּת תְּחַיּוּן.

וְאֶת לַחֲצֵנוּ. זֶה הַדְּחַק, כְּמָה שֶׁנֶּאֱמַר (שמות ג:ט): וְגַם־רָאִיתִי אֶת־הַלַּחַץ אֲשֶׁר מִצְרַיִם לֹחֲצִים אֹתָם.

וְאֶת עֲמָלֵנוּ - **And our travail:** The support text explains, "this [refers to the killing of the] sons." Greater than personal pain is seeing our children suffer. The support text recalls Pharaoh's decree that every boy born should be thrown in the Nile, but the girls will live.

One of the earliest moments of resistance was the midwives' refusal to follow Pharaoh's orders. One wonders, who were these midwives? Their identity is critical because they deserve a tremendous amount of credit. At great personal risk, they "did not do as the king of Egypt commanded them, but saved the boys."

Rashi insists that the midwives were Jewish women. Sforno disagrees. Rashi, living during the Crusades, could never imagine that gentiles would stand up against the Pharaoh and save Jews. Sforno similarly mirrors the time in which he lived. As part of Renaissance Italy in the fifteenth century, he was a universalist. He believed that gentiles would stand up and risk their lives to help Jews.

Without this watershed moment in our history of standing up in the face of evil, there might never have been a nation of Israel. Yet there is no consensus as to the identity of these heroines. Sometimes, it is God alone who really knows.

In my decades of spiritual activism, I've met extraordinary gentiles who stood with us courageously, like the elderly psychologist from Linz University whose name I unfortunately do not know. Having heard that Austrian police had encircled us with

וְאֶת עֲמָלֵנוּ - **"And our travail"** - this refers to the killing of the sons, as it is said (Exodus 1:22), "Every boy that is born, throw him into the Nile and every girl you shall allow to live."

וְאֶת לַחֲצֵנוּ - **"And our duress"** - this refers to the pressure, as it is said (Exodus 3:9), "And I also saw the duress that the Egyptians are applying on them."

guns drawn as we protested Pope John Paul II's embrace of Kurt Waldheim (June 1988), he made his way to our group, telling the police, "We did too little to save Jews during the Holocaust, I will not move from here until I know these men are safe."

Or Octavia, whom I met in 2015 at the AME Church in Charleston during our solidarity visit after nine parishioners were murdered in cold blood. Octavia was kind enough to give me a lift to a local synagogue so I could say Kaddish for my father who had recently died. Thanking her profusely, she said, "No need to thank, but I want you to know, Rabbi, had it been necessary, I would have carried you on my back so you could say a prayer for your father."

וְאֶת לַחֲצֵנוּ - **And our duress:** The attack against the Jews came from every direction. While Pharaoh commanded the midwives to kill the infant boys, he fully hoped, as the support text indicates, that the general populous would expand the decree and freely murder Jews. This was Pharaoh's *modus operandi* – he did not wish to be seen as anti-Jewish, even as he orchestrated the sweeping antisemitism. During the Shoah, this ploy was repeated. While leaders of the Third Reich were directly responsible for Kristallnacht, the Night of the Broken Glass, they tried to make it appear as if the attack was spontaneous, coming from grassroots Germans, angry that a junior German official had been killed in France. Antisemites often "kick the blame down"; our task is to go after the big guy, the leader at the top who bears the primary responsibility.

וַיּוֹצִאֵנוּ יהוה מִמִּצְרַיִם בְּיָד חֲזָקָה, וּבִזְרֹעַ נְטוּיָה, וּבְמֹרָא גָּדֹל, וּבְאֹתוֹת וּבְמֹפְתִים.

(דברים כו:ח).

וַיּוֹצִאֵנוּ יהוה מִמִּצְרַיִם. לֹא עַל־יְדֵי מַלְאָךְ, וְלֹא עַל־יְדֵי שָׂרָף, וְלֹא עַל־יְדֵי שָׁלִיחַ, אֶלָּא הַקָּדוֹשׁ בָּרוּךְ הוּא בִּכְבוֹדוֹ וּבְעַצְמוֹ. שֶׁנֶּאֱמַר (שמות יב:יב): וְעָבַרְתִּי בְאֶרֶץ־מִצְרַיִם בַּלַּיְלָה הַזֶּה, וְהִכֵּיתִי כָל־בְּכוֹר בְּאֶרֶץ מִצְרַיִם מֵאָדָם וְעַד־בְּהֵמָה, וּבְכָל־אֱלֹהֵי מִצְרַיִם אֶעֱשֶׂה שְׁפָטִים, אֲנִי יהוה.

וְעָבַרְתִּי בְאֶרֶץ־מִצְרַיִם בַּלַּיְלָה הַזֶּה – אֲנִי וְלֹא מַלְאָךְ; וְהִכֵּיתִי כָל־בְּכוֹר בְּאֶרֶץ־מִצְרַיִם. אֲנִי וְלֹא שָׂרָף; וּבְכָל־אֱלֹהֵי מִצְרַיִם אֶעֱשֶׂה שְׁפָטִים. אֲנִי וְלֹא הַשָּׁלִיחַ; אֲנִי יהוה. אֲנִי הוּא וְלֹא אַחֵר.

Vayotzi'enu: Freedom

וַיּוֹצִאֵנוּ ה' מִמִּצְרַיִם - **And the Lord took us out from Egypt:** When born, everything must be done for the new arrival. In fact, there is no life more helpless at birth than human life. So, too, with Am Yisrael. When coming into being, as emphasized in the support text, God and God alone unilaterally cared for us. In time, much like a child who matures, we, as a people, assumed greater responsibility. And so the name of Moses does not appear in the Haggadah: God did it all.

Millennia later, in the Purim Megillah story, God's name is not mentioned. Having matured, we're expected to do the bulk of the work. It must be added, however, that while God is then less visible, He is more present. Hence, the word *hamelech* in the Megillah, literally King Achashverosh, may refer to God, *HaMelech*, working in the background, helping weave the tapestry toward redemption. Indeed, there are *HaMelech* Megillot, whose every column (except the first) begin with the word *HaMelech* to underscore this very point.

~~~~~

While Moses' name is not mentioned in the Haggadah, as he is eclipsed by God who miraculously

Vayotzi'einu: Freedom - וַיּוֹצִאֵנוּ

"And the Lord took us out from Egypt with a mighty hand and with an outstretched arm and with great awe and with signs and with wonders" (Deuteronomy 26:8).

וַיּוֹצִאֵנוּ - **"And the Lord took us out from Egypt"** - not through an angel and not through a seraph and not through a messenger, but directly by the Holy One, blessed be He, Himself, as it is said (Exodus 12:12), "And I will pass through the Land of Egypt on that night and I will smite every firstborn in the Land of Egypt, from men to animals; and with all the gods of Egypt, I will make judgments, I am the Lord."

"And I will pass through the Land of Egypt" - I and not an angel. "And I will smite every firstborn" - I and not a seraph. "And with all the gods of Egypt, I will make judgments" - I and not a messenger. "I am the Lord" - I am He and there is no other.

intervened, his heroism should be remembered.

After being raised in the Egyptian palace, Moses goes into the field and sees an Egyptian smiting a Jew. In the words of the Torah, "He looked this way and that way, and when he saw there was no man [*ish*], he smote the Egyptian" (Exodus 2:12).

Taken literally, it seems that Moses looked to see if anyone was watching. With the coast clear, Moses defends the Jew. But this interpretation is difficult because, in the midst of a busy working field, it's doubtful that no one was there.

The Netziv, Rabbi Naftali Zvi Yehudah Berlin, in his *Ha'amek Davar*, reads this phrase differently. In his view, Moses, seeing a Jew beaten, looked to see if any Egyptian would stand up for him. Moses looks this way and that way but sees no one who seems to care. In the absence of Egyptian justice, Moses acts. Things are not so different today. All too frequently, the world is silent as Jews are attacked.

Rav Yaakov Zvi Mecklenberg, in his *Hak'tav v'Hakabbalah*, has another take. Moses knew that no Egyptian would come forward. He looked, however, to see whether any Jew would care enough to save his own brother. When no Jew did, Moses killed the Egyptian. Once again, this dynamic plays out today. Tragically, too often, Jews don't respond to the suffering of their fellow Jews.

There is yet another possible interpretation. Moses was raised in an Egyptian home but nursed by his biological Jewish mother. As a consequence, perhaps Moses was still unsure who he really was. When seeing an Egyptian smiting a Jew, he looked within himself to ascertain whether he should help the Egyptian or defend the Jew. Even more: The meaning of "he looked this way and that way" is that Moses looked within himself to see who he really was, Egyptian or Jewish. When he fully grasped that he had not firmly established his identity, he made a decision: He smote the Egyptian, symbolically eliminating a part of himself, declaring unequivocally that he was a Jew.

At a certain point, it's crucial for each of us to stop wavering and to stand up and identify ourselves boldly and clearly. When we find ourselves in a place where there is no person (*ish*), as so many of us often do, it's crucial that each of us steps up as Moses did to make the difference. To paraphrase our rabbis, in a place where there is no *ish*, stand up and be one.

After running for his life, making his way to Midian, Moses hears the voice of God from the burning *s'neh*: "Moses! Moses!" Heroically, Moses responds, "*Hineni* — here I am." In a certain sense, Moses' *hineni* is a response to the first question asked in the Torah. After Adam eats of the forbidden tree, God asks him, "*Ayeka? Where are you?*" Now, of course, the omnipotent, omnipresent God knew where Adam was. The question was deeper. With Adam defying God, God asks, Where are you, what have you done?

Adam is not just Adam. Adam represents the nature of the human being. To all people, at all times, God calls out, "*Ayeka?* Where are you? Are you doing your share to redeem the Jewish People, to fix the world? In that sense, *ayeka* is a calling that comes from within us. It is the inner voice of God, encouraging, imploring, insisting we do more.

The proper response to "*Ayeka?* Where are you?" is "*Hineni!* Here I am!" Moses, unlike Adam, answered God's question correctly. The power of *hineni* is that it is the promise to be present, to show up. While Moses, like many leaders, questions whether he can succeed, his *hineni* ultimately prevails.

Each one of us, too, has the capacity to do the same – to hear the call of *ayeka* and respond, "Here I am," ready to do, to give, to sacrifice, to make a difference. To declare with humble strength, "*Hineni!*"

After Moses convinces the Jewish elders to join him in demanding of Pharaoh to free the Jews, he and his brother Aaron arrive at Pharaoh's palace alone. Where were the elders? Rashi's explanation: "One by one, they dropped out." Only Moses and Aaron had the courage to show up; they stood alone.

The great leaders like Moses and Aaron speak out as lonely voices, setting their minds to do all they can to navigate the choppy waters and bring the reluctant public along.

בְּיָד חֲזָקָה. זוֹ הַדֶּבֶר, כְּמָה שֶׁנֶּאֱמַר (שמות ט:ג): הִנֵּה יַד־יְהוָה הוֹיָה בְּמִקְנְךָ אֲשֶׁר בַּשָּׂדֶה, בַּסּוּסִים, בַּחֲמֹרִים, בַּגְּמַלִּים, בַּבָּקָר וּבַצֹּאן, דֶּבֶר כָּבֵד מְאֹד.

וּבִזְרֹעַ נְטוּיָה. זוֹ הַחֶרֶב, כְּמָה שֶׁנֶּאֱמַר (דברי הימים א כא:טז): וְחַרְבּוֹ שְׁלוּפָה בְּיָדוֹ, נְטוּיָה עַל־יְרוּשָׁלָיִם.

וּבְמוֹרָא גָּדֹל. זוֹ גִּלּוּי שְׁכִינָה, כְּמָה שֶׁנֶּאֱמַר (דברים ד:לד): אוֹ הֲנִסָּה אֱלֹהִים לָבוֹא לָקַחַת לוֹ גוֹי מִקֶּרֶב גּוֹי בְּמַסֹּת בְּאֹתֹת וּבְמוֹפְתִים וּבְמִלְחָמָה וּבְיָד חֲזָקָה וּבִזְרוֹעַ נְטוּיָה וּבְמוֹרָאִים גְּדֹלִים כְּכֹל אֲשֶׁר־עָשָׂה לָכֶם יְהוָה אֱלֹהֵיכֶם בְּמִצְרַיִם לְעֵינֶיךָ.

The Haggadah now adopts two interpretive approaches to this verse's end.

First Interpretive Approach: God's Intercession throughout Jewish History

בְּיָד חֲזָקָה, וּבִזְרֹעַ נְטוּיָה, וּבְמוֹרָא גָּדֹל - With a mighty hand… and with an outstretched arm… and with great awe: While the first approach is generally understood to illustrate God's unilateral punishing of the Egyptians (pestilence, slaying of the firstborn, blood) an alternative interpretation may be considered that reads the end of this verse in a way that goes beyond the Egypt story.

Note that the Haggadah defines the first three phrases as "pestilence," "sword" and "God's revelation." There is an event going back to the days of King David hundreds of years after the exodus from Egypt, that deals with this progression (II Samuel 24). After David mistakenly counts Israel, God punishes King David and Am Yisrael with pestilence. Matters become worse when an angel is seen

First Interpretive Approach:
God's Intercession throughout Jewish History

בְּיָד חֲזָקָה - "With a mighty hand" - this refers to the pestilence, as it is said (Exodus 9:3); "Behold the hand of the Lord is upon your herds that are in the field, upon the horses, upon the donkeys, upon the camels, upon the cattle and upon the flocks, there will be a very heavy pestilence."

וּבִזְרֹעַ נְטוּיָה - "And with an outstretched arm" - this refers to the sword, as it is stated (I Chronicles 21:16); "And his sword was drawn in his hand, leaning over Jerusalem."

וּבְמֹרָא גָּדֹל - "And with great awe" - this refers to the revelation of God's omnipresence, as it is stated (Deuteronomy 4:34), "Has any alien god taken for himself a nation from within a nation with miracles, with signs and with wonders and with war and with a mighty hand and with an outstretched arm and with great and awesome acts, like all that the Lord, your God, did for you in Egypt in front of your eyes?"

stretching a sword over Jerusalem, bent on its destruction. At the last moment, "God reveals Himself" by interceding and stopping the imminent attack, saving Jerusalem. Soon after, King David purchases Jerusalem.

On its face, the story is similar to the *Akeidah*, the Binding of Isaac. There, Abraham stretches out his knife to kill his son, only to have an angel of God intervene at the last moment. Soon after, Abraham purchases the holy city of Chevron. Both narratives are followed with parallel phrases – Abraham (Genesis) and David (1 Kings) grew old, becoming preoccupied with matters related to their successor; in Abraham's case, the marriage of Isaac, in David's case, the king who would follow his rulership.

וּבְאֹתוֹת. זֶה הַמַּטֶּה, כְּמָה שֶׁנֶּאֱמַר (שמות ד:יז): וְאֶת־הַמַּטֶּה הַזֶּה תִּקַּח בְּיָדֶךָ, אֲשֶׁר תַּעֲשֶׂה־בּוֹ אֶת־הָאֹתוֹת.

וּבְמֹפְתִים. זֶה הַדָּם, כְּמָה שֶׁנֶּאֱמַר (יואל ג:ג): וְנָתַתִּי מוֹפְתִים בַּשָּׁמַיִם וּבָאָרֶץ –

כשאומר דם ואש ותימרות עשן, ישפוך באצבעו מן הכוס מעט יין.

דָּם וָאֵשׁ וְתִימְרוֹת עָשָׁן.

וּבְאֹתוֹת - **And with signs:** The Haggadah's progression of pestilence, sword, and God's revelation is followed by interpreting the *ot* (sign) as a *mateh*, a rod, symbol of God's power.

וּבְמֹפְתִים - **And with wonders:** Even as God steps in, it is only a matter of time until savage enemies attempt to attack, destroy and annihilate the Jewish people. For me, the imagery of the Haggadah with its support text explicating wonders as "blood and fire and a pillar of smoke" may evoke remembrances of the Holocaust, when our blood was spilled as our lives were taken in gas chambers, leading to our being cast into the oven fire with its accompanying smoke.

Just a few years after the Shoah, a wondrous intervention – with God's help, the State of Israel is born. Here, God no longer acts unilaterally. Having matured as a people, we are expected to partner with God to realize the dream of the Jewish State. Thus, "blood" "fire" "smoke" may represent in a dramatically different way, the battles Israel fought and continues to fight to defend itself. As God through the prophet Joel declared: "On that day, [I shall lay waste the enemy]…because of the innocent Jewish blood they spilled… But Judah shall be forever settled, Jerusalem to the end of time" (4:18-20).

From this perspective, the spilling of wine from the Seder cup as we call out "blood, and fire, and a pillar of smoke" may symbolize for our generation the spilling of Jewish blood when we were victimized during the Shoah, and the spilling of blood over the years as thousands of soldiers and victims of terror gave and lost their lives for Israel.

~~~~~

While nothing, even the establishment of Israel, is worth the murder of the six million, there is some connection between the two. Former prime minister Menachem

וּבְאֹתוֹת - "And with signs" - this refers to the staff, as it is stated (Exodus 4:17); "And this staff you shall take in your hand, with which you will perform signs."

וּבְמֹפְתִים - "And with wonders" - this refers to the blood, as it is stated (Joel 3:3); "And I will place my wonders in the skies and in the earth:

When saying "blood and fire and pillars of smoke" we dip a finger in the second cup of wine, removing for each a drop.

Blood ~ And Fire ~ And Pillars of Smoke"

Begin said it well: Standing before the first gathering of survivors at Jerusalem's Western Wall, he cried out with deep emotion, "*mir zenen da* – we are here." With all my heart and soul, I believe that the modern State of Israel would have been born even if there was no Shoah; in the same breath, there never would have been a Shoah had the State of Israel then existed.

Here, my thoughts are with my father, of blessed memory, who was raised in the town of Oświęcim, which ultimately became the notorious Auschwitz death camp. In 1959, he was one of the first to return to Poland to visit the remnants of Jewish communities that remained after the Shoah. Overcome by what he saw there and seeking a measure of comfort and healing, he flew to Israel for the first time. While in Israel he composed a beautiful poem that speaks of the interfacing of the Holocaust and the reborn State of Israel.

In his poem, my father pictures himself standing on a hill in the Auschwitz death camp overlooking the barracks, surrounded by white snow, ash, and bone. Recalling the question of the prophet Ezekiel, my father also asks, "Can these bones live?" As if in a vision, there is a great noise and shaking. Bones come together with bones, covered by sinew and flesh and skin. Breath enters them and they live. They stand up on their feet, come out of their graves, and are brought to the Land of Israel.

The scene then shifts from darkness to light, death to life. My father now finds himself standing on a mountaintop in Jerusalem. Below, the vast host of the Jewish people is spread out – in schoolrooms, cities, factories, villages – in peace, and yes, also in battle. My father concludes his poem with this prayer: "God, remember the souls of the departed, and guard over the resurrected children of Israel in the Land of Israel."

דבר אחר: מכות

דָּבָר אַחֵר:

בְּיָד חֲזָקָה – שְׁתַּיִם,

וּבִזְרֹעַ נְטוּיָה – שְׁתַּיִם,

וּבְמֹרָא גָּדֹל – שְׁתַּיִם,

וּבְאֹתוֹת – שְׁתַּיִם,

וּבְמֹפְתִים – שְׁתַּיִם.

Second Interpretive Approach: Ten Plagues

בְּיָד חֲזָקָה… וּבִזְרֹעַ נְטוּיָה… וּבְמֹרָא גָּדֹל… וּבְאֹתוֹת… וּבְמֹפְתִים - With a mighty hand…and with an outstretched arm…and with great awe.. and with signs… and with wonders: The second interpretive approach focuses on the plagues and only the plagues unleashed on the Egyptians. At the outset, they are paired: A mighty hand makes two of the plagues, outstretched arm, another two. All told, five descriptions, 10 *makkot*.

A good exercise for Seder attendees is to try to decipher how the pairing works – that is, what is the connection between blood and frogs? Lice and beasts? Pestilence and boils? Hail and Locusts? Darkness and the Slaying of the Firstborn?

Second Interpretive Approach: Ten Plagues

Another explanation:

בְּיָד חֲזָקָה - "With a mighty hand" corresponds to two plagues;

"and with an outstretched arm" corresponds to two plagues;

"and with great awe" corresponds to two plagues;

"and with signs" corresponds to two plagues;

"and with wonders" corresponds to two plagues.

אֵלּוּ עֶשֶׂר מַכּוֹת שֶׁהֵבִיא הַקָּדוֹשׁ בָּרוּךְ הוּא עַל־הַמִּצְרִים בְּמִצְרַיִם, וְאֵלּוּ הֵן:

כשמונים את המכות ואת הסימנים דצ"ך אד"ש באח"ב, מטפטפים עם האצבע מעט יין.

דָּם

צְפַרְדֵּעַ

כִּנִּים

עָרוֹב

דֶּבֶר

שְׁחִין

בָּרָד

אַרְבֶּה

חֹשֶׁךְ

מַכַּת בְּכוֹרוֹת

אֵלּוּ עֶשֶׂר מַכּוֹת - **These are the ten plagues that the Holy One, blessed be He, brought on the Egyptians in Egypt and they are:** Although the plagues may seem like random punishments, they are actually a divine plan to teach the Egyptians fundamental lessons. For example, the first plague of water turning into blood can, as the Midrash points out, be seen as an attack on the Egyptian god: the Nile River. The point of this plague was to demonstrate to the Egyptians the impotency of their god.

Alternatively, the plague of blood can be viewed as a measure-for-measure punishment. Since the Egyptians drowned Jewish children, shedding their blood in water, their water was turned into blood.

The Maharal (Rabbi Judah Loew ben Bezalel, ca. 1512–1609)

Ten Plagues

These are the ten plagues that the Holy One, blessed be He, brought on the Egyptians in Egypt and they are:

When reciting the plague and its mnemonic, we dip a finger into the cup of wine, removing for each a drop

Blood

Frogs

Lice

The Mixture of Wild Animals

Pestilence

Boils

Hail

Locusts

Darkness

Slaying of the Firstborn

The story of Genesis is the story of God unleashing His power to create the world "with ten sayings" in the words of the Rabbis. The narrative of the ten plagues deals with the world unraveling on all levels. As creation was carefully carried out by God, so, too, were the plagues a carefully designed plan by God to undo part of that creation that had gone wrong.

insists that the plagues reveal God's unlimited power. The first three (blood, frogs, and lice) are attacks from below – turning the depths of the earth and sea against the Egyptians. The next three (beasts, pestilence, and boils) are attacks from the ground level. And the last three before the final plague of the firstborn (hail, locusts, and darkness) emerge from the heavens.

רַבִּי יְהוּדָה הָיָה נוֹתֵן בָּהֶם סִמָּנִים: דְּצַ"ךְ עֲדַ"שׁ בְּאַחַ"ב.

Plagues and Spilling Drops of Wine

The most commonly offered reason for spilling wine when listing the ten plagues and their mnemonic, relates to wine, especially red wine, being a symbol of blood. When recalling the punishment meted out to the Egyptians, wine is spilled as a reminder that the loss of any life, even enemy life, is not to be celebrated. More expansively, perhaps it refers to the distress, even in self-defense, of killing our enemy. As Golda Meir once said, "We cannot forgive them [the Arabs] for forcing us to kill their children."

After October 7, the spilling of wine may also symbolize our disgust for the barbaric Hamas murderers, rapists and decapitators, for losing their image of God, every shred of their humanity – if you will, losing and spilling their own blood (see Radak, Genesis 9:6).

As pointed out, the first spilling of wine when reciting "blood and fire and a pillar of smoke" may refer to the spilling of Jewish blood.

Limiting the Number of Plagues

רַבִּי יְהוּדָה הָיָה נוֹתֵן בָּהֶם סִמָּנִים: דְּצַ"ךְ עֲדַ"שׁ בְּאַחַ"ב - **Rabbi Yehuda would give [the plagues] mnemonics: DETZACH ADASH BE'ACHAV:** Perhaps concerned with the brutality of the plagues, Rabbi Yehuda seems to offer a softer approach, understanding them in three triplets, culminating with the slaying of the first born. Note that each triplet moves from the outer places in Egypt to inner places – the river turning into blood, to the frogs that swarmed into Egyptian homes, to locusts, which attacked the very bodies of the Egyptians. One would have expected that the fourth plague somehow would be more severe, and yet it is not. *Arov*, the mixture of animals, primarily manifests itself in the fields; pestilence comes indoors; boils affect Egyptian bodies. The pattern is repeated in the

Limiting the Number of Plagues

Rabbi Yehuda would give the plagues mnemonics: *Detzach* the Hebrew initials of the first three plagues, *Adash* the Hebrew initials of the second three plagues, *Be'achav* the Hebrew initials of the last four plagues .

last triplet, from the outer hail to the indoor locust, to darkness, so dark the Egyptians were immobilized, unable to move.

In fact, some claim there were only three main plagues, the third, sixth and ninth – those that attacked the Egyptians directly. Indeed, the Torah has Moses issuing a warning in the first two of each triplet, with the third happening without warning – the warning being implicit in the first two.

Only when refusing to change their ways does the slaying of the firstborn occur. This was a focused response, what is called in modern times a "targeted killing," as the firstborn were the Egyptian priests, the wicked visionaries responsible for advising Pharaoh and planning the brutal enslavement of the Jews. Hence, they alone are attacked.

מנין

רַבִּי יוֹסֵי הַגְּלִילִי אוֹמֵר: מִנַּיִן אַתָּה אוֹמֵר שֶׁלָּקוּ הַמִּצְרִים בְּמִצְרַיִם עֶשֶׂר מַכּוֹת וְעַל הַיָּם לָקוּ חֲמִשִּׁים מַכּוֹת?

בְּמִצְרַיִם מַה הוּא אוֹמֵר? וַיֹּאמְרוּ הַחַרְטֻמִּם אֶל-פַּרְעֹה, אֶצְבַּע אֱלֹהִים הִוא (שמות ח:טו). וְעַל הַיָּם מָה הוּא אוֹמֵר? וַיַּרְא יִשְׂרָאֵל אֶת-הַיָּד הַגְּדֹלָה אֲשֶׁר עָשָׂה יְהוָה בְּמִצְרַיִם, וַיִּירְאוּ הָעָם אֶת-יְהוָה, וַיַּאֲמִינוּ בַּיהוָה וּבְמֹשֶׁה עַבְדּוֹ (שמות יד:לא).

כַּמָּה לָקוּ בְאֶצְבַּע? עֶשֶׂר מַכּוֹת. אֱמוֹר מֵעַתָּה: בְּמִצְרַיִם לָקוּ עֶשֶׂר מַכּוֹת וְעַל הַיָּם לָקוּ חֲמִשִּׁים מַכּוֹת.

Expanding the Number of Plagues

מִנַּיִן - **Rabbi Yossi Haglili, Rabbi Eliezer, Rabbi Akiva:** Here begin three of the strangest teachings in the Haggadah, with each of these great rabbis one-upping the other, insisting that in Egypt God brought more plagues – ten or forty or fifty, while at the sea, the numbers quintupled – fifty, two hundred, two hundred fifty. Not coincidentally, these positions are juxtaposed to Rabbi Yehuda's mnemonic, which may be limiting the number of plagues. The pushback is expanding the number of plagues, seeing in the ten not less, but more.

My sense, too, is that no matter how supernatural an historical event, in time people look back and see it as part of a natural happening. The plagues, as mentioned by British Chief Rabbi Dr. J.H. Hertz in his Bible commentary, could very well have occurred when the Nile became especially polluted during the summer months, turning the waters heavily red (*dam*). Through a natural process, this led to swarms of frogs (*tz'fardeya*), and lice (*kinim*), a mixture of beasts (*arov*) and pestilence (*dever*) swamping the area, ultimately infecting Egyptians with boils (*sh'chin*). In a natural hailstorm (*barad*), locusts (*arbeh*) descended so thickly it led to a fog of darkness (*choshech*) hovering everywhere, making it impossible to see.

Even the splitting of the sea is understood by Rashbam as a result of a strong east wind. In his words: "God brought about the marvelous event in a natural way. He caused

Expanding the Number of Plagues - מִנַּיִן

רַבִּי יוֹסֵי הַגְּלִילִי - Rabbi Yossi HaGelili says, "From where can you derive that the Egyptians were struck with ten plagues in Egypt and struck with fifty plagues at the Sea?

In Egypt, what does it state? 'Then the magicians said unto Pharaoh: "This is the finger of God' (Exodus 8:15). And at the Sea, what does it state? 'And Israel saw the Lord's great hand that he used upon the Egyptians, and the people feared the Lord; and they believed in the Lord, and in Moses, His servant' (Exodus 14:31).

How many were they struck with the finger? Ten plagues. You can say from here that in Egypt, they were struck with ten plagues and at the Sea, they were struck with fifty plagues."

a strong east wind to blow, which dried up and congealed the waters."

Precisely because the plagues could be explained away naturally, the Rabbis in the Haggadah, like a pendulum swinging in the extreme opposite direction, insisted that they were supernatural, so supernatural that they were multiples, many multiples of what the naked eye could see. God's involvement was everywhere.

Not coincidentally, these rabbis insist that at the sea the hand of God was fivefold more. In Egypt, Jews were passive, God is the sole Actor. At the sea, Jews became involved. They were personally invested as they jumped in, trying to swim across. Only then did God intervene, splitting the waters. When invested in an enterprise, one may more clearly realize God's critical role every step of the way and hence perceive more miracles unfolding. And, as Rabbi Ahron Soloveichik suggests, only at the sea did they sing. Song is spontaneous, coming from the inner heart. Only when our ancestors were actively involved did they raise their voices in poetic melody.

The Hebrew word "*nes*" (miracle) says it all. *Nes* literally means a banner; a banner is symbolic of something beyond itself. The power of the *nes* is looking at what appear to be natural phenomena and seeing within them the supernatural hand of God.

רַבִּי אֱלִיעֶזֶר אוֹמֵר: מִנַּיִן שֶׁכָּל־מַכָּה וּמַכָּה שֶׁהֵבִיא הַקָּדוֹשׁ בָּרוּךְ הוּא עַל הַמִּצְרִים בְּמִצְרַיִם הָיְתָה שֶׁל אַרְבַּע מַכּוֹת?

שֶׁנֶּאֱמַר (תהלים עח:מט): יְשַׁלַּח־בָּם חֲרוֹן אַפּוֹ, עֶבְרָה וָזַעַם וְצָרָה, מִשְׁלַחַת מַלְאֲכֵי רָעִים. עֶבְרָה – אַחַת,

וָזַעַם – שְׁתַּיִם,

וְצָרָה – שָׁלֹשׁ,

מִשְׁלַחַת מַלְאֲכֵי רָעִים – אַרְבַּע.

אֱמוֹר מֵעַתָּה: בְּמִצְרַיִם לָקוּ אַרְבָּעִים מַכּוֹת וְעַל הַיָּם לָקוּ מָאתַיִם מַכּוֹת.

רַבִּי עֲקִיבָא אוֹמֵר: מִנַּיִן שֶׁכָּל־מַכָּה וּמַכָּה שֶׁהֵבִיא הַקָּדוֹשׁ בָּרוּךְ הוּא עַל הַמִּצְרִים בְּמִצְרַיִם הָיְתָה שֶׁל חָמֵשׁ מַכּוֹת?

שֶׁנֶּאֱמַר (תהלים עח:מט): יְשַׁלַּח־בָּם חֲרוֹן אַפּוֹ, עֶבְרָה וָזַעַם וְצָרָה, מִשְׁלַחַת מַלְאֲכֵי רָעִים.

חֲרוֹן אַפּוֹ – אַחַת,

עֶבְרָה – שְׁתַּיִם,

וָזַעַם – שָׁלֹשׁ,

וְצָרָה – אַרְבַּע,

מִשְׁלַחַת מַלְאֲכֵי רָעִים – חָמֵשׁ.

אֱמוֹר מֵעַתָּה: בְּמִצְרַיִם לָקוּ חֲמִשִּׁים מַכּוֹת וְעַל הַיָּם לָקוּ חֲמִשִּׁים וּמָאתַיִם מַכּוֹת.

רַבִּי אֱלִיעֶזֶר - Rabbi Eliezer says, "From where can you derive that every plague that the Holy One, blessed be He, brought upon the Egyptians in Egypt was composed of four plagues?

As it is said (Psalms 78:49): 'He sent upon them the fierceness of His anger, wrath, and fury, and trouble, a sending of messengers of evil.' 'Wrath' corresponds to one; 'and fury' brings it to two; 'and trouble' brings it to three; 'a sending of messengers of evil' brings it to four.

You can say from here that in Egypt, they were struck with forty plagues and at the Sea, they were struck with two hundred plagues."

רַבִּי עֲקִיבָא - Rabbi Akiva says, says, "From where can you derive that every plague that the Holy One, blessed be He, brought upon the Egyptians in Egypt was composed of five plagues?

As it is said (Psalms 78:49): 'He sent upon them the fierceness of His anger, wrath, and fury, and trouble, a sending of messengers of evil.'

'The fierceness of His anger' corresponds to one;

'wrath' brings it to two;

'and fury' brings it to three;

'and trouble' brings it to four;

'a sending of messengers of evil' brings it to five.

You can say from here that in Egypt, they were struck with fifty plagues and at the Sea, they were struck with two hundred and fifty plagues."

דיינו

כַּמָּה מַעֲלוֹת טוֹבוֹת לַמָּקוֹם עָלֵינוּ!

אִלּוּ הוֹצִיאָנוּ מִמִּצְרַיִם וְלֹא עָשָׂה בָהֶם שְׁפָטִים, דַּיֵּנוּ.

אִלּוּ עָשָׂה בָהֶם שְׁפָטִים, וְלֹא עָשָׂה בֵאלֹהֵיהֶם, דַּיֵּנוּ.

אִלּוּ עָשָׂה בֵאלֹהֵיהֶם, וְלֹא הָרַג אֶת־בְּכוֹרֵיהֶם, דַּיֵּנוּ.

אִלּוּ הָרַג אֶת־בְּכוֹרֵיהֶם וְלֹא נָתַן לָנוּ אֶת־מָמוֹנָם, דַּיֵּנוּ.

אִלּוּ נָתַן לָנוּ אֶת־מָמוֹנָם וְלֹא קָרַע לָנוּ אֶת־הַיָּם, דַּיֵּנוּ.

אִלּוּ קָרַע לָנוּ אֶת־הַיָּם וְלֹא הֶעֱבִירָנוּ בְתוֹכוֹ בֶּחָרָבָה, דַּיֵּנוּ.

Dayenu

Many feel that redemption requires complete change. *Dayenu* reminds us that redemption or self-improvement is a process. Each line of the *Dayenu* makes this very point. For example, we say that had God taken us out of Egypt and not executed judgment upon the Egyptians, *Dayenu* – it would have been enough. One should be perpetually moving toward self-improvement. The process is sometimes more valuable than the end result.

The process is often gradual. Note that the Dayenu is made up of fifteen *ma'alot* – fifteen steps that we ascend one by one, as each is an accomplishment on its own. This reminds us that redemption comes slowly. So, too, in our personal lives – each small step along the way in our own process of self-improvement is a Dayenu milestone, worthy of recognition in its own right.

I remember, during some of the

Dayenu - דיינו

כַּמָה מַעֲלוֹת טוֹבוֹת לַמָּקוֹם עָלֵינוּ - How many degrees of good did the God bestow upon us!

If God had taken us out of Egypt but not made judgements on them; it would have been enough.

If God had made judgments on them but had not made them on their gods; it would have been enough.

If God had made them on their gods but had not killed their firstborn; it would have been enough.

If God had killed their firstborn but had not given us their money; it would have been enough.

If God had given us their money but had not split the Sea for us; it would have been enough.

If God had split the Sea for us but had not taken us through it on dry land; it would have been enough.

most difficult times of the Soviet Jewry Movement, standing outside Soviet government buildings and chanting *Dayenu*. Our message was clear. We were saying "Enough of the suffering that our sisters and brothers in the Soviet Union are experiencing." We would spell out what we meant using the structure of the *Dayenu* itself. "Had the Soviets only prevented the baking of *matzot*, and not imprisoned Prisoners of Zion, it would have been enough…."

But in reality *Dayenu* teaches the opposite message. It tells us that had God only done one favor for us, it would have been enough. *Dayenu* is not a song of complaint; it is rather a song of acknowledging God.

Dayenu is an artful way to bring the learning in the Maggid section to a higher level. As we complete an in-depth study of the exodus, we cannot contain ourselves as we say: Thank you, God. Thank you for allowing us to ascend and come step by step closer to full redemption.

אִלּוּ הֶעֱבִירָנוּ בְתוֹכוֹ בֶּחָרָבָה וְלֹא שִׁקַּע צָרֵנוּ בְּתוֹכוֹ דַּיֵּנוּ.

אִלּוּ שִׁקַּע צָרֵנוּ בְּתוֹכוֹ וְלֹא סִפֵּק צָרְכֵּנוּ בַּמִּדְבָּר אַרְבָּעִים שָׁנָה דַּיֵּנוּ.

אִלּוּ סִפֵּק צָרְכֵּנוּ בַּמִּדְבָּר אַרְבָּעִים שָׁנָה וְלֹא הֶאֱכִילָנוּ אֶת־הַמָּן דַּיֵּנוּ.

אִלּוּ הֶאֱכִילָנוּ אֶת־הַמָּן וְלֹא נָתַן לָנוּ אֶת־הַשַּׁבָּת, דַּיֵּנוּ.

אִלּוּ נָתַן לָנוּ אֶת־הַשַּׁבָּת, וְלֹא קֵרְבָנוּ לִפְנֵי הַר סִינַי, דַּיֵּנוּ.

אִלּוּ קֵרְבָנוּ לִפְנֵי הַר סִינַי, וְלֹא נָתַן לָנוּ אֶת־הַתּוֹרָה. דַּיֵּנוּ.

אִלּוּ נָתַן לָנוּ אֶת־הַתּוֹרָה וְלֹא הִכְנִיסָנוּ לְאֶרֶץ יִשְׂרָאֵל, דַּיֵּנוּ.

אִלּוּ הִכְנִיסָנוּ לְאֶרֶץ יִשְׂרָאֵל וְלֹא בָנָה לָנוּ אֶת־בֵּית הַבְּחִירָה דַּיֵּנוּ.

If God had taken us through it on dry land but had not pushed down our enemies in the Sea ; it would have been enough.

If God had pushed down our enemies in the Sea but had not supplied our needs in the wilderness for forty years; it would have been enough.

If God had supplied our needs in the wilderness for forty years but had not fed us the manna; it would have been enough.

If God had fed us the manna but had not given us the Shabbat; it would have been enough.

If God had given us the Shabbat but had not brought us close to Mount Sinai; it would have been enough.

If God had brought us close to Mount Sinai but had not given us the Torah; it would have been enough.

If God had given us the Torah but had not brought us into the land of Israel; it would have been enough.

If God had brought us into the land of Israel but had not built us the 'Chosen House' the Temple; it would have been enough.

עַל אַחַת, כַּמָּה וְכַמָּה, טוֹבָה כְפוּלָה וּמְכֻפֶּלֶת לַמָּקוֹם עָלֵינוּ:

שֶׁהוֹצִיאָנוּ מִמִּצְרַיִם, וְעָשָׂה בָהֶם שְׁפָטִים, וְעָשָׂה בֵאלֹהֵיהֶם, וְהָרַג אֶת־בְּכוֹרֵיהֶם, וְנָתַן לָנוּ אֶת־מָמוֹנָם, וְקָרַע לָנוּ אֶת־הַיָּם, וְהֶעֱבִירָנוּ בְתוֹכוֹ בֶּחָרָבָה, וְשִׁקַּע צָרֵינוּ בְּתוֹכוֹ, וְסִפֵּק צָרְכֵּנוּ בַּמִּדְבָּר אַרְבָּעִים שָׁנָה, וְהֶאֱכִילָנוּ אֶת־הַמָּן, וְנָתַן לָנוּ אֶת־הַשַּׁבָּת, וְקֵרְבָנוּ לִפְנֵי הַר סִינַי, וְנָתַן לָנוּ אֶת־הַתּוֹרָה, וְהִכְנִיסָנוּ לְאֶרֶץ יִשְׂרָאֵל, וּבָנָה לָנוּ אֶת־בֵּית הַבְּחִירָה לְכַפֵּר עַל־כָּל־עֲוֹנוֹתֵינוּ.

Al Achat Kamah v'Kamah

עַל אַחַת, כַּמָּה וְכַמָּה - **How much more so are the favors that God doubled and quadrupled upon us:** This paragraph repeats the *Dayenu* with an important caveat: Whereas every sentence of *Dayenu* includes a hypothetical of what God did not do for us, here, only God's positive contributions are listed. This may be the meaning of the words in our paragraph's preamble "double and quadrupled." The first double is the goodness of God's acts; the second double is the goodness that we do not recall what God did not do for us.

In this spirit I recite every morning this personal prayer:

How Much More So - עַל אַחַת, כַּמָּה וְכַמָּה

עַל אַחַת, כַּמָּה וְכַמָּה - How much more so are the favors that God doubled and quadrupled upon us:

He took us out of Egypt, And made judgments with them, And made them with their gods, And killed their firstborn, And gave us their money, And split the Sea for us, And brought us through it on dry land, And pushed down our enemies in the Sea, And supplied our needs in the wilderness for forty years, and fed us the manna, And gave us the Shabbat, And brought us close to Mount Sinai, And gave us the Torah, And brought us into the land of Israel And built us the 'Chosen House' the Temple to atone upon all of our sins.

My Beloved Love Precious One of my soul	יְדִידִי אֲהוּבִי מַחְמַד נַפְשִׁי	Yedidi ahuvi, machmad nafshi:
Please help me thank You for all the blessings you've bestowed upon me	אָנָּא עֲזֹר לִי לְהוֹדוֹת לְךָ עַל כָּל הַבְּרָכוֹת שֶׁהֶעֱנַקְתָּ לִי	ana azor li l'hodot lecha al kol hab'rachot shehe'enakta li,
And not allow my heart to be weighed down by blessings I lack.	וְלֹא לָתֵת אֶת לִבִּי עַל בְּרָכוֹת שֶׁחֲסֵרוֹת לִי.	v'lo latet et libi al b'rachot shechaserot li.
My Beloved Love Precious One of my soul	יְדִידִי אֲהוּבִי מַחְמַד נַפְשִׁי	Yedidi ahuvi, machmad nafshi:
Please help me embrace with love the day before me A holy day overflowing with value and meaning.	אָנָּא עֲזֹר לִי לְקַבֵּל בְּאַהֲבָה אֶת הַיּוֹם שֶׁעוֹמֵד לְפָנַי יוֹם קָדוֹשׁ וְרַב עֶרֶךְ.	ana azor li lekabel be'ahavah et hayom she'omed lefanai yom kadosh v'rav orech.

REENACTING

We recall the exodus from Egypt in every day's prayers. At the Seder, we take it to the next level, telling the story, studying its meaning, and then, as Rabban Gamliel teaches, reenacting the exodus history by pointing to the key Passover symbols on the Seder table.

Truth be told, nothing in Jewish history is remembered unless ritualized. We remember our victory over Haman through the ritual of the Purim festival. So, too, Chanukah is part of our consciousness because of the menorah ritual. Similarly, the biblical Egypt story is infused into our consciousness because of the Passover Seder ritual, reenacting the event, "as if we were enslaved, as if we were redeemed."

In this spirit, I have argued that the only way the Holocaust will be remembered is through ritual. And so, we at the Bayit wrote and published a Haggadah for the Yom Hashoah Seder. That Haggadah is divided into four sections — physical destruction; spiritual devastation; murder of children; and resistance. It includes rituals of reenactment: eating potato peels; burning paper with the Hebrew *alef-bet* written on it; sending children to a roped-off corner of the room; and hearing the words of Ezekiel's prophecy that the valley of dry bones will rise to become a strong army in Israel.

In Israel today, the modern ritual of standing still as the siren sounds on Yom Hashoah in memory of the six million helps assure they will not be forgotten. In the same breath, the siren sounded on Yom Hazikaron in memory of the soldiers who sacrificed their lives as well as for victims of terror forever keeps their memories alive.

פסח מצה ומרור

רַבָּן גַּמְלִיאֵל הָיָה אוֹמֵר: כָּל שֶׁלֹּא אָמַר שְׁלֹשָׁה דְבָרִים אֵלּוּ בַּפֶּסַח,
לֹא יָצָא יְדֵי חוֹבָתוֹ, וְאֵלּוּ הֵן:

פֶּסַח,

מַצָּה,

וּמָרוֹר.

מצביע על הזרוע ואין לאחוז אותו ביד:

פֶּסַח שֶׁהָיוּ אֲבוֹתֵינוּ אוֹכְלִים בִּזְמַן שֶׁבֵּית הַמִּקְדָּשׁ הָיָה קַיָּם,
עַל שׁוּם מָה?

עַל שׁוּם שֶׁפָּסַח הַקָּדוֹשׁ בָּרוּךְ הוּא עַל בָּתֵּי אֲבוֹתֵינוּ בְּמִצְרַיִם, שֶׁנֶּאֱמַר (שמות יב:כו):
וַאֲמַרְתֶּם זֶבַח-פֶּסַח הוּא לַיהוה,
אֲשֶׁר פָּסַח עַל-בָּתֵּי בְנֵי-יִשְׂרָאֵל בְּמִצְרַיִם בְּנָגְפּוֹ אֶת-מִצְרַיִם,
וְאֶת-בָּתֵּינוּ הִצִּיל, וַיִּקֹּד הָעָם וַיִּשְׁתַּחֲווּ.

Rabban Gamliel's Three Things

The custom is to point to the roasted bone (*zeroa*) and lift the matza and bitter herbs (*maror*) when reciting their respective paragraphs. The pointing and lifting, my father once explained to me, was meant to build into the "saying" mandate of Rabban Gamliel, a gesture of reenactment.

פסח מצה ומרור - Pesach, Matza, Maror: The sequence seems out of order. *Maror* should be first, as it reenacts bitter slavery; in time God intervened, passing over Jewish homes as we consumed the paschal lamb, leading to our eating the *matzot* as we fled Egypt.

But the Haggadah's order may remind us that the pattern of the exodus would be repeated throughout Jewish history. *Maror* is mentioned after the paschal lamb, because our coming forth from Egypt did not end all of our bitterness. In time, in a different place, facing a different

Reenacting - פסח מצה ומרור

Rabban Gamliel's Three Things

רַבָּן גַּמְלִיאֵל הָיָה אוֹמֵר - Rabban Gamliel was accustomed to say, "Anyone who has not said these three things on Pesach has not fulfilled her or his obligation, and these are them: the Pesach sacrifice, matza, and maror."

Pesach Sacrifice - פֶּסַח

Pointing to the roasted bone (zeroa) representative of the Pesach sacrifice, we say:

The **Pesach sacrifice** that our ancestors would eat when the Temple existed, for the sake of what was it?

To commemorate that the Holy One, blessed be He, passed over the homes of our ancestors in Egypt, as it is said (Exodus 12:27), "And you shall say: 'It is the Pesach sacrifice to the Lord, for that He passed over the homes of the Children of Israel in Egypt, when He smote the Egyptians, and our homes He saved.' And the people bowed their heads and prostrated themselves."

enemy, we would be victimized again.

Note too, that each of these symbols has a deeper meaning. Such is the way of ritual – elastic, always open to new interpretation.

Pesach may be a play on the word "*pise'ach* – one who is lame." Who is free? Who is it that passes over, almost flying in freedom? One who is sensitive to those who are less fortunate, those with disabilities, those who cannot walk on their own, dependent on others for help.

Matza can be connected to the word *matzui*, literally meaning to be present. When fleeing Egypt, we hardly had the time to feel what was unfolding. Matza as *matzui* reminds us as we reenact the exodus to pause, stop, take in the moment.

Maror, as already noted, may be associated with the word "*mohr*," frankincense used in the Temple to sweeten the sacrificial offering. Who is free? Only one who is able to turn bitterness into sweetness, paving the way to build on the past – a glorious inviting future.

מרימים את המצות ומראים אותן מסביב:

מַצָּה זוֹ שֶׁאָנוּ אוֹכְלִים, עַל שׁוּם מַה?

עַל שׁוּם שֶׁלֹּא הִסְפִּיק בְּצֵקָם שֶׁל אֲבוֹתֵינוּ לְהַחֲמִיץ עַד שֶׁנִּגְלָה עֲלֵיהֶם מֶלֶךְ מַלְכֵי הַמְּלָכִים, הַקָּדוֹשׁ בָּרוּךְ הוּא, וּגְאָלָם, שֶׁנֶּאֱמַר (שמות יב:לט): וַיֹּאפוּ אֶת־הַבָּצֵק אֲשֶׁר הוֹצִיאוּ מִמִּצְרַיִם עֻגֹת מַצּוֹת, כִּי לֹא חָמֵץ, כִּי גֹרְשׁוּ מִמִּצְרַיִם וְלֹא יָכְלוּ לְהִתְמַהְמֵהַּ, וְגַם־צֵדָה לֹא־עָשׂוּ לָהֶם.

מרימים את המרור ומראים אותו מסביב:

מָרוֹר זֶה שֶׁאָנוּ אוֹכְלִים, עַל שׁוּם מַה?

עַל שׁוּם שֶׁמֵּרְרוּ הַמִּצְרִים אֶת־חַיֵּי אֲבוֹתֵינוּ בְּמִצְרַיִם, שֶׁנֶּאֱמַר (שמות א:יד): וַיְמָרֲרוּ אֶת־חַיֵּיהֶם בַּעֲבֹדָה קָשָׁה, בְּחֹמֶר וּבִלְבֵנִים וּבְכָל־עֲבֹדָה בַּשָּׂדֶה אֵת כָּל־עֲבֹדָתָם אֲשֶׁר־עָבְדוּ בָהֶם בְּפָרֶךְ.

Matza - מַצָּה

Lifting the matza we say:

This matza that we are eating, for the sake of what is it?

To commemorate that our ancestors' dough was not yet able to rise, before the Ruler of rulers, the Holy One, blessed be He, revealed Himself to them and redeemed them, as it is said (Exodus 12:39), "And they baked the dough which they brought out of Egypt into matza cakes, since it did not rise; because they were expelled from Egypt, and could not tarry, nor did they make provisions for themselves."

Maror - מָרוֹר

Lifting the maror we say:

This maror bitter greens that we are eating, for the sake of what is it?

To commemorate that the Egyptians embittered the lives of our ancestors in Egypt, as it is said (Exodus 1:14), "And they made their lives bitter with hard service, in mortar and in brick, and in all manner of service in the field; in all their service, wherein they made them serve with rigor."

בְּכָל־דּוֹר וָדוֹר חַיָּב אָדָם לִרְאוֹת אֶת־עַצְמוֹ כְּאִלּוּ הוּא יָצָא מִמִּצְרַיִם,
שֶׁנֶּאֱמַר (דברים ו:כג): וְהִגַּדְתָּ לְבִנְךָ בַּיּוֹם הַהוּא לֵאמֹר,
בַּעֲבוּר זֶה עָשָׂה יהוה לִי בְּצֵאתִי מִמִּצְרָיִם.
לֹא אֶת־אֲבוֹתֵינוּ בִּלְבַד גָּאַל הַקָּדוֹשׁ בָּרוּךְ הוּא,
אֶלָּא אַף אוֹתָנוּ גָּאַל עִמָּהֶם, שֶׁנֶּאֱמַר:
וְאוֹתָנוּ הוֹצִיא מִשָּׁם, לְמַעַן הָבִיא אוֹתָנוּ,
לָתֶת לָנוּ אֶת־הָאָרֶץ אֲשֶׁר נִשְׁבַּע לַאֲבֹתֵינוּ.

B'chol Dor Vador

בְּכָל־דּוֹר וָדוֹר - **In each and every generation, a person should see her or himself as if they left Egypt:** Maimonides replaces the word "*lir'ot* – to see" with "*l'har'ot* – to show oneself," that is, to personally replicate the story. The Haggadah makes this point by declaring "it was not our ancestors alone who the Holy One, blessed be he, redeemed, but we ourselves were redeemed with them." We were not there, but we act out the story as if we were.

Over the years, an empty chair was set up representing prisoners of Zion in the Former Soviet Union,

In Every Generation

בְּכָל־דּוֹר וָדוֹר - In each and every generation, a person should see him or herself as if they left Egypt, as it is stated (Exodus 13:8), "And you shall explain to your child on that day: For the sake of this, did the Lord do this for me in my going out of Egypt." Not only our ancestors did the Holy One, blessed be He, redeem, but rather also us together with them did He redeem, as it is stated (Deuteronomy 6:23), "And He took us out from there, in order to bring us in, to give us the land which He swore unto our fathers."

and most recently, Israeli hostages with whom we empathize. Today, the chair awaits the freedom of the hostages, including Edan Alexander, a *chayal boded*, an American lone soldier who enlisted in the IDF, putting his life on the line for Israel, for all of us. He did so not out of obligation, but out of choice. This is a time around the Seder table to raise our voice and, in the spirit of Moses speaking truth to power, call out "Let Our Hostages Go Now." Participants may consider reciting the prayer on the following page for all those affected by the war.

A Prayer for Israel
Please Please Please   אָנָּא אָנָּא אָנָּא

Master of the world	רִבּוֹנוֹ שֶׁל עוֹלָם
Please please please	אָנָּא אָנָּא אָנָּא
Do not forsake us	אַל תַּעַזְבֵנוּ

Master of the world	רִבּוֹנוֹ שֶׁל עוֹלָם
Please please please	אָנָּא אָנָּא אָנָּא
Stand with us	עֲזֹר לָנוּ

Bless our people with victory	לְבָרֵךְ עַמֵּנוּ בְּנִצָּחוֹן
Bring our soldiers home, wholly	לְהַחֲזִיר חַיָּלֵינוּ לְשָׁלוֹם
Free our captives to their families	לְשַׁחְרֵר חֲטוּפֵינוּ לְמִשְׁפְּחוֹתֵיהֶם
Return the evacuees to their homes	לְהָשִׁיב הַמְפֻנִּים לְבָתֵּיהֶם

Heal the wounded fully	לְרַפֵּא פְּצוּעֵינוּ בִּשְׁלֵמוּת
Lay the slain to rest gently	לִקְבֹּר חֲלָלֵינוּ בַּעֲדִינוּת
Comfort the mourners sensitively	לְנַחֵם אֲבֵלֵינוּ בִּרְגִישׁוּת
Please please please	אָנָּא אָנָּא אָנָּא

Master of the world	רִבּוֹנוֹ שֶׁל עוֹלָם
Please please please	אָנָּא אָנָּא אָנָּא
Do not forget us	אַל תִּשְׁכָּחֵנוּ

Master of the world	רִבּוֹנוֹ שֶׁל עוֹלָם
Please please please	אָנָּא אָנָּא אָנָּא
Help us transform –	עֲזֹר לָנוּ לַהֲפֹךְ

Division to unity	פֵּרוּד לְאִחוּד
Bitterness to friendship	מְרִירוּת לְרֵעוּת
Distance to closeness	רָחוֹק לְקָרוֹב
Hatred to love	שִׂנְאָה לְאַהֲבָה

Sorrow to solace	צָרָה לִרְוָחָה
Darkness to light	אֲפֵלָה לְאוֹרָה
Assault to redemption	מִתְקָפָה לִגְאֻלָּה
Now, swiftly and soon	הַשְׁתָּא בַּעֲגָלָא וּבִזְמַן קָרִיב

Please please please	אָנָּא אָנָּא אָנָּא

THANKSGIVING

The Maggid reaches its crescendo as we offer praises and thanksgiving (*shevach v'hoda'ah*) to the Lord.

There are two types of thank-yous.

The first is perfunctory, thanking another for opening the door for us or giving up his or her seat. Truth be told, we would have survived without that gesture.

The second is far deeper. It is the *hoda'ah* associated with the word *modim*, literally making an admission that we could not have done it without you. The latter is much more difficult to offer as it includes a recognition of limitation, of dependency upon others and, more importantly, on God.

חצי הלל

מגביהים את הכוס, מכסים את המצות ואומרים:

לְפִיכָךְ אֲנַחְנוּ חַיָּבִים לְהוֹדוֹת, לְהַלֵּל, לְשַׁבֵּחַ, לְפָאֵר, לְרוֹמֵם, לְהַדֵּר, לְבָרֵךְ, לְעַלֵּה, וּלְקַלֵּס לְמִי שֶׁעָשָׂה לַאֲבוֹתֵינוּ וְלָנוּ אֶת־כָּל־הַנִּסִּים הָאֵלּוּ: הוֹצִיאָנוּ מֵעַבְדוּת לְחֵרוּת, מִיָּגוֹן לְשִׂמְחָה, וּמֵאֵבֶל לְיוֹם טוֹב, וּמֵאֲפֵלָה לְאוֹר גָּדוֹל, וּמִשִּׁעְבּוּד לִגְאֻלָּה. וְנֹאמַר לְפָנָיו שִׁירָה חֲדָשָׁה: הַלְלוּ יָהּ.

מניחים את הכוס ומגלים את המצות:

הַלְלוּ עַבְדֵי יהוה, הַלְלוּ אֶת־שֵׁם יהוה.
יְהִי שֵׁם יהוה מְבֹרָךְ מֵעַתָּה וְעַד־עוֹלָם.
מִמִּזְרַח־שֶׁמֶשׁ עַד־מְבוֹאוֹ מְהֻלָּל שֵׁם יהוה.
רָם עַל־כָּל־גּוֹיִם יהוה, עַל הַשָּׁמַיִם כְּבוֹדוֹ.

Lefichach

לְפִיכָךְ - **Therefore:** Overflowing with gratitude, we pour forth, using every variant of the word thank you: "We are therefore obligated to thank, praise, laud, glorify, exalt, beautify, bless, raise high…" This leads in turn to poetic expressions of our journey to freedom: "from sorrow to joy, from mourning to celebration, from darkness to great light, and from servitude to redemption."

Hallelu

Here, we begin reciting the first two paragraphs of the Hallel service, lifted from the Book of Psalms, dealing with the exodus.

אֶת־שֵׁם ה׳ - **The Name of the Lord:** *Shem Hashem* spells out our mission – as enunciated by Abraham, our first patriarch, to bring the Name of the Lord into the world. In time, God presents its specifics, "[To] observe the way of the Lord, to perform righteousness and justice."

First Half of Hallel

We lift the cup as the matzot are covered and say:

לְפִיכָךְ - Therefore we are obligated to thank, praise, laud, glorify, exalt, beautify, bless, raise high, and acclaim He who made all these miracles for our ancestors and for us: He brought us out from slavery to freedom, from sorrow to joy, from mourning to celebration, from darkness to great light, and from servitude to redemption. And let us sing a new song before Him, Hallelujah!

The cup is put down, the matzot uncovered:

הַלְלוּ - Hallelu!
Praise, servants of the Lord,
praise the name of the Lord.
May the Name of the Lord be blessed from now and forever.
From the rising sun to its setting, praise be the name of the Lord.
Above all nations is the Lord, His honor is above the heavens.

Note, the key word of the Kaddish prayer is *Shmeih*, a composite of *Shem Hashem*. Here, the mourner reciting the prayer declares, his/her beloved brought the Name of God into the world, leaving the world a better place. Note, too, the Kaddish is in the future tense. In other words, the legacy, the impact, the influence of the beloved who has passed from this world – the *Shem Hashem* promulgated – will continue to make a difference for years and decades and more to come.

מֵעַתָּה וְעַד עוֹלָם - **From now and forever:** God's involvement knows no boundaries of time; it is eternal – was, is, will always be.

מִמִּזְרַח-שֶׁמֶשׁ - **From the rising sun to its setting, praise be the name of the Lord:** Witnessing the rising and setting of the sun, one feels the awesome holiness of God. One of the most beautiful presentations of such a moment is Chaim Nachman Bialik's description of the sun setting as the Shabbat begins. I have vivid memories of my mother, dressed in white – in the upstate New York camp my parents ran – singing these beautiful words welcoming the Sabbath bride.

מִי כַּיהוָה אֱלֹהֵינוּ הַמַּגְבִּיהִי לָשָׁבֶת.
הַמַּשְׁפִּילִי לִרְאוֹת בַּשָּׁמַיִם וּבָאָרֶץ.
מְקִימִי מֵעָפָר דָּל,
מֵאַשְׁפֹּת יָרִים אֶבְיוֹן.
לְהוֹשִׁיבִי עִם־נְדִיבִים,
עִם נְדִיבֵי עַמּוֹ.
מוֹשִׁיבִי עֲקֶרֶת הַבַּיִת,
אֵם־הַבָּנִים שְׂמֵחָה, הַלְלוּ־יָהּ. (תהלים קיג)

The sun has set from the tops of the trees	הַחַמָּה מֵרֹאשׁ הָאִילָנוֹת נִסְתַּלְקָה.	Hachama merosh ha'ilanot nistakla
Come, let us go out to greet the Shabbat bride	בֹּאוּ וְנֵצֵא לִקְרַאת שַׁבָּת הַמַּלְכָּה.	Bo'u ve'netzei likrat Shabbat hamalkah
She is already descending, the holy, the blessed	הִנֵּה הִיא יוֹרֶדֶת הַקְּדוֹשָׁה הַבְּרוּכָה.	Hinei hi yoredet hak'dosha hab'rucha
And with her angels, a host of peace and rest	וְעִמָּהּ מַלְאָכִים צְבָא שָׁלוֹם וּמְנוּחָה:	Ve'imah mal'achim tz'va shalom umnucha
Come, come, O Queen	בֹּאִי בֹּאִי הַמַּלְכָּה.	Bo'i, bo'i hamalkah
Come, come, O Bride	בֹּאִי בֹּאִי הַכַּלָּה.	Bo'i, bo'i hakallah
Welcome to you, ministering angels, angels of peace.	שָׁלוֹם עֲלֵיכֶם מַלְאֲכֵי הַשָּׁלוֹם:	Shalom Aleichem mal'achei hashalom

מִי כַּה' אֱלֹהֵינוּ - Who is like the Lord, our God, enthroned on high; Who looks down upon the heavens and the earth? God is transcendent, above, beyond, as expressed in the formula God minus world equals God (G-w=G). In the same breath, God has imminence, He is near, close, reflected in the formula world minus God equals nothing (w-G=nothing). In other words, God doesn't create the world and withdraw as the Deists proclaim but is involved in every minute detail.

מְקִימִי מֵעָפָר דָּל - He lifts the poor out of the dirt: We take off our masks and say it as it is: O God, thank you for lifting us from the lowly dust. Perhaps this speaks to extreme moments when we feel close to death, close to being covered by earth – only to be swept up at the last

Who is like the Lord, our God, enthroned on high;
Who looks down upon the heavens and the earth?
He lifts the poor out of the dust;
from the refuse piles, He raises the destitute.
To seat them with the nobles,
with the nobles of God's people.
God seats the childless woman at home
As a joyful mother of children.
Hallelujah! (Psalms 113)

moment to live and flourish.

מֵאַשְׁפֹּת יָרִים אֶבְיוֹן - **From the refuse piles, He raises the destitute:** The first daily task of the priest is to remove the remains of the ashes of yesterday's sacrificial service (*t'rumat hadeshen*). Too often, those who rise to important, lofty positions separate themselves from the people and withdraw from everyday menial tasks. The Torah – through the laws of *t'rumat hadeshen* – insists on a different model, emphasizing ongoing commitment through quotidian responsibilities.

A story reflects this point. Years ago, a husband and wife appeared before Rabbi Mordechai Gifter, *rosh yeshivah* of Telz, asking him to rule on a family dispute. The husband, who was studying at Rabbi Gifter's yeshiva, felt that it was beneath his dignity as a Torah scholar to take out the garbage. His wife felt otherwise. The rabbi concluded that while the husband should in fact help his wife, he had no religio-legal obligation to remove the refuse. The next morning, before the early prayer service, the *rosh yeshivah* knocked at the couple's door. Startled, the young man asked him in. "No," he responded, "I've not come to socialize, but to take out your garbage. You may believe it's beneath your dignity, but it's not beneath mine."

מוֹשִׁיבִי עֲקֶרֶת הַבַּיִת - **God seats the childless woman at home as a joyful mother of children:** When all seems hopeless, God has the capacity to make possible the impossible. As we emerged from the depths of Egyptian slavery to reach high, so, too, throughout our history, throughout our lives.

Well before its time, this psalm shows an understanding of those struggling to conceive. The Seder, often attended by children, many children, is the perfect time to be especially sensitive to those who are not so blessed.

בְּצֵאת יִשְׂרָאֵל מִמִּצְרַיִם,
בֵּית יַעֲקֹב מֵעַם לֹעֵז.
הָיְתָה יְהוּדָה לְקָדְשׁוֹ,
יִשְׂרָאֵל מַמְשְׁלוֹתָיו.

B'tzeit Yisrael

בְּצֵאת יִשְׂרָאֵל מִמִּצְרַיִם, בֵּית יַעֲקֹב מֵעַם לֹעֵז - **When Israel went out of Egypt, The house of Jacob from a people of foreign speech:** Alienated and separated from his brother Esau for more than two decades, Jacob – accompanied by his family – makes final preparations to rendezvous with him (Esau), when suddenly, the Torah tells us, he (Jacob) is alone. Alone? Does this mean Jacob abandoned his family when they needed him most? Rashbam radically suggests, that this is precisely what happened.

Up to this point, when faced with a challenge, Jacob always ran. He ran after he took the blessings from Esau. He hardly protested when he found Leah and not Rachel the morning after his wedding. He tolerated his father-in-law Laban's dishonesty in their business dealings. And he fled from Laban's house in the dead of night.

Just hours before confronting Esau, it seemed that Jacob finally had no choice but to stand strong as he prepared his family and larger camp to face Esau. At the last moment, however, Rashbam insists, Jacob separated from his family, as he once again was running away. As much as Jacob had carefully prepared for the inevitable confrontation with Esau, his nature took over – he saw fleeing as the only solution.

For Rashbam, the mysterious being who struggled with Jacob that night was an emissary of God sent to Jacob. In the end, the emissary wounds Jacob, making it difficult for him to walk. This was God's way of telling Jacob that he no longer could run. When facing an adversary, it's important to stand fast.

Thus, the next day when Esau sees Jacob standing tall with pride,

When Israel Went Out of Egypt

בְּצֵאת יִשְׂרָאֵל מִמִּצְרָיִם - When Israel went out of Egypt,
The house of Jacob from a people of foreign speech.
Judah became God's holy one,
Israel, God's dominion.

unwilling to run and be pushed around, he gains respect for him and embraces him. Sometimes, the only way to gain respect from others is if one first has self-respect. According to this view, that new resolve on Jacob's part caused Esau to embrace Jacob rather than fight him.

Interestingly, after struggling with the mysterious man, Jacob is given another name, Israel. No longer is he only Jacob, from the word *akev* (heel), one who, when challenged, turns and even runs on his heels. Now he is also Israel, meaning the fighter (*sarita*), who has the strength to stand strong and prevail.

As reflected in our psalm, Jacob retains both names, which departs from the previous pattern when other Torah figures' names are changed (Berachot 12b). For example, Abraham and Sarah's old names, Avram and Sarai, are never used again after the divine bestowing of their new names.

The message of the Jacob-Israel dual name is clear: both the "Jacob" approach of avoiding conflict, negotiating and compromising with the enemy, and the "Israel" approach of more assertive, strident action are crucial. They work in tandem, each complementing the other to achieve the goal of securing the safety of our people.

הָיְתָה יְהוּדָה לְקָדְשׁוֹ - **Judah became God's holy one:** Judah became God's holy one when he and his progeny consistently led the Jewish people, thereby sanctifying God's name. To wit: Only after Nachshon from the tribe of Judah jumps into the sea does it split. And the tribe of Judah is first, showing the way as Israel treks through the desert. Being first requires a readiness to take chances. This was Judah, the epitome of heroic courage, a model of kiddush Hashem.

הַיָּם רָאָה וַיָּנֹס,
הַיַּרְדֵּן יִסֹּב לְאָחוֹר.
הֶהָרִים רָקְדוּ כְאֵילִים,
גְּבָעוֹת כִּבְנֵי צֹאן.

מַה-לְּךָ הַיָּם כִּי תָנוּס, הַיַּרְדֵּן – תִּסֹּב לְאָחוֹר.
הֶהָרִים – תִּרְקְדוּ כְאֵילִים, גְּבָעוֹת כִּבְנֵי-צֹאן.

מִלִּפְנֵי אָדוֹן חוּלִי אָרֶץ,
מִלִּפְנֵי אֱלוֹהַּ יַעֲקֹב.

הַהֹפְכִי הַצּוּר אֲגַם-מָיִם,
חַלָּמִישׁ לְמַעְיְנוֹ-מָיִם. (תהלים קיד)

הַיָּם רָאָה וַיָּנֹס - **The sea saw and fled… What is happening to you, sea, that you are fleeing?… From before the Master, tremble O earth:** Note the Psalmist's formulation: First a statement of fact. Then, in the spirit of the Haggadah, a question: Why, O sea, did you split? Finally, the answer: It all happened at God's behest. In the end, whatever we do, whatever unfolds is only with God's indispensable help.

הַיַּרְדֵּן יִסֹּב לְאָחוֹר - **The Jordan, that you ran backwards:** We recall not only the exodus and the splitting of the sea, but the splitting of the Jordan River as we entered Israel forty years later. Here again, the Land of Israel plays a central role in the Egypt story, reminding us that it is not enough to

The sea saw and fled,
The Jordan turned to the rear.
The mountains danced like rams,
The hills like young sheep.

What is happening to you, sea, that you are fleeing,
Jordan, that you ran backwards;
Mountains, that you danced like rams,
Hills like young sheep?

From before the Master, tremble O earth,
From the presence of the Lord of Jacob.

Who transformed the rock into a pool of water,
The flint into a spring. (Psalms 114)

"leave from," but we must also "enter into" a new noble future.

הַהֹפְכִי הַצּוּר אֲגַם־מָיִם - **Who transformed the rock into a pool of water**: Not only does God have the capacity to turn water into dry land, but the reverse – God can turn dry land, even rocks, into water. My dear friend Dr. Gaya Aranoff Bernstein, in her magnificent volume *Psalmsongs*, sees this as an expression of hope that God do His share to cure cancer. On the words "transformed the rock into... water," she writes: "to melt a rock-hard cancer mass converting it to water…," a profound expression of shaking free from the shackles of sickness.

כוס שניה

מגביהים את הכוס ומברכים ברכת גאל ישראל.

בָּרוּךְ אַתָּה יהוה אֱלֹהֵינוּ מֶלֶךְ הָעוֹלָם, אֲשֶׁר גְּאָלָנוּ וְגָאַל אֶת־אֲבוֹתֵינוּ מִמִּצְרַיִם, וְהִגִּיעָנוּ הַלַּיְלָה הַזֶּה לֶאֱכָל־בּוֹ מַצָּה וּמָרוֹר. כֵּן יהוה אֱלֹהֵינוּ וֵאלֹהֵי אֲבוֹתֵינוּ יַגִּיעֵנוּ לְמוֹעֲדִים וְלִרְגָלִים אֲחֵרִים הַבָּאִים לִקְרָאתֵנוּ לְשָׁלוֹם, שְׂמֵחִים בְּבִנְיַן עִירֶךָ וְשָׂשִׂים בַּעֲבוֹדָתֶךָ. וְנֹאכַל שָׁם מִן הַזְּבָחִים וּמִן הַפְּסָחִים אֲשֶׁר יַגִּיעַ דָּמָם עַל קִיר מִזְבַּחֲךָ לְרָצוֹן, וְנוֹדֶה לְךָ שִׁיר חָדָשׁ עַל גְּאֻלָּתֵנוּ וְעַל פְּדוּת נַפְשֵׁנוּ. בָּרוּךְ אַתָּה יהוה, גָּאַל יִשְׂרָאֵל.

מברכים ושותים את הכוס בהסיבת שמאל.

בָּרוּךְ אַתָּה יהוה, אֱלֹהֵינוּ מֶלֶךְ הָעוֹלָם בּוֹרֵא פְּרִי הַגָּפֶן.

Asher Ge'alanu

גָּאַל יִשְׂרָאֵל - **Blessed are You, Lord… who redeemed Israel**: Raising the second cup of wine, we recite the blessing of redemption, interweaving the ritual of the exodus with the hope it will be a precursor to peace in Jerusalem, Israel and the world. Still, its conclusion, "Blessed are You, O Lord, who redeemed Israel," is the final line of the Haggadah's discussion of our past redemption from Egypt.

בּוֹרֵא פְּרִי הַגָּפֶן - **Who creates the fruit of the vine**: We celebrate our past redemption by raising a cup of wine – symbol of joy – drinking while reclining.

Second Cup of Wine

We raise the cup and recite the Maggid's final blessing of past redemption.

אֲשֶׁר גְּאָלָנוּ - Blessed are You, Lord our God, Ruler of the universe, who redeemed us and redeemed our ancestors from Egypt, and brought us on this night to eat matza and maror; So too, Lord our God, and God of our ancestors, bring us to other appointed times and holidays that will come to greet us in peace, joyful in the building of Your city and happy in Your worship; that we shall eat there from the offerings and from the Pesach sacrifices, the blood of which shall reach the wall of Your altar for favor, and we shall thank You with a new song upon our redemption and upon the restoration of our souls. Blessed are you, Lord, who redeemed Israel.

We say the blessing over wine and drink, reclining to the left.

Blessed are You, Lord our God, who creates the fruit of the vine.

PRESENT

The Seder meal and its introductory ritual elevate the memory of the exodus to a new level. Beyond simply telling, relearning, and reenacting the events that unfolded for our ancestors, we actively live them in the present by ritually ingesting the symbols of that experience and reflecting on how events of today may echo things past.

רָחְצָה

נוטלים את הידים ומברכים:

בָּרוּךְ אַתָּה יהוה, אֱלֹהֵינוּ מֶלֶךְ הָעוֹלָם, אֲשֶׁר קִדְּשָׁנוּ בְּמִצְוֹתָיו וְצִוָּנוּ עַל נְטִילַת יָדָיִם.

Rachtza

Food is essential to life. And so, as already noted, we wash hands before eating as water celebrates life. Water, too, reminds us of the necessity to suffuse our lives with love. Indeed, in the Bible, water is frequently associated with love.

✦ Isaac's wife, Rebecca, is found at the well.

✦ Jacob meets Rachel as flocks gather around the water.

✦ Moses comes in contact with his wife to be, Tziporah, after saving her and her siblings at the river.

Not coincidentally, water and love have much in common. Without

RACHTZAH

We wash the hands and make a blessing.

עַל נְטִילַת יָדָיִם - Blessed are You, Lord our God, Ruler of the Universe, who has sanctified us with His commandments and has commanded us on the washing of the hands.

water, one cannot live. Without love, life is virtually impossible. But, like water, love can be fleeting. As water slips through one's fingers, so too can love; if not nurtured, it can easily slip away.

As Rabba Sara Hurwitz points out, "The very word *mayim* can be vocalized *mah im* (what if). It is a nexus of possibility where complete transformation is suddenly imaginable." *Mah im*: ritually washing our hands can serve as an external manifestation of an internal message charging all of us to push away hate with love.

מוֹצִיא מַצָּה

לוקחים את שלושת המצות ביד ומברכים "המוציא". מניחים את המצה התחתונה ומברכים על המצה העליונה והאמצעית "על אכילת מצה".

בָּרוּךְ אַתָּה יהוה, אֱלֹהֵינוּ מֶלֶךְ הָעוֹלָם, הַמּוֹצִיא לֶחֶם מִן הָאָרֶץ.

בָּרוּךְ אַתָּה יהוה, אֱלֹהֵינוּ מֶלֶךְ הָעוֹלָם, אֲשֶׁר קִדְּשָׁנוּ בְּמִצְוֹתָיו וְצִוָּנוּ עַל אֲכִילַת מַצָּה.

יבצע מן העליונה השלמה ומן הפרוסה, ויטבלם במלח, ויאכל בהסיבה.

Motzi Matza

In reality, *Motzi Matza* comprises two distinct sections of the Haggadah. *Motzi* refers to the blessing *Hamotzi lechem min ha'aretz* said over the two and a half matzot on the table (the other half was set aside for the afikoman). Thus, the blessing is recited over the minimal two full pieces.

Matza refers to the second blessing, *al achilat matza*, recited over the top one and a half matzot (the bottom matza having been put down before the *al achilat matza* blessing is said). Thus, it is recited over less than the minimal two pieces. What does all of this symbolize? While *hamotzi* is said before *al achilat matza* in deference to it being the more standard (*tadir*) blessing, their juxtaposition calls for analyzing *al achilat matza* first.

עַל אֲכִילַת מַצָּה - **On the eating of matzah:** Reciting this blessing over fewer than two loaves sends a message that our struggles, symbolized by the less than two complete *matzot*, continue today. In many ways, it parallels breaking the glass under the *chuppah*. It is not only the destruction of the Temples that we remember then, but the six million temples murdered during the Holocaust… and Israeli soldiers and victims of terror throughout the decades, reaching the horror of horrors on October 7.

הַמּוֹצִיא לֶחֶם מִן הָאָרֶץ - **Who brings forth bread from the ground:** The hamotzi said over the two full matzot (actually two and a half) reminds us never to give up. Homiletically, this teaches that the central idea of breaking the matzot, like the breaking of the glass under the chuppah

MOTZI MATZA

We lift the matza in the order we placed them, the broken one between the two whole ones and recite the first blessing, "ha-motzi." We then place the lower matza on the table, and, lifting the top one-and-a-half pieces, recite the second blessing, "al achilat matza."

הַמּוֹצִיא - Blessed are You, Lord our God, Ruler of the Universe, who brings forth bread from the ground.

עַל אֲכִילַת מַצָּה - Blessed are You, Lord our God, Ruler of the Universe, who has sanctified us with His commandments and has commanded us on the eating of matza.

We eat from the top and middle matza, sprinkled with salt, while reclining.

– mystically the *sh'virat hakeilim*, breaking of the vessels – is the *tikkun*, our resolve to fix the shattered pieces, turning servitude into freedom, night into day, agony into joy. Such is the miracle of rebirth. No matter the brokenness, redemption is built in.

More broadly, in times of challenge, rather than ask "Why?" a better question is "What now?" "Why" relates to the past, which cannot be undone; it is philosophical, concerning which God understands and we do not. "What now" is a future-oriented, pragmatic query that we, on some level, can control.

Not only should we ask, "What can we do about it?" but we should ask, "What will God do about it?" God gives us inner strength to overcome, to do things we never thought we could.

Sometimes I think there are no great people in this world – only great challenges. Faced with these challenges, God from above helps us to do the impossible. And as God is limitless, so are we, created in the image of God, given the strength to reach toward limitlessness.

When confronted with inexplicable suffering, we all ought to remember the words of Esther Wachsman, mother of Nachshon, the young Israeli soldier murdered by Arab terrorists in the early 1990s. Asked how she continued on, Esther, paraphrasing Rabbi Yosef Dov Soloveitchik, said, "I had to ask myself, will I be a victim of my fate, or will I initiate a new destiny?"

This idea has helped me face many challenges in my life. The motto I strive to live by is *never allow what you cannot do to control what you can do.*

מָרוֹר

לוקחים מרור, טובלים בחרוסת, מנערים את החרוסת, מברכים "על אכילת מרור" ואוכלים ללא הסבה.

בָּרוּךְ אַתָּה יהוה, אֱלֹהֵינוּ מֶלֶךְ הָעוֹלָם,
אֲשֶׁר קִדְּשָׁנוּ בְּמִצְוֹתָיו וְצִוָּנוּ
עַל אֲכִילַת מָרוֹר.

Maror

Maror (bitter herbs) is dipped into *charoset*, representing the mortar used by Jewish slaves to build Egyptian pyramids right there in the open. In this sense, it also refers to the bystanders, the masses of Egyptians who stood by, failing to intervene. In fact, Jews may have suffered more deeply from the bystanders who remained silent as the persecution intensified.

Elie Wiesel makes this point in his *Legends of our Time*. There, he argues that the victims of the Holocaust were more broken by the silence of the onlookers than the brutality of the murderers. The victims knew their foes – they had come to expect nothing from the evil Nazis. It was the mute non-response of those who chose to remain uninvolved that broke them.

Today, we expect nothing from evil terrorists like Hamas and Hezbollah and the Iranian Mullahs. However, to paraphrase Wiesel, it is the cruel silence and indifference of the bystanders who should know better. Those "whom we believe are our friends" are the ones that cruelly

MAROR

We take the maror, dip it into charoset. We recite the following blessing, and then eat without reclining.

עַל אֲכִילַת מָרוֹר - Blessed are You, Lord our God, Ruler of the Universe, who has sanctified us with His commandments and has commanded us on the eating of maror.

break our hearts.

For me, this teaching resonates powerfully. As a rabbi-human rights activist for sixty years, I'm proud of the myriad of Jews who stood beside the Black community, the LGBT community, feminists and environmentalists, joining in their righteous struggles. Our participation in these struggles was, is, and will always be unconditional. Today, however, many Jews feel abandoned. We wonder – for the larger world – do we count? Do we matter? *Mar li* – how bitter the maror dipped into *charoset*.

Al Achilat Maror

עַל אֲכִילַת מָרוֹר - **On the eating of maror:** Eating bitter herbs powerfully brings home our responsibility to empathize with those living broken lives in the present. The *maror* is dipped in *charoset* – tempering its bitterness – teaching that even at the worst of times, we believe redemption will come.

כּוֹרֵךְ

לוקחים מן המצה השלישית עם מרור, כורכים ביחד, אוכלים בהסבה ואומרים:

זֵכֶר לְמִקְדָּשׁ כְּהִלֵּל. כֵּן עָשָׂה הִלֵּל בִּזְמַן שֶׁבֵּית הַמִּקְדָּשׁ הָיָה קַיָּם:
הָיָה כּוֹרֵךְ מַצָּה וּמָרוֹר וְאוֹכֵל בְּיַחַד, לְקַיֵּם מַה שֶּׁנֶּאֱמַר (במדבר ט:יא):
עַל מַצּוֹת וּמְרוֹרִים יֹאכְלֻהוּ.

Korech

We take the *maror*, symbolic of challenging times – and we pack it between *matzot*, the food consumed immediately after leaving Egypt, and eat it as one – moments of highs and lows, mixed, fused. Truth be told, bad and good experiences most often are not compartmentalized. Often the two mesh.

In this spirit, I'll be thinking of Alon, a jewelry manufacturer, who lost his son, Adir, in Gaza. Although in deep mourning, Alon was moved by weddings that took place on army bases in the midst of the war. As he explains, "I decided I'm going to donate a ring. On Facebook I wrote the first soldier who is ready to propose I will give a ring. When a second called, I couldn't turn him away. Since then it's 81 rings. They pick it up and the best part is to get a hug from the soldiers. Hamas wanted to take our life to prevent the building of a house in Israel. And what I'm doing is the opposite. Adir won't build a home in Israel, but because of him a lot of people will. Adir is still with us. And this is my win."

Yehuda Amichai said it well:

KORECH

We take the maror and put it between two pieces broken from the bottom matza, wrap them together "sandwich style" and eat them while reclining. Before doing so, we recite:

זֵכֶר לְמִקְדָּשׁ כְּהִלֵּל This is what Hillel did when the Temple existed: He would wrap the matza and maror and eat them together, in order to fulfill what is said, (Numbers 9:11): "You should eat it (the Pesach sacrifice) on matzot and maror."

A man doesn't have time in his life to have time for everything.
He doesn't have seasons enough to have a season for every purpose.
Ecclesiastes was wrong about that.
A man needs to love and hate at the same moment,
To laugh and cry with the same eyes.
With the same hands to throw stones
And gather them in,
To make love in war and war in love,
And to hate and forgive, and remember and forget,
To arrange and confuse, to eat and digest,
What history takes years and years to do.
A man doesn't have time.
As he loses he seeks,
As he finds he forgets,
As he forgets he loves,
And as he loves he begins to forget

(translation by Chana Bloch and Stephen Mitchell)

שֻׁלְחָן עוֹרֵךְ
אוכלים ושותים.

Shulchan Orech

We all look forward to the sumptuous Seder meal. However, doesn't eating and drinking lavishly run contrary to the deep and uplifting Haggadah analyses on exile and redemption, past and future? Doesn't it degrade the spiritual moment?

A similar interruption occurred at the zenith of religious ecstasy, revelation at Sinai. There, too, the Torah tells us that the people "ate and drank." While some commentators insist such behavior was wrongful, others like Nachmanides believe it was perfectly appropriate. They ate the peace offering and drank joyously, making it "an occasion for rejoicing and festival….such is one's duty to rejoice at the receiving of the Torah."

Similarly, the Seder meal (*Shulchan Orech*) does not disturb the story of the exodus, but enhances its meaning. This teaching reflects mainstream Jewish philosophical thought. While some insist that the pathway to spirituality is suppression of the body, Judaism maintains that the pathway to godliness is to sanctify the physical. In fact, the very essence of halachah teaches that the body is not to be extolled or repressed but sanctified, lifting earth to heaven and bringing heaven down to earth. The Jewish goal is to meld spirituality and earthliness.

In this spirit, the students of Rabbi Avraham Yitzchak Hakohen Kook have quoted their teacher as saying, "There is no such thing as the unholy.

SHULCHAN ORECH

The Seder meal is served.

There is only the holy and the not yet holy." For Rabbi Kook, the way one eats, engages in business, or makes love has the same capacity for holiness as fasting, meditation, or prayer. Every act of life has the potential to be suffused with *kedushah* – with godly spirituality.

The Seder meal teaches – eating and drinking can become holy experiences. More broadly, the Seder, Shabbat and all other holiday meals follow the pattern of the sacrificial service. We begin the festive meal with kiddush over wine, reminiscent of the wine libation; break challah (on Passover, matza), reminiscent of the meal offering; sprinkle salt, reminiscent of the "covenant of salt;" and then sit down for a meal reminiscent of the ancient offerings.

Other similarities exist as well: we wash hands before the meal, as hands were washed at the *kiyor* (Temple laver); we sing *zemirot* (songs), as the Levites lifted their voices in melodic praise of God. Finally, we recite the Grace after Meals, which includes the hope that the Messiah come, heralded by the rebuilding of the Temple.

In no small measure, the festive meals turn our homes into mini-temples where we celebrate our love for God and God's love for us, proclaiming that our covenantal relationship with God was, is, and will always be.

צָפוּן

מחלקים לכל אחד מהסועדים מהמצה שהייתה צפונה לאפיקומן ואוכלים ממנה בהסבה.

לפני אכילת האפיקומן אומרים:

זֵכֶר לְקָרְבַּן פֶּסַח הַנֶּאֱכָל עַל הַשָֹבַע.

Tzafun

The last food eaten while reclining is the *afikoman*, the larger piece of matza put aside to introduce the last half of the Seder – the half dealing with the hope for future redemption

This part of the Seder is called *tzafun*, meaning "hidden." On its surface, this refers to the hidden matza. But more deeply, the term *tzafun* teaches that the time of future redemption is hidden. That is, we have no specific knowledge of when the Messiah will come.

In fact, *tzafun* as hidden is always used in some form when a text deals with redemption. For example, the savior of Egypt, Joseph, is called *"tzaf'nat pa'ne'ach."* When Moses, the future leader of our people, is born, the Torah says: *"Vatitzpeneihu,"* and he was hidden three months. Note the prophecy "from the north the evil (leading to messianic times) will come." The term in Hebrew for north – *tzafon* – is similar in sound to *tzafun*, the redemptive hidden time.

TZAFUN

At the end of the meal, we take the matza that was hidden for the afikoman, and eat it while reclining.

Before doing so, we say:

זֵכֶר לְקָרְבַּן פֶּסַח - This matza is a reminder of the Pesach sacrifice that was eaten in the Temple upon being satiated.

בָּרֵךְ

מוזגים כוס שלישי שרים שיר המעלות ומברכים ברכת המזון.

Barech

We recite the Grace After Meals. Within this Grace is the microcosm of the entire Haggadah. This becomes clear when noting when and by whom the four distinct sections of the Grace were introduced (Berachot 48b).

First Blessing: This blessing – Blessed are You, O Lord our God who feeds the entire world – was introduced by Moses when the Israelites received the manna, the food that sustained our people in the desert. Here, the Grace After Meals picks up our history soon after we leave Egypt, a bit beyond the end point of the story as told by Shmuel in the Maggid.

Second Blessing: Forty years later, after liberating Israel, Joshua composes the second blessing, "For the land and its food." This is very much aligned with the timetable of Rav, the second Maggid storyteller, who uses as a primary quote Joshua's farewell address after Israel was liberated.

Third Blessing: Decades later, after the periphery cities in Israel are conquered, David liberates Jerusalem and, soon after, his son Solomon builds the Temple. In gratitude, they write the third blessing of the Grace: "Blessed are You, O God, builder of Jerusalem." This is implicit in the sentences we studied in the Learning Section of the Maggid,

BARECH

We pour the third cup, sing the Song of Ascents and recite the Grace After Meals.

sentences quoted from the Book of Deuteronomy, outlining what a farmer says when bringing his first fruits to Jerusalem.

Fourth Blessing: Centuries later, after Jerusalem was vanquished and the Temple destroyed not once but twice, the Jews again rebelled against their oppressor in the time of Rabbi Akiva — only to be slaughtered en masse. When, long after the final battle, the Jews were allowed to bury the dead, the rabbis composed this blessing, praising " God who does good (*hatov*) and continues to do good (*umeitiv*)." Here, the story of our past has moved well beyond our first entry into Israel and liberation of Jerusalem. Much like the Reenacting Section of the Maggid – which ends in Maror, forecasting other exiles – the fourth blessing relates to other historical lows and highs.

Addendum: As an addendum, the closing paragraphs of the Grace After Meals relate to the hope the Messiah will arrive bringing our full redemption – the central theme of the Hallel and Nirtzah sections of the Haggadah said after the meal.

In sum, compressed into the Grace After Meals (Barech) is the whole of the Haggadah: our past history, and future hopes that Israel will prevail. With the establishment of the modern State of Israel, our generation has been blessed to witness and participate in a redemptive miracle.

שיר המעלות

שִׁיר הַמַּעֲלוֹת,
בְּשׁוּב יהוה אֶת־שִׁיבַת צִיּוֹן
הָיִינוּ כְּחֹלְמִים.
אָז יִמָּלֵא שְׂחוֹק פִּינוּ וּלְשׁוֹנֵנוּ רִנָּה,

Shir Hama'alot

שִׁיר הַמַּעֲלוֹת - A Song of Ascents: The power of song is that it reaches beyond itself. Song is a uniting force that brings together people of disparate backgrounds. Even those who do not know each other join, arm in arm. As different as we are, we become sisters and brothers.

Song not only moves outward but inward, touching the inner core, our inner goodness and godliness. And although sometimes we are unaware of that potential purity, song can stir and awaken our inner souls.

Song also moves upward. The distance between the lower world and upper world is great. How can we bridge the chasm? With the connecting ladder of song, which brings heaven down to earth and earth up to heaven. The song ascends.

בְּשׁוּב ה' אֶת שִׁיבַת צִיּוֹן - When the Lord will bring back the captivity of Zion: Homiletically, this can be read as saying the Lord returns *with* those returning to Zion, as the Torah states, "the Lord will return *with* your captivity." From this perspective, God feels the pain of Israel so deeply that when we are exiled, so is He. In other words, God dwells with us in our suffering; when we return, God returns with us.

הָיִינוּ כְּחֹלְמִים - We will be like dreamers: But every dream, even the dream of returning to Zion, includes inevitable setbacks. How, then, does one deal with dreams that have gone awry? The key is to recognize the difference between dream and reality. Dream is the hope of a glorious, almost perfect future. Reality, by definition, includes disappointments.

The challenge, when reality and disappointment set in, is to never forget the dream. Once you forget the dream, you won't be able to handle the reality; only by keeping the dream alive can we survive the difficulties we face.

This is important relative to what's happening in Israel today. Israel is *reishit tz'michat ge'ulatenu*, the dream of the dawn of redemption. But

שִׁיר הַמַּעֲלוֹת - A Song of Ascents:
When the Lord will bring back the captivity of Zion,
We will be like dreamers.
Then our mouths will be full of laughter
And our tongues with joyful melody;

once there, we face reality. There are internal and external divisions, terrorist bombings, political and social strife… And yet, with all of these problems, Israel is a remarkable, holy country as long as the dream is still in place.

In our personal lives, too, we witness the tension between dream and reality. Built into dreams are disappointments – a marriage, health, a profession gone sour. But we can persevere if we keep dreaming. If we stop dreaming, we stop living.

אָז יִמָּלֵא שְׂחוֹק פִּינוּ - **Then our mouths will be full of laughter:** Despite all he had endured, Natan Sharansky, the heroic Soviet prisoner of Zion, was blessed with the ability to see the lighter side of things. He never forgot the power of laughter. One memorable moment occurred when he was at New York's Kennedy Airport about to return to Israel from an early trip to the United States.

A short man, even shorter than Natan, approached us. Placing his black yarmulke on Natan's head, he said with a deep Yiddish accent, "*Gib mir a bracha* [Give me a blessing]."

Natan seemed confused. And so, I turned to him and said, "Natan, you're not going to believe this, but you've become a Chassidic rebbe. This man wants a blessing from you."

"You don't understand," Natan told the man, "I'm not a rebbe." Pointing to me, he said, "He is a rabbi. He'll bless you."

"No," the man firmly replied. "I have no interest in his blessing – only yours. And Mr. Sharansky," he added lovingly, "I will not move from here until you give me a *bracha*."

"Natan," I said, "you may have overcome the KGB, but you're not going to beat him. You've got a plane to catch. Just put your hands on his head and give him a *bracha* and let's go."

With a twinkle in his eye, Natan placed his hands on the gentleman's head and said, "*Baruch atah Hashem, Elokeinu melech ha'olam, hamotzi lechem min ha'aretz*," which is the blessing recited before eating bread.

אָז יֹאמְרוּ בַגּוֹיִם,
הִגְדִּיל יְהוָה לַעֲשׂוֹת עִם־אֵלֶּה.
הִגְדִּיל יְהוָה לַעֲשׂוֹת עִמָּנוּ, הָיִינוּ שְׂמֵחִים.
שׁוּבָה יְהוָה אֶת־שְׁבִיתֵנוּ כַּאֲפִיקִים בַּנֶּגֶב.
הַזֹּרְעִים בְּדִמְעָה, בְּרִנָּה יִקְצֹרוּ.
הָלוֹךְ יֵלֵךְ וּבָכֹה נֹשֵׂא מֶשֶׁךְ־הַזָּרַע,
בֹּא־יָבוֹא בְרִנָּה נֹשֵׂא אֲלֻמֹּתָיו. (תהלים קכו)

It was Natan's way of laughing at himself and declaring his unworthiness to give a blessing.

Even more humorous was the man's reaction. Taking back his yarmulke, he walked off ecstatic, absolutely delighted. While Natan may have thought his blessing was worth nothing, this man thought it was worth everything.

For spiritual activists, laughter is particularly important. It reminds us not to take ourselves too seriously. This is especially helpful in uneven situations involving direct confrontation with power. Laughter in such settings teaches humility and restores one's sense of proportion.

Interestingly, the Hebrew word *litz'ok*, "to cry," is similar to the word *litzchok*, which can be translated as "to laugh." In the Hebrew language, the guttural letters *ayin* and *het* often interchange, rendering *litz'ok* and *litzchok* the same, thus illustrating the fundamental connection between tears and laughter. Perhaps the association between the words for crying and laughing can also teach a lesson about conquering despair. No matter how bleak the situation, no matter how dark the circumstances, no matter how profound the tears, laughter is not far away. One should never give up.

Laughter is an important tool in the spiritual activist's arsenal. So important is laughter that the second of our three patriarchs is called Yitzchak, which literally means "will laugh." And so laughter accompanies us as we protest, as we cry out. It is our way of declaring that in the end, despite the odds, *Am Yisrael* will prevail.

הִגְדִּיל ה' לַעֲשׂוֹת עִמָּנוּ, הָיִינוּ שְׂמֵחִים - **The Lord has done great things with us; We are happy**: How is happiness attained? The answer to this question lies in our definition

Then the nations will say;
"The Lord has done great things for them."
The Lord has done great things for us;
We are happy.
Lord, return our captivity
Like streams in the desert.
Those who sow with tears
Will reap with joyful song.
Those who walk and cry,
Carrying the measure of seed,
Will surely return
Singing for joy, carrying their sheaves. (Psalms 126)

of happiness, and, here, Judaism parts company with what I see as the pervasive culture of America. For most Americans, the goal in life is a feeling that is achieved by taking as much as one can for oneself. In too many circles, self-indulgence equals happiness.

Judaism sees this term differently. The aim of Judaism is not happiness in this self-indulgent sense. Rather, it is a commitment to the performance of good deeds. This goal is spelled out clearly in the Torah, where God, in just a few words, lays out the mission of Judaism: "*V'asita hayashar v'hatov b'einei Hashem*" (and you shall do that which is upright and good in the eyes of the Lord).

There you have it. The goal of Judaism is not to be happy but to do that which is upright and good. But – and this is the key – from living a life of uprightness, from living a life of goodness and good deeds, from leading a life of serving others, of reaching out rather than reaching in, happiness flows. In Torah, happiness is not the goal to which we aspire but the result of leading a good life.

הַזֹּרְעִים בְּדִמְעָה, בְּרִנָּה יִקְצֹרוּ - **Those who sow in tears (*dimah*) will reap with joyous song (*rinah*)**: In Chassidic literature, *dimah* and *rinah* are read in one breath; that is, one can sow and reap with tears and joy all at once. In other words, emotions may not come in absolutes; they may overlap. Such is the way of life, crying and laughing all at once.

הָלוֹךְ יֵלֵךְ וּבָכֹה - **Who walk and cry**: Crying and walking stirs the heart these days, as we recall the countless funerals of IDF soldiers who gave

שלשה שאכלו כאחד מזמנים

המזמן פותח: חֲבֵרִים וְחַבְרוֹת נְבָרֵךְ:

המסבים עונים: יְהִי שֵׁם יהוה מְבֹרָךְ מֵעַתָּה וְעַד-עוֹלָם. (תהלים קיג:ב)

המזמן אומר: בִּרְשׁוּת מָרָנָן וְרַבָּנָן וְרַבּוֹתַי, נְבָרֵךְ [אֱלֹהֵינוּ] שֶׁאָכַלְנוּ מִשֶּׁלּוֹ.

המסבים עונים: בָּרוּךְ [אֱלֹהֵינוּ] שֶׁאָכַלְנוּ מִשֶּׁלּוֹ וּבְטוּבוֹ חָיִינוּ.

המזמן חוזר ואומר: בָּרוּךְ [אֱלֹהֵינוּ] שֶׁאָכַלְנוּ מִשֶּׁלּוֹ וּבְטוּבוֹ חָיִינוּ.

their lives for Israel. With many hundreds present – and sometimes more – a rabbi reads out the Yoshev Be'seter Elyon, the psalm recited to begin the burial. Behind him are soldiers carrying the coffin. And behind them, walking ever so slowly, the next of kin, walking, walking, walking while crying, crying while walking – sobs piercing.

בִּרְשׁוּת - With the permission: While thanking God for food, we emphasize our responsibility to our fellow person. And so, the leader declares, "With the permission of all present, let us bless [our God] from whom we have eaten."

This parallels a picturesque prayer said daily about angels paying homage to God. But which angel is privileged to speak first? One would expect cut-throat competition for this honor. Yet the liturgy records that each angel steps back, declaring: You go first (*v'notnim reshut zeh lazeh*). Finally, all as one proclaim

Three who ate together introduce the Grace After Meals with the leader opening as follows:

חֲבֵרִים וְחַבֵרוֹת - Friends, dear friends, let us offer blessings:

All those present answer: May the Name of the Lord be blessed from now and forever. (Psalms 113:2)

The leader says: With the permission of all present, let us bless [our God] from whom we have eaten.

Those present answer: Blessed is [our God] from whom we have eaten and from whose goodness we live.

The leader repeats and says: Blessed is [our God] from whom we have eaten and from whose goodness we live.

His holiness, saying in awe: "Holy, holy, holy is the Lord of hosts; the whole earth is full of His glory" (Isaiah 6:3).

The formula of "Holy, holy, holy" is repeated during the repetition of the Amidah. It is introduced with the words: "We [human beings] will sanctify Your name on earth, as they sanctify it in the highest heavens, as it is written by Your prophet, 'And they [the angels] call to one another, saying Holy, holy, holy….'"

Here we pray to acknowledge God as the angels do, without competitiveness, reaching out to each other in peaceful, loving coexistence. In a world too often consumed with causeless hatred, this posture of stepping back and making space for others is desperately needed.

Like in the prayer service, the *zimun*, the call to recite the Grace After Meals, is not limited to encountering God; it also expresses a call to love our fellow person.

כלם אומרים:

הזן את הכל

בָּרוּךְ אַתָּה יהוה, אֱלֹהֵינוּ מֶלֶךְ הָעוֹלָם, הַזָּן אֶת הָעוֹלָם כֻּלּוֹ בְּטוּבוֹ בְּחֵן בְּחֶסֶד וּבְרַחֲמִים, הוּא נוֹתֵן לֶחֶם לְכָל בָּשָׂר כִּי לְעוֹלָם חַסְדּוֹ. וּבְטוּבוֹ הַגָּדוֹל תָּמִיד לֹא חָסַר לָנוּ, וְאַל יֶחְסַר לָנוּ מָזוֹן לְעוֹלָם וָעֶד. בַּעֲבוּר שְׁמוֹ הַגָּדוֹל, כִּי הוּא אֵל זָן וּמְפַרְנֵס לַכֹּל וּמֵטִיב לַכֹּל, וּמֵכִין מָזוֹן לְכָל בְּרִיּוֹתָיו אֲשֶׁר בָּרָא. בָּרוּךְ אַתָּה יהוה, הַזָּן אֶת הַכֹּל.

על הארץ ועל המזון

נוֹדֶה לְּךָ יהוה אֱלֹהֵינוּ עַל שֶׁהִנְחַלְתָּ לַאֲבוֹתֵינוּ אֶרֶץ חֶמְדָּה טוֹבָה וּרְחָבָה, וְעַל שֶׁהוֹצֵאתָנוּ יהוה אֱלֹהֵינוּ מֵאֶרֶץ מִצְרַיִם, וּפְדִיתָנוּ מִבֵּית עֲבָדִים, וְעַל בְּרִיתְךָ שֶׁחָתַמְתָּ בִּבְשָׂרֵנוּ, וְעַל תּוֹרָתְךָ שֶׁלִּמַּדְתָּנוּ, וְעַל חֻקֶּיךָ שֶׁהוֹדַעְתָּנוּ, וְעַל חַיִּים חֵן וָחֶסֶד שֶׁחוֹנַנְתָּנוּ, וְעַל אֲכִילַת מָזוֹן שָׁאַתָּה זָן וּמְפַרְנֵס אוֹתָנוּ תָּמִיד, בְּכָל יוֹם וּבְכָל עֵת וּבְכָל שָׁעָה.

Birkat Hamazon

Thanksgiving for Food

הַזָּן אֶת הַכֹּל - **Blessed are you, Lord, who feeds the entire world:** God creates the world with potential for humans to provide food for everyone. That billions go to sleep hungry is our failure, a failure to distribute food properly to all corners of the earth.

Thanksgiving for Israel

עַל הָאָרֶץ וְעַל הַמָּזוֹן - **Blessed are you, Lord, for the land and its food:** The question arises: Thanking God for food is completely understandable, but why include blessings for Israel? Perhaps we are not only thanking God for the food that we've eaten, but we are also expressing confidence that food will be provided in the future. The place where this confidence is

Thanksgiving for Food

הַזָּן אֶת הַכֹּל - Blessed are You, Lord our God, Ruler of the Universe, who nourishes the entire world in His goodness, in grace, in kindness and in mercy. He gives bread to all flesh since His kindness is forever. And in His great goodness, we have never lacked, and may we never lack nourishment, because of His great name. For He is the Lord that feeds and provides for all and does good to all and prepares nourishment for all of his creatures that he created. Blessed are You, Lord, who feeds the entire world.

Thanksgiving for Israel

עַל הָאָרֶץ וְעַל הַמָּזוֹן - We thank you, Lord our God, that you have given as an inheritance to our ancestors a lovely, good and spacious land, and that You took us out, Lord our God, from the land of Egypt and that You redeemed us from a house of slaves, and for Your covenant which You have sealed in our flesh, and for Your Torah that You have taught us, and for Your statutes which You have made known to us, and for life, grace and kindness that You have granted us, and for the eating of nourishment that You feed and provide for us always, on all days, and at all times and in every hour.

greatest is in Israel. In the diaspora, even the most comfortable of diasporas – and, when appropriate, we must always express gratitude to countries wherein we reside – we can never be sure how we will be treated in the future; hence, there is a level of uncertainty about where the next morsel will come from.

Indeed, Jews today keep holidays for two days in the diaspora out of concern that antisemitism could once again spiral, resulting in the confiscation of Bibles, prayerbooks, and even Jewish calendars. To ensure Jews would know how to conduct themselves in such a circumstance, two days are still kept as was done millennia ago when calendars were not available.

In the words of the Talmud, "Be careful with the custom of your ancestors…for it might happen that the government may issue a decree and it will cause confusion [concerning holiday observance]" (Beitza 4b).

וְעַל הַכֹּל יהוה אֱלֹהֵינוּ, אֲנַחְנוּ מוֹדִים לָךְ וּמְבָרְכִים אוֹתָךְ,
יִתְבָּרַךְ שִׁמְךָ בְּפִי כָּל חַי תָּמִיד לְעוֹלָם וָעֶד.
כַּכָּתוּב (דברים ח:י): וְאָכַלְתָּ וְשָׂבָעְתָּ וּבֵרַכְתָּ אֶת־יהוה אֱלֹהֶיךָ
עַל־הָאָרֶץ הַטֹּבָה אֲשֶׁר נָתַן־לָךְ.
בָּרוּךְ אַתָּה יהוה, עַל הָאָרֶץ וְעַל הַמָּזוֹן.

בונה ירושלים

רַחֵם נָא יהוה אֱלֹהֵינוּ עַל יִשְׂרָאֵל עַמֶּךָ וְעַל יְרוּשָׁלַיִם עִירֶךָ
וְעַל צִיּוֹן מִשְׁכַּן כְּבוֹדֶךָ וְעַל מַלְכוּת בֵּית דָּוִד מְשִׁיחֶךָ
וְעַל הַבַּיִת הַגָּדוֹל וְהַקָּדוֹשׁ שֶׁנִּקְרָא שִׁמְךָ עָלָיו.
אֱלֹהֵינוּ אָבִינוּ, רְעֵנוּ זוּנֵנוּ פַּרְנְסֵנוּ וְכַלְכְּלֵנוּ וְהַרְוִיחֵנוּ,
וְהַרְוַח לָנוּ יהוה אֱלֹהֵינוּ מְהֵרָה מִכָּל צָרוֹתֵינוּ.
וְנָא אַל תַּצְרִיכֵנוּ יהוה אֱלֹהֵינוּ, לֹא לִידֵי מַתְּנַת בָּשָׂר וָדָם
וְלֹא לִידֵי הַלְוָאָתָם,
כִּי אִם לְיָדְךָ הַמְּלֵאָה הַפְּתוּחָה הַקְּדוֹשָׁה וְהָרְחָבָה,
שֶׁלֹּא נֵבוֹשׁ וְלֹא נִכָּלֵם לְעוֹלָם וָעֶד.

בשבת מוסיפין:

רְצֵה וְהַחֲלִיצֵנוּ יהוה אֱלֹהֵינוּ בְּמִצְוֹתֶיךָ וּבְמִצְוַת יוֹם הַשְּׁבִיעִי הַשַּׁבָּת הַגָּדוֹל
וְהַקָּדוֹשׁ הַזֶּה. כִּי יוֹם זֶה גָּדוֹל וְקָדוֹשׁ הוּא לְפָנֶיךָ לִשְׁבָּת בּוֹ וְלָנוּחַ בּוֹ בְּאַהֲבָה
כְּמִצְוַת רְצוֹנֶךָ. וּבִרְצוֹנְךָ הָנִיחַ לָנוּ יהוה אֱלֹהֵינוּ שֶׁלֹּא תְהֵא צָרָה וְיָגוֹן וַאֲנָחָה
בְּיוֹם מְנוּחָתֵנוּ. וְהַרְאֵנוּ יהוה אֱלֹהֵינוּ בְּנֶחָמַת צִיּוֹן עִירֶךָ וּבְבִנְיַן יְרוּשָׁלַיִם עִיר
קָדְשֶׁךָ כִּי אַתָּה הוּא בַּעַל הַיְשׁוּעוֹת וּבַעַל הַנֶּחָמוֹת.

Thanksgiving for Jerusalem

הַשַּׁבָּת הַגָּדוֹל וְהַקָּדוֹשׁ הַזֶּה - **This great and holy Shabbat**: Shabbat is the highest expression of *kedushat zman*, the holiness of time. Purposefully it's mentioned here in the paragraph dealing with Jerusalem, the epitome of *kedushat makom*, holiness of space. The confluence of both – the holiness of time and space – is the ideal we aspire for in our daily lives.

And for everything, Lord our God, we thank You and bless You; may Your name be blessed by the mouth of all life, constantly forever and always, as it is written (Deuteronomy 8:10); "And you shall eat and you shall be satiated and you shall bless the Lord your God for the good land that He has given you." Blessed are You, Lord, for the land and for its food.

Thanksgiving for Jerusalem

רַחֵם נָא - Please have mercy, Lord our God, upon Israel, Your people; and upon Jerusalem, Your city; and upon Zion, the dwelling place of Your Glory; and upon the royal House of David, Your appointed one; and upon the great and holy house that Your name is called upon. Our God, our Father, shepherd us, sustain us, provide for us, nourish us and give us quick relief, Lord our God, from all of our troubles. And please do not make us needy, Lord our God, not for the gifts of others, and not for their loans, but rather from Your full, open, holy and broad hand, so that we not be embarrassed and we not be shamed forever and always.

On Shabbat, we add the following paragraph:

> רְצֵה - May You be pleased to strengthen us, Lord our God, in your commandments and in the command of the seventh day, of this great and holy Shabbat, since this day is great and holy before You, to cease work upon it and to rest upon it, with love, according to the commandment of Your will. And with Your will, allow us, Lord our God, that we should not have trouble, and grief and sighing on the day of our rest. And may You show us, Lord our God, the consolation of Zion, Your city; and the building of Jerusalem, Your holy city; for You are the Master of salvation and consolation.

אֱלֹהֵינוּ וֵאלֹהֵי אֲבוֹתֵינוּ, יַעֲלֶה וְיָבֹא וְיַגִּיעַ וְיֵרָאֶה וְיֵרָצֶה וְיִשָּׁמַע וְיִפָּקֵד וְיִזָּכֵר זִכְרוֹנֵנוּ וּפִקְדּוֹנֵנוּ, וְזִכְרוֹן אֲבוֹתֵינוּ, וְזִכְרוֹן מָשִׁיחַ בֶּן דָּוִד עַבְדֶּךָ, וְזִכְרוֹן יְרוּשָׁלַיִם עִיר קָדְשֶׁךָ, וְזִכְרוֹן כָּל עַמְּךָ בֵּית יִשְׂרָאֵל לְפָנֶיךָ, לִפְלֵיטָה לְטוֹבָה לְחֵן וּלְחֶסֶד וּלְרַחֲמִים, לְחַיִּים וּלְשָׁלוֹם בְּיוֹם חַג הַמַּצּוֹת הַזֶּה זָכְרֵנוּ יהוה אֱלֹהֵינוּ בּוֹ לְטוֹבָה וּפָקְדֵנוּ בוֹ לִבְרָכָה וְהוֹשִׁיעֵנוּ בוֹ לְחַיִּים. וּבִדְבַר יְשׁוּעָה וְרַחֲמִים חוּס וְחָנֵּנוּ וְרַחֵם עָלֵינוּ וְהוֹשִׁיעֵנוּ, כִּי אֵלֶיךָ עֵינֵינוּ, כִּי אֵל מֶלֶךְ חַנּוּן וְרַחוּם אָתָּה.

וּבְנֵה יְרוּשָׁלַיִם עִיר הַקֹּדֶשׁ בִּמְהֵרָה בְיָמֵינוּ. בָּרוּךְ אַתָּה יהוה, בּוֹנֵה בְרַחֲמָיו יְרוּשָׁלָיִם. אָמֵן.

הטוב והמטיב

בָּרוּךְ אַתָּה יהוה, אֱלֹהֵינוּ מֶלֶךְ הָעוֹלָם, הָאֵל אָבִינוּ מַלְכֵּנוּ אַדִּירֵנוּ בּוֹרְאֵנוּ גּוֹאֲלֵנוּ יוֹצְרֵנוּ קְדוֹשֵׁנוּ קְדוֹשׁ יַעֲקֹב רוֹעֵנוּ רוֹעֵה יִשְׂרָאֵל הַמֶּלֶךְ הַטּוֹב וְהַמֵּטִיב לַכֹּל שֶׁבְּכָל יוֹם וָיוֹם הוּא הֵטִיב, הוּא מֵטִיב, הוּא יֵיטִיב לָנוּ. הוּא גְמָלָנוּ הוּא גוֹמְלֵנוּ הוּא יִגְמְלֵנוּ לָעַד, לְחֵן וּלְחֶסֶד וּלְרַחֲמִים וּלְרֶוַח הַצָּלָה וְהַצְלָחָה, בְּרָכָה וִישׁוּעָה נֶחָמָה פַּרְנָסָה וְכַלְכָּלָה וְרַחֲמִים וְחַיִּים וְשָׁלוֹם וְכָל טוֹב, וּמִכָּל טוּב לְעוֹלָם אַל יְחַסְּרֵנוּ.

יַעֲלֶה וְיָבֹא - May there ascend and come and reach: Manifold verbs are found here, reminding us – as the Sefat Emet would say – to walk, keep walking, one step after another (*mi'madreiga le'madreiga*). A rebbe turned to his students asking, who is higher – the person on the 47th or 25th rung of a ladder? Of course, the 47th, the students responded. No, the rebbe replied: it depends which way you're going.

וְזִכְרוֹן מָשִׁיחַ - And the remembrance of the Messiah: Remembrances are normatively associated with past occurrences. But there are remembrances of the future – as mentioned here, the promise that one day redemption will come, the Messiah will be here, encouraging us to reinvigorate our efforts to reach for that goal.

יַעֲלֶה וְיָבֹא - God and God of our ancestors, may there ascend and come and reach and be seen and be acceptable and be heard and be recalled and be remembered - our remembrance and our recollection; and the remembrance of our ancestors; and the remembrance of the Messiah, the son of David, Your servant; and the remembrance of Jerusalem, Your holy city; and the remembrance of all Your people, the house of Israel – before You – for survival, for good, for grace, and for kindness, and for mercy, for life and for peace on this day of the Festival of Matzot. On this day, remember us, Lord our God, for good, and recall us for blessing and save us for life. With salvation and mercy, spare us, be gracious to us and have mercy on us and save us, for our eyes yearn for You, since You are gracious and merciful.

בּוֹנֵה בְרַחֲמָיו יְרוּשָׁלָיִם - And may You build Jerusalem, the holy city, speedily and in our days. Blessed are You, Lord, builder of Jerusalem. Amen.

Thanksgiving for God's Goodness

הַטּוֹב וְהַמֵּטִיב - Blessed are You, Lord our God, Ruler of the Universe, God, our Father, our Ruler, our Mighty One, our Creator, our Redeemer, our Shaper, our Holy One, the Holy One of Jacob, our Shepherd, the Shepherd of Israel, the good Ruler, who does good to all, since on every single day He has done good, He does good, He will continue to do good for us. He has granted us, He grants us, He will grant us forever - in grace and in kindness, and in mercy, and in relief - rescue and success, blessing and salvation, consolation, provision and nourishment and mercy and life and peace and all good; and may we never lack any good.

בּוֹנֵה בְרַחֲמָיו יְרוּשָׁלָיִם - Blessed are you, Lord, builder of Jerusalem, Amen: Lest we think that the focus of Israel is only land, the physical protection of Jews, we add the blessing of Jerusalem, symbolic of the spirituality of Israel so necessary for its survival. A land without a spiritual mission is like a body without a soul.

Thanksgiving for God's Goodness

הַטּוֹב וְהַמֵּטִיב - Blessed are you, Lord our God... who does good to all: The Talmud explains that even after the destruction of the Second

שאיפה לגאולה

הרחמן

הָרַחֲמָן הוּא יִמְלוֹךְ עָלֵינוּ לְעוֹלָם וָעֶד.

הָרַחֲמָן הוּא יִתְבָּרַךְ בַּשָּׁמַיִם וּבָאָרֶץ.

הָרַחֲמָן הוּא יִשְׁתַּבַּח לְדוֹר דּוֹרִים, וְיִתְפָּאַר בָּנוּ לָעַד וּלְנֵצַח נְצָחִים, וְיִתְהַדַּר בָּנוּ לָעַד וּלְעוֹלְמֵי עוֹלָמִים.

הָרַחֲמָן הוּא יְפַרְנְסֵנוּ בְּכָבוֹד.

הָרַחֲמָן הוּא יִשְׁבּוֹר עֻלֵּנוּ מֵעַל צַוָּארֵנוּ, וְהוּא יוֹלִיכֵנוּ קוֹמְמִיּוּת לְאַרְצֵנוּ.

הָרַחֲמָן הוּא יִשְׁלַח לָנוּ בְּרָכָה מְרֻבָּה בַּבַּיִת הַזֶּה, וְעַל שֻׁלְחָן זֶה שֶׁאָכַלְנוּ עָלָיו.

Temple, a period of devastation, Jews expressed thanks to God for allowing the bodies of those who fell in the rebellion against Rome to be returned. Miraculously, the remains were intact. Thus, the word *tov* is repeated.

This is an important message to all of us to do everything we can to make certain that the bodies of slain Israeli soldiers and civilians are returned for proper burial.

It can also be suggested that the double *tov* is a microcosm of all of Jewish history: No matter the challenge, no matter the setback, Jews never lost hope that one day things would again be "good," even "better" – Israel would be redeemed.

Yearning for Redemption

הָרַחֲמָן הוּא יִמְלוֹךְ עָלֵינוּ לְעוֹלָם וָעֶד **- May the Merciful One rule over us forever and ever:** Concluding paragraphs were added to the Grace After Meals reflecting our yearning for the Messiah, the time of redemption, when God and the system of ethical monotheism will reign supreme. Note, the God who rules the world (*Yimloch*) is described as *Harachaman* – the Merciful One. When creating the world, God's appellative title was *Elohim* – the God of strict judgment (Genesis 1). When it becomes clear, says the Midrash, that the world could not

Yearning for Redemption

הָרַחֲמָן - May the Merciful One rule over us forever and ever.

May the Merciful One be blessed in the heavens and in the earth.

May the Merciful One be praised for all generations,
and exalted among us forever and ever,
and glorified among us always for eternity.

May the Merciful One sustain us honorably.

May the Merciful One break our yoke from upon our necks
and bring us upright to our land.

May the Merciful One send multiple blessings,
to this home and upon this table on which we have eaten.

---

be sustained on strict law alone, an added description was introduced – *Hashem Elohim*, the God who tempers judgement (*Elohim*) with mercy (*Hashem*; Genesis 2). So, too, the second Ten Declarations, unlike the first, was given in the framework of the Thirteen Attributes of Mercy, "The Lord, the Lord is a God of mercy and graciousness." Thus, the first *Harachaman* in the Grace After Meals shows the way for all others, speaking of God as Ruler (*Yimloch*) who rules mercifully (*Harachaman*). In the spirit of *imitatio Dei*, we should do the same, whenever possible, tempering justice with mercy.

הָרַחֲמָן הוּא יִתְבָּרַךְ בַּשָּׁמַיִם וּבָאָרֶץ - **May the Merciful One be blessed in the heavens and in the earth:** An evidence of God's existence is the teleological argument, the argument of order. For the heavens and the earth to be, billions of conditions are necessary, pointing to God, the Architect, the Artist who brings it all together. Presenting this position in my first year in the rabbinate more than a jubilee ago, Dr. Ron Burde, who went on to become a renown neuro-ophthalmologist strengthened this teaching, sharing that as an expert of the eye, he understood that there are billions of conditions necessary for the eye to be. For the mystics, the eye is the gateway to the soul; for Dr. Burde, of blessed memory, the eye was his gateway to God.

הָרַחֲמָן הוּא יִשְׁלַח לָנוּ אֶת אֵלִיָּהוּ הַנָּבִיא זָכוּר לַטּוֹב, וִיבַשֶּׂר לָנוּ בְּשׂוֹרוֹת טוֹבוֹת יְשׁוּעוֹת וְנֶחָמוֹת.

הָרַחֲמָן הוּא יְבָרֵךְ אֶת מְדִינַת יִשְׂרָאֵל, רֵאשִׁית צְמִיחַת גְּאֻלָּתֵנוּ.

הָרַחֲמָן הוּא יְבָרֵךְ אֶת חַיָּלֵי צְבָא הַהֲגַנָּה לְיִשְׂרָאֵל הָעוֹמְדִים עַל מִשְׁמַר אַרְצֵנוּ.

הָרַחֲמָן הוּא יְבָרֵךְ אֶת מִשְׁפַּחְתִּי וְאֶת כָּל הַמְסוּבִּין כָּאן.

הָרַחֲמָן הוּא יְבָרֵךְ אֶת בַּעַל הַבַּיִת הַזֶּה, וְאֶת בַּעֲלַת הַבַּיִת הַזֶּה, אוֹתָם וְאֶת בֵּיתָם וְאֶת זַרְעָם וְאֶת כָּל אֲשֶׁר לָהֶם.

אוֹתָנוּ וְאֶת כָּל אֲשֶׁר לָנוּ, כְּמוֹ שֶׁנִּתְבָּרְכוּ אֲבוֹתֵינוּ אַבְרָהָם יִצְחָק וְיַעֲקֹב בַּכֹּל מִכֹּל כֹּל, כֵּן יְבָרֵךְ אוֹתָנוּ כֻּלָּנוּ יַחַד בִּבְרָכָה שְׁלֵמָה. וְנֹאמַר, אָמֵן.

בַּמָּרוֹם יְלַמְּדוּ עֲלֵיהֶם וְעָלֵינוּ זְכוּת שֶׁתְּהֵא לְמִשְׁמֶרֶת שָׁלוֹם. וְנִשָּׂא בְרָכָה מֵאֵת יהוה, וּצְדָקָה מֵאֱלֹהֵי יִשְׁעֵנוּ, וְנִמְצָא-חֵן וְשֵׂכֶל-טוֹב בְּעֵינֵי אֱלֹהִים וְאָדָם.

בשבת: הָרַחֲמָן הוּא יַנְחִילֵנוּ יוֹם שֶׁכֻּלּוֹ שַׁבָּת וּמְנוּחָה לְחַיֵּי הָעוֹלָמִים.

הָרַחֲמָן הוּא יַנְחִילֵנוּ יוֹם שֶׁכֻּלּוֹ טוֹב.

הָרַחֲמָן הוּא יְזַכֵּנוּ לִימוֹת הַמָּשִׁיחַ וּלְחַיֵּי הָעוֹלָם הַבָּא.

וִיבַשֶּׂר לָנוּ בְּשׂוֹרוֹת טוֹבוֹת יְשׁוּעוֹת וְנֶחָמוֹת - **And may He announce good tidings of salvation and consolation:** These days, it is difficult to read, listen or watch the news as it is so fraught with evil. But the day will come when the news will be glorious, with everyone sharing "good tidings of salvation and consolation." Sometimes, a word's sound offers commentary on its meaning. *Viy'vaser* with emphasis on the "vvss" sounds like a whisper; a viral, quiet spreading from person to person that the Great Day is coming.

May the Merciful One send us Elijah the prophet - may he be remembered for good - and may he announce good tidings of salvation and consolation.

May the Merciful One bless the State of Israel, which marks the dawn of our redemption.

May the Merciful One bless the Israeli Defense Forces, who stand guard over our land.

May the Merciful One bless my family (mother, father, spouse, children, grandparents, grandchildren…) and all who are with us.

May the Merciful One bless our hosts, their families and all that is theirs.

Just as our patriarchs Abraham, Isaac and Jacob, (and our matriarchs Sarah, Rebecca, Rachel and Leah) were blessed in everything, from everything, with everything, so too may all of us be blessed, and let us say, Amen.

From above, may they advocate upon them and upon us merit, that should protect us in peace; and may we carry a blessing from the Lord and charity from the God of our salvation; and find grace and good understanding in the eyes of God and humankind.

On Shabbat, we say:
> May the Merciful One grant us to inherit the time when every day will be Shabbat, with inner everlasting peace.

May the Merciful One give us to inherit the day that will be all good.

May the Merciful One help us merit to experience the Messianic Period and life in the World to Come.

מגדול

מִגְדּוֹל יְשׁוּעוֹת מַלְכּוֹ וְעֹשֶׂה-חֶסֶד לִמְשִׁיחוֹ לְדָוִד וּלְזַרְעוֹ עַד-עוֹלָם (שמואל ב כב:נא). עֹשֶׂה שָׁלוֹם בִּמְרוֹמָיו, הוּא יַעֲשֶׂה שָׁלוֹם עָלֵינוּ וְעַל כָּל יִשְׂרָאֵל. וְאִמְרוּ, אָמֵן.

יראו

יְראוּ אֶת-יהוה קְדֹשָׁיו, כִּי-אֵין מַחְסוֹר לִירֵאָיו. כְּפִירִים רָשׁוּ וְרָעֵבוּ, וְדֹרְשֵׁי יהוה לֹא-יַחְסְרוּ כָל-טוֹב (תהלים לד:י-יא). הוֹדוּ לַיהוה כִּי-טוֹב כִּי לְעוֹלָם חַסְדּוֹ (תהלים קיח:א). פּוֹתֵחַ אֶת-יָדֶךָ, וּמַשְׂבִּיעַ לְכָל-חַי רָצוֹן (תהלים קמה:טז). בָּרוּךְ הַגֶּבֶר אֲשֶׁר יִבְטַח בַּיהוה, וְהָיָה יהוה מִבְטַחוֹ (ירמיהו יז:ז). נַעַר הָיִיתִי גַּם-זָקַנְתִּי, וְלֹא רָאִיתִי צַדִּיק נֶעֱזָב, וְזַרְעוֹ מְבַקֶּשׁ-לָחֶם (תהלים לז:כה). יהוה עֹז לְעַמּוֹ יִתֵּן, יהוה יְבָרֵךְ אֶת-עַמּוֹ בַשָּׁלוֹם (תהלים כט:יא).

כוס שלישית

בָּרוּךְ אַתָּה יהוה, אֱלֹהֵינוּ מֶלֶךְ הָעוֹלָם, בּוֹרֵא פְּרִי הַגָּפֶן.

ושותים בהסיבה ואינו מברך ברכה אחרונה.

מִגְדּוֹל - A tower (*migdol*): On a non-holiday (or non-Shabbat) we vocalize the *mem* with a *patach* – *magdil* – He makes greater. The two *mems* conflate – only when we are trying to improve (*magdil*) are we blissfully in the *migdol*, in the tower of salvation. The journey is as important as arrival at the destination.

נַעַר הָיִיתִי גַּם-זָקַנְתִּי - I was a youth and I have also aged and I have not seen a righteous person forsaken and his or her offspring seeking bread: Many authorities insist that even in messianic, redemptive times, the world will be governed by natural law. In those days, as the Grace After Meals concludes, no one will be forsaken, no one will be begging for food, as caring people will step up to make sure there is no more hunger in the world. From this perspective, the *Na'ar Ha'yiti* sentence may be read as elliptically alluding to our obligations: "I was a youth and I have also aged and I have not seen a righteous person forsaken and his or her offspring seeking bread… **and I did nothing about it.**"

מִגְדּוֹל - A tower of salvations is our Ruler; may He do kindness with His Messiah, with David and his offspring, forever (II Samuel 22:51). The One who makes peace above, may He make peace upon us and upon all of Israel; and say, Amen.

יְראוּ - Fear the Lord, His holy ones, since there is no lacking for those that fear Him. Young lions may grow weak and hungry, but those who seek the Lord will not lack any good thing (Psalms 34:10-11). Thank the Lord, since He is good, since His kindness is forever (Psalms 118:1). You open Your hand and satisfy the will of all living things (Psalms 146:16). Blessed is the person that trusts in the Lord and the Lord is his security (Jeremiah 17:7). I was a youth and I have also aged and I have not seen a righteous person forsaken and his or her offspring seeking bread (Psalms 37:25). The Lord will give courage to His people. The Lord will bless His people with peace (Psalms 29:11).

Third Cup of Wine

בּוֹרֵא פְּרִי הַגָּפֶן - Blessed are You, Lord our God, Ruler of the universe, who creates the fruit of the vine.

We drink while reclining.

Third Cup of Wine

בּוֹרֵא פְּרִי הַגָּפֶן - **Who creates the fruit of the vine:** We drink a cup of wine as is our custom at the end of reciting the Grace After Meals on festivals or Shabbat. Additionally, the drinking celebrates the joyous completion of the Shulchan Orech "present" section of the Seder.

FUTURE

The last half of the Seder begins by reflecting on the future. With all the challenges we face, we believe that someday redemption will come.

Appropriately, we introduce this section by inviting in the prophet Elijah. After all, the prophet Malachi prophesizes that before the Messiah comes, Elijah the prophet will announce his arrival:

> Behold, I will send you Elijah the prophet before the coming of the great and awesome day of the Lord. And he shall turn the heart of the fathers to the children and the heart of the children to their fathers. (Malachi 3:23)

One wonders, as my son Dov once asked as a little boy, "Abba, if Elijah miraculously can fly over oceans, mountains, deserts in an instant, if he can drink all that wine at the Seder and not get drunk, shouldn't he be able to squeeze through the cracks of the windows or doors of any home. Why must we open the door?"

A child's question has enormous depth as it reveals much about the Messiah. If we want the Messiah to come, we must do our share, get off our hands, walk to the door, open it wide, and proactively, with open arms, welcome him in. Who knows? Maybe he's been knocking at the door, waiting for an invitation to enter.

In a word, as much as we search for God, God searches for us. As much as we yearn for redemption, redemption yearns for us. As much as we await the Messiah, the Messiah waits for us.

שפוך חמתך

מוזגים כוס של אליהו ופותחים את הדלת.

שְׁפֹךְ חֲמָתְךָ אֶל־הַגּוֹיִם אֲשֶׁר לֹא יְדָעוּךָ וְעַל־מַמְלָכוֹת אֲשֶׁר בְּשִׁמְךָ לֹא קָרָאוּ. כִּי אָכַל אֶת־יַעֲקֹב וְאֶת־נָוֵהוּ הֵשַׁמּוּ (תהלים עט:ו-ז).

שְׁפָךְ־עֲלֵיהֶם זַעְמֶךָ וַחֲרוֹן אַפְּךָ יַשִּׂיגֵם (תהלים סט:כה).

תִּרְדֹּף בְּאַף וְתַשְׁמִידֵם מִתַּחַת שְׁמֵי יהוה (איכה ג:סו).

Sh'foch Chamat'cha

שְׁפֹךְ חֲמָתְךָ - **Pour your wrath:** Harsh words, so harsh that some suggest an alternative text – שְׁפֹךְ אַהֲבָתְךָ – pour out your love. And yet, it says, "chamat'cha" – your wrath.

Historically, the chamat'cha text becomes understandable. At the end of the Seder meal, when participants often went outside for a breather, they found at their doorsteps a dead Christian child, whom they (the Jews) were accused of killing to use the child's blood to bake matzot or color the wine. An ancient blood libel that has surfaced these days with a vengeance, as Israel is falsely accused of genocide (sic), an accusation so abhorrent it deserves the response of sh'foch chamat'cha. The lie is compounded as it is our Torah that prohibits the consumption of blood. So important is this law, that it becomes one of the Seven Laws of Noah, the foundational, ethical principles incumbent on all of humankind.

תִּרְדֹּף בְּאַף וְתַשְׁמִידֵם מִתַּחַת שְׁמֵי ה' - **You will pursue them with anger and eradicate them from under the heavens of the Lord:** The ritual of opening the door to invite Elijah in as we recite Sh'foch is not part of the Barech or Hallel sections of the Seder. It stands on its own, in a vacuum. This speaks to Elijah's persona. Indeed, Elijah in the Book

Pour Out Your Wrath - שְׁפֹךְ חֲמָתְךָ

We open the door for Elijah, lifting his cup we recite:

שְׁפֹךְ חֲמָתְךָ - Pour your wrath upon the nations that did not know You and upon the kingdoms that did not call upon Your Name! For they have consumed Jacob and laid waste his habitation (Psalms 79:6-7).

Pour out Your fury upon them and the fierceness of Your anger shall reach them (Psalms 69:25)!

You will pursue them with anger and eradicate them from under the heavens of the Lord (Lamentations 3:66).

of Kings has no pedigree, appearing out of nowhere. Unlike most other prophets, his father is not even listed. Moreover, Elijah flits from place from place; he is everywhere. The Elijah of the Seder, like Elijah in Tanach, is not rooted.

The language here, requesting Elijah to obliterate our enemy, is the Elijah of *kana'ut* (zealotry), the modus operandi of Elijah in Tanach. This characteristic surfaces most clearly when Elijah tells God (1 Kings 19), "I have been very zealous for You…and I am the only believer left." God responds that He is not in the "whirlwind" (*ruach*), not in the "earthquake" (*ra'ash*), and not in the "fire" (*eish*), but in the "still small voice" (*kol demamah dakah*). This is the voice of the spirit, the voice of humility, the voice that hears others and inspires reconciliation. God then asks Elijah for a second time, "What are you doing here, Elijah?" When Elijah again responds, "I have been very zealous for the Lord," God tells him that He will appoint Elisha in his stead. In effect, God says, "Elijah, you have missed the point. You have failed to realize that what endures, what lasts, is the 'still, small voice,' the little things; that is what makes the real difference."

Despite being reprimanded and told he'll be replaced, Elijah adamantly clings to the approach of zealotry. It reaches a crescendo when Elijah ascends in a chariot of fire, *eish*, and in a *se'arah*, which in the Hebrew is the reverse spelling of *ra'ash* (as *samech* and *shin* are often interchangeable; see Judges 12:5,6). All this occurs as Elijah's students watch from Yericho (Jericho) – a play on *ruach*. This is no mere coincidence. Elijah leaves this world as the prophet of zealotry, the prophet of *ruach*, *ra'ash* and *eish* – whirlwind, earthquake and fire – the very mediums rejected by God as representing His voice.

While Elijah of Tanach was a prophet – in many ways an unsuccessful prophet of zealotry – the Elijah of Rabbinic literature becomes a remarkably different figure. He appears sometimes in the garb of a beggar; sometimes in the garb of a scholar who brings together different sides; sometimes in the guise of a persona who comes from nowhere to save someone in need. What all these images of Elijah have in common is that they reflect a figure of *kol demamah dakah* – a still small voice.

This, I believe, is the other face of Elijah that we encounter at the Seder. Unlike in the paragraph "Pursue them in anger," where Elijah's name is missing, Elijah appears in the Grace After Meals – the only time his name is found in the Haggadah. Indeed, immediately after praying that the "All Merciful send the prophet Elijah to us," we beseech the "All Merciful One" to bless our parents and children, reminding us of the last sentences of Malachi:

Behold! I will send the prophet Elijah to you before the coming of the great and awesome day of the Lord. He shall restore the hearts of parents to children and children to parents" (Malachi 3:23-24).

This is the Elijah who patiently and softly brings together generations.

It would be a good idea at this point to consider reading these sentences from Malachi and to read as well from the Book of Ben Sira, the second century BCE sage who described Elijah this way:

> You were taken on high by a whirlwind, by fiery legions to heaven. Ready, it is written, for the time to put [divine] wrath to rest, before the Day of the Lord, to turn back the hearts of fathers to their children, and to re-establish the tribes of Israel. (48:9-11).

In other words, Elijah will not only bring generations together; he will bring the people together; he will bring back and restore the ten tribes. The Elijah of the Book of Kings who only speaks to the North and speaks disparagingly of them will merge the northern kingdom with the southern one. The divider will become a uniter. To achieve this unity, one requires the "still, small voice" that is reflective of the ability to make space for the other, to listen to the other, to dialogue with the other, to generously give and graciously receive from the other, to bring people of different religious and political perspectives together.

הַלֵּל

מוזגים כוס רביעי וגומרים עליו את ההלל.

לֹא לָנוּ, יהוה, **לֹא** לָנוּ, כִּי-לְשִׁמְךָ תֵּן כָּבוֹד, עַל-חַסְדְּךָ עַל-אֲמִתֶּךָ. לָמָּה יֹאמְרוּ הַגּוֹיִם אַיֵּה-נָא אֱלֹהֵיהֶם. וֵאלֹהֵינוּ בַשָּׁמָיִם, כֹּל אֲשֶׁר-חָפֵץ עָשָׂה. עֲצַבֵּיהֶם כֶּסֶף וְזָהָב מַעֲשֵׂה יְדֵי אָדָם. פֶּה-לָהֶם וְלֹא יְדַבֵּרוּ, עֵינַיִם לָהֶם וְלֹא יִרְאוּ. אָזְנַיִם לָהֶם וְלֹא יִשְׁמָעוּ, אַף לָהֶם וְלֹא יְרִיחוּן. יְדֵיהֶם וְלֹא יְמִישׁוּן, רַגְלֵיהֶם וְלֹא יְהַלֵּכוּ, לֹא יֶהְגּוּ בִּגְרוֹנָם.

Hallel

The appearance of Elijah at the Seder segues into the Hallel. Whereas the first two paragraphs of this Hallel recited before the Seder meal speak of the past exodus, i.e. "when Israel left Egypt," the latter part of the Hallel, recited now, points to our future redemption. And so, we declare: "May God [into the future] bless the House of Israel."… "Blessed is the one who comes in the name of the Lord, we bless you from the House of the Lord (the Holy Temple)."

We then broaden our petitions and resolve to seek redemption for the world. We do so by reading and singing what is called the Hallel Hagadol, the Great Hallel, referring to this universal quest. This is followed by the opening paragraphs of the Shabbat morning service, containing a similar even more intense yearning.

HALLEL

Second Half of Hallel: National Redemption
We pour the fourth cup and complete the Hallel

Lo Lanu - לֹא לָנוּ

Not for our sake, O Lord, not for our sake, but rather for Your name, give glory for your kindness and for your truth. Why should the nations say, "Where is their God?" But our God is in the heavens, all that He wanted, He has done. Their idols are silver and gold, the work of human hands. They have a mouth but do not speak; eyes but do not see. Ears but do not hear; a nose but do not smell. Hands, but they do not feel; feet, but do not walk; they do not make a sound from their throat.

National Redemption

The Hallel HaMitzri focuses on our particularistic agenda. A strong sense of national consciousness does not contradict our universal striving, but is a prerequisite to it.

Lo Lanu

לֹא לָנוּ - **Not for our sake:** Perhaps this should be interpreted, "Not *only* for our sake." In other words, we, too, need to live and breathe Your teachings.

כִּי לְשִׁמְךָ תֵּן כָּבוֹד - **But rather for Your Name, give glory:** This doesn't only refer to the Name of God but to His characteristics. God doesn't seek glory for Himself. He's not concerned for His Name, but the world desperately needs His teachings.

עַל חַסְדְּךָ עַל אֲמִתֶּךָ - **For Your kindness and for Your truth:** Truth is foundational to the world, but as important is kindness, as the Psalmist says, the world is built on kindness. The Rabbis make this point when declaring, "When God created the world, He did so with strict judgement. Seeing that the world could not subsist on justice alone, He infused it with kindness – only then can humankind survive, even thrive."

פֶּה לָהֶם וְלֹא יְדַבֵּרוּ - **Mouths but do not speak:** As we present the impotence of heathen gods, we might consider asking ourselves, how

כְּמוֹהֶם יִהְיוּ עֹשֵׂיהֶם, כֹּל אֲשֶׁר-בֹּטֵחַ בָּהֶם.
יִשְׂרָאֵל בְּטַח בַּיהוה, עֶזְרָם וּמָגִנָּם הוּא.
בֵּית אַהֲרֹן בִּטְחוּ בַיהוה, עֶזְרָם וּמָגִנָּם הוּא.
יִרְאֵי יהוה בִּטְחוּ בַיהוה, עֶזְרָם וּמָגִנָּם הוּא.

יהוה זְכָרָנוּ יְבָרֵךְ,
יְבָרֵךְ אֶת בֵּית יִשְׂרָאֵל, יְבָרֵךְ אֶת בֵּית אַהֲרֹן.
יְבָרֵךְ יִרְאֵי יהוה, הַקְּטַנִּים עִם הַגְּדֹלִים.
יֹסֵף יהוה עֲלֵיכֶם, עֲלֵיכֶם וְעַל בְּנֵיכֶם.
בְּרוּכִים אַתֶּם לַיהוה, עֹשֵׂה שָׁמַיִם וָאָרֶץ.

effective are we? Even if we're blessed with the ability to speak, do our words help or hurt? Do our eyes only see, or do they also empathize? Do our ears only hear, or do they listen as well? Do we only move our hands and feet, or do we move them with moral purpose and direction?

יִשְׂרָאֵל בְּטַח בַּה' - **Israel, trust in the Lord:** Trusting in God also involves our constant recollection that God trusts in us – only if we do our share will God do His. In partnership, redemption comes. There's a story I like to tell about this:

Two friends were discussing some of the more difficult issues of life. One said, "Sometimes I would like to ask God why He allows poverty, famine, and injustice, when He could do something about it." The other replied, "Well, why don't you ask Him?" The response came quickly: "Because I am afraid that God might ask me the same question."

Adonai Zecharanu

ה' זְכָרָנוּ - **The Lord who remembers us:** Virtually all people are forgotten. How many of us know the names of our great-

Like them will be their makers, all those that trust in them.
Israel, trust in the Lord; He is their help and shield.
House of Aaron, trust in the Lord; He is their help and shield.
Those that fear the Lord, trust in the Lord; He is their help and shield. (Psalms 115:1-11)

Yevarech Et Beit Yisrael - יְהוָה זְכָרָנוּ יְבָרֵךְ

The Lord who remembers us,
He will bless the House of Israel; He will bless the House of Aaron;
He will bless those that fear the Lord, the small ones with the great ones.
May the Lord bring increase to you, to you and to your children.
Blessed are you to the Lord, the maker of heavens and earth.

grandparents? And considering the sweep of history, they lived a short time ago. In the end, who remembers? Only God. Thus, like our Psalm, the Memorial Prayer begins with "Yizkor Elohim" – May the Lord remember.

יְבָרֵךְ יִרְאֵי ה' - **He will bless those that fear the Lord:** Who in life doesn't fear? We all fear something – aging, sickness, loss of job, or standing. But, Rabbi Soloveitchik teaches, there is one fear that removes all these lesser fears, and that is the fear of God. In that sense, fear of God expresses God's love, as it diminishes other fears.

יֹסֵף ה' עֲלֵיכֶם - **May the Lord bring increase to you:** In all the biblical countings of Israel, special attention is given to each individual. No one is objectified. Everyone plays an indispensable, unique role. Thus, the increase of numbers is more qualitative than quantitative.

So critical is everyone to the *Knesset Yisrael* (the community of Israel) that we become, as Rabbi Soloveitchik points out, a "community persona." If one person is missing, the collective whole has been forever altered. While no one is indispensable, no one is dispensable. Without that individual, our wholeness as a people is never the same.

הַשָּׁמַיִם שָׁמַיִם לַיהוה וְהָאָרֶץ נָתַן לִבְנֵי־אָדָם.
לֹא הַמֵּתִים יְהַלְלוּ־יָהּ
וְלֹא כָּל־יֹרְדֵי דוּמָה.
וַאֲנַחְנוּ נְבָרֵךְ יָהּ מֵעַתָּה וְעַד־עוֹלָם. הַלְלוּ־יָהּ. (תהלים קטו)

הַשָּׁמַיִם שָׁמַיִם לַה' וְהָאָרֶץ נָתַן לִבְנֵי אָדָם - **The heavens are the Lord's heavens, while the earth He gave to humankind:** And yet, the Torah tells us that Moses ascended heavenward, and elsewhere we're told that God descended in a cloud. The Talmud suggests that humans and God simultaneously move towards each other, stopping a short distance apart. In that sense, God is in the heaven, mortals on earth. It's in that liminal space that the deepest love between humans and God manifests, reaching but not touching (Sukkah 5a).

וְהָאָרֶץ נָתַן לִבְנֵי אָדָם - **While the earth He gave to humankind:** As a sacred responsibility, to Adam and Eve, God says, "Be fruitful and multiply and fill the earth and conquer it [*v'kivshuha*]." After the deluge, God uses similar terminology when telling Noah, "Be fruitful and multiply and fill the earth."

Notably, the word *v'kivshuha* is missing, as it may have initially been misunderstood to mean that humans can do with the earth what they wish

The heavens, are the Lord's heavens, while the earth He gave to humankind.
The dead will not praise the Lord,
nor do those who go down to the grave in silence.
But we will bless the Lord from now and forever.
Hallelujah! (Psalms 115:12-18)

— and this, of course, is not the case.

The environmental focus coheres with the Torah's glorious depiction of God's placing Adam in the Garden of Eden to "serve it and protect it." While the ground produces food for our benefit, we have the sacred responsibility of guarding and caring for its welfare.

From my perspective, one of the most pressing issues we face today is the degradation of the environment. If this colossal challenge is not addressed, other issues will be forever unaddressed as the world will no longer exist.

לֹא הַמֵּתִים יְהַלְלוּ יָהּ - **The dead will not praise the Lord:** We place emphasis on this world, not the next. It's in this world, when alive, that we can partner with God to help create a better world. In death, Rabbi Soloveitchik notes, we're dormant. We may enjoy the afterlife, but we no longer can play an active role in "doing," in redeeming the world.

אָהַבְתִּי כִּי-יִשְׁמַע יהוה אֶת-קוֹלִי תַּחֲנוּנָי.
כִּי-הִטָּה אָזְנוֹ לִי וּבְיָמַי אֶקְרָא.
אֲפָפוּנִי חֶבְלֵי-מָוֶת וּמְצָרֵי שְׁאוֹל מְצָאוּנִי, צָרָה וְיָגוֹן אֶמְצָא.
וּבְשֵׁם יהוה אֶקְרָא, אָנָּא יהוה מַלְּטָה נַפְשִׁי.
חַנּוּן יהוה וְצַדִּיק, וֵאלֹהֵינוּ מְרַחֵם. שֹׁמֵר פְּתָאִים יהוה, דַּלּוֹתִי וְלִי יְהוֹשִׁיעַ.

Ahavti

אָהַבְתִּי כִּי יִשְׁמַע ה' אֶת קוֹלִי תַּחֲנוּנָי - I love the Lord since He listens to my voice, my supplicatory prayers: Here, the Psalmist posits that God listens to our prayers, not that He accepts them. While prayer can impact the decree, this is not its primary purpose.

The foundation of prayer is the reaching out to God in our times of greatest loneliness and despair. Whatever the outcome, prayer allows us the possibility of forging an intimate relationship with God. Whatever the future brings, we are no longer alone – we are in fellowship with God.

The idea that the essence of prayer can be found in the individual's feeling close to God rather than in God's response finds expression in the words of Rabbi Dr. Eliezer Berkovits in his classic work *Prayer*:

> In its original form, prayer is not asking God for anything; it is not a request. It is a cry; an elementary outburst of woe, a spontaneous call in need; a hurt, a sorrow, given voice. It is the call of human helplessness directed to God. It is not asking, but coming with one's burden before God. It is like the child's running to the mother because it hurts. It is not the bandage that the child seeks instinctively but the nearness of the mother, to unburden his heart to the one of whose love he is certain.

Ahavti - אֲהַבְתִּי

I love the Lord since He listens to my voice, my supplicatory prayers. Since He inclined His ear to me - and in my days, I will call out. The pangs of death have encircled me and the straits of the grave have found me. As I encountered distress and sorrow I called out in the name of the Lord, "Please Lord, Spare my soul." Gracious is the Lord and righteous, and our God acts mercifully. The Lord watches over the fools; I was lowly and He has saved me.

From this perspective, the Hebrew term for prayer – *tefillah* – may be associated with *nafal* (fall), falling before God, seeking His embrace. This is "prayer as feeling God's love."

כִּי הִטָּה אָזְנוֹ לִי - **Since He inclined His ear to me:** When searching for God, God is searching for us – already inclining His ear to listen intently. Even more: while God is independent, self-existent, to be manifest in the world humans need to accept the Divine. Thus, to be whole, God not only searches for us, He needs us. So says the prophet Zachariah: Today God is not wholly manifest, but "On that day God will be One and His name will be One." On which day? On the day God is embraced by humankind.

So important is this idea it becomes the finale of the *Al Kein* (said after *Aleinu*), concluding most prayer services.

צָרָה וְיָגוֹן אֶמְצָא. וּבְשֵׁם ה' אֶקְרָא - **As I encountered distress and sorrow, I called out in the name of the Lord:** "Distress" and "sorrow" may speak of God's hiddenness, as the Torah states, "And I will certainly conceal [*haster astir*] My face on that day." Counterintuitively, it can be suggested that even then, in that darkness of darkness, we have the capacity to search for and find God. This attitude reflects the thinking of the eighteenth-century Chassidic master Rav Nachman of Breslov, who says that if, somehow, we penetrate worldly and existential suffering and

שׁוּבִי נַפְשִׁי לִמְנוּחָיְכִי, כִּי-יהוה גָּמַל עָלָיְכִי.
כִּי חִלַּצְתָּ נַפְשִׁי מִמָּוֶת,
אֶת-עֵינִי מִן-דִּמְעָה,
אֶת-רַגְלִי מִדֶּחִי.

אֶתְהַלֵּךְ לִפְנֵי יהוה בְּאַרְצוֹת הַחַיִּים.
הֶאֱמַנְתִּי כִּי אֲדַבֵּר, אֲנִי עָנִיתִי מְאֹד.
אֲנִי אָמַרְתִּי בְחָפְזִי כָּל הָאָדָם כֹּזֵב.

do all within our power to try to reach out to God, we will find Him. In his words, "Even in the hiddenness within the hiddenness, even there, God, may He be blessed, is found."

As my son Dr. Dov Weiss posits in his book *Pious Irreverence*, while the Christian critique of Judaism millennia ago suggests that, with the destruction of the Temple, we have been cast away by God, the Rabbis emphatically respond no. *Shechinah bagolah*. God is with us – even in the exile of exiles.

This is one of the deepest challenges of faith. Can we find closeness in distance, revelation in concealment? In times of abandonment, can we feel God's unconditional love even in the hidden of the hiddenness?

אֶתְהַלֵּךְ לִפְנֵי ה' - **I will walk before the Lord:** At times, like the biblical Noah, we walk *with* God. At other moments, much like Abraham, we walk *before* God, showing the way, sometimes respectfully urging God to do better. This, as my son points out, is not a sign of disrespect but of love: a love so great I feel open enough to share my deepest feelings – even if a critique – with God.

אֲנִי אָמַרְתִּי בְחָפְזִי כָּל הָאָדָם כֹּזֵב - **I said in my haste, all people are deceitful:** If we would only slow down to assess our neighbor more compassionately, we would find that most people possess inner goodness

Return, my soul to tranquility, for the Lord has favored you.
For You have rescued my soul from death,
my eyes from tears,
my feet from stumbling.

I will walk before the Lord in the land of the living.
I trust in God, even when I am afflicted.
I said in my haste, all people are deceitful. (Psalms 116:1-11)

– an inner pure holy spark waiting to be lit. In our very fast world, slowing down can be spiritually uplifting, as magically laid out in this poem variously credited to Wilfred A. Peterson or Orin L. Crain:

> Slow me down, Lord,
> Ease the pounding of my heart
> By the quieting of my mind.
> Steady my hurried pace
> With a vision of the eternal reach of time....
>
> Break the tensions of my nerves
> With the soothing music
> Of singing streams....
>
> Slow me down, Lord,
> And inspire me to send my own roots deep
> Into the soil of life's enduring values
> That I may grow toward the stars
> Of my greater destiny.

מָה-אָשִׁיב לַיהוה כָּל-תַּגְמוּלוֹהִי עָלָי.
כּוֹס-יְשׁוּעוֹת אֶשָּׂא וּבְשֵׁם יהוה אֶקְרָא.
נְדָרַי לַיהוה אֲשַׁלֵּם נֶגְדָה-נָּא לְכָל-עַמּוֹ.

יָקָר בְּעֵינֵי יהוה הַמָּוְתָה לַחֲסִידָיו.

אָנָּה יהוה כִּי-אֲנִי עַבְדֶּךָ, אֲנִי-עַבְדְּךָ בֶּן-אֲמָתֶךָ, פִּתַּחְתָּ לְמוֹסֵרָי.

לְךָ-אֶזְבַּח זֶבַח תּוֹדָה וּבְשֵׁם יהוה אֶקְרָא.
נְדָרַי לַיהוה אֲשַׁלֵּם נֶגְדָה-נָּא לְכָל-עַמּוֹ.
בְּחַצְרוֹת בֵּית יהוה, בְּתוֹכֵכִי יְרוּשָׁלַיִם,

הַלְלוּ-יָהּ. (תהלים קטז)

Mah Ashiv

מָה אָשִׁיב - **What shall I give to the Lord for all He's given me?** When considering all that God does for us, the countless blessings in our day-to-day lives we so often take for granted, there would be no way to repay the Lord.

יָקָר בְּעֵינֵי ה' - **Piercingly painful in the eyes of the Lord is the death of His devoted ones:** As the number of terror victims in Israel mounts, I lovingly challenge God with the plea: Why?

Never will I forget a mother's eulogy for her son who fell in the Gaza war. Quoting Bruriah (the Talmudic Rav Meir's wife), she cried out, "The Lord gives, and the Lord takes." Strikingly, she stopped there, not concluding Bruriah's statement: "May the Name of the Lord be blessed." As she told me during shiva, in her heart she just couldn't bring herself to say those words.

פִּתַּחְתָּ לְמוֹסֵרָי - **You have loosened my bonds:** You have freed me not only to relieve my suffering, but also, You can be more gentle, more kind in Your *mussar*, in Your criticism of each of us.

לְךָ אֶזְבַּח זֶבַח תּוֹדָה - **To You I will offer thanksgiving sacrifices, calling out in the name of the Lord:** Sacrifices were meant to be an external manifestation of what a person feels internally. Indeed, the

Mah Ashiv - מָה אָשִׁיב

What shall I give to the Lord for all He's given me? A cup of salvations I will raise up and I will call out in the name of the Lord. My vows to the Lord I will pay, publicly before His entire people.

Piercingly painful in the eyes of the Lord is the death of His devoted ones.

Please Lord, since I am Your servant, the child of Your maidservant; You have loosened my bonds.

To You I will offer a thanksgiving sacrifice, calling out in the name of the Lord. My vows to the Lord I will pay, publicly before all His people. In the courtyards of the house of the Lord, in your midst, Jerusalem.

Hallelujah! (Psalms 116:12-19)

first animal sacrifice accepted was that of Abel. The Torah states that "Abel also brought of the firstlings of his flock and of the fat thereof." The Hebrew for "also brought" is *gam hu* (literally, "also him"), which the Sefat Emet understands to mean that Abel literally brought himself. His sacrifice was accepted because it reflected his sincere inner feelings of bring himself to and connecting with God.

As important as the sacrificial service was during ancient times, prophets spoke out against sacrifices that were not sincere. And so, when King Saul tried to defend himself to the prophet Samuel (1 Samuel 15), pointing out that the soldiers "took sheep and cattle from the plunder…in order to sacrifice them to the Lord," the prophet gloriously responds, "Does the Lord delight in burnt offerings and sacrifices as much as in obeying the Lord? To obey is better than sacrifice (*shemoa mizevach tov*), and to heed is better than the fat of rams."

Today, prayer has replaced sacrifices. But its efficacy, too, depends upon the purity of the heart, the goodness and sincerity of the supplicant.

בְּתוֹכֵכִי יְרוּשָׁלָיִם - **In your midst, Jerusalem:** We pray that Jerusalem soon be a city reflecting the meaning of its Hebrew name – Yerushalayim. *Yeru* is Aramaic for city (similar to the word *ir*, city in Hebrew); *shalayim*

הַלְלוּ אֶת-יהוה כָּל גּוֹיִם,
שַׁבְּחוּהוּ כָּל-הָאֻמִּים.
כִּי גָבַר עָלֵינוּ חַסְדּוֹ,
וֶאֱמֶת יהוה לְעוֹלָם, הַלְלוּ-יָהּ. (תהלים קיז)

הוֹדוּ לַיהוה כִּי-טוֹב כִּי לְעוֹלָם חַסְדּוֹ.
יֹאמַר-נָא יִשְׂרָאֵל כִּי לְעוֹלָם חַסְדּוֹ.
יֹאמְרוּ-נָא בֵית-אַהֲרֹן כִּי לְעוֹלָם חַסְדּוֹ.
יֹאמְרוּ-נָא יִרְאֵי-יהוה כִּי לְעוֹלָם חַסְדּוֹ.

has several meanings:
- It may be associated with Shalom, upper case (a name of God). Thus, Jerusalem has the capacity to be a godly city.
- Or it may reflect the word *shalem* ("whole" or "one"). Thus, Jerusalem has the potential to be a city of unity for all Jews, and for that matter, for all Jews and gentiles.
- Or it may refer to *shalom*, lower case (peace). Thus, Jerusalem represents a constant yearning and reaching for peace – outer peace, inner peace.

Hallelu et Adonai

הַלְלוּ אֶת ה' כָּל גּוֹיִם - **Praise the name of the Lord, all nations:** This aligns with the prophet's declaration, "For My House is a House of Prayer for all nations."

כִּי גָבַר עָלֵינוּ חַסְדּוֹ - **Since His kindness has overwhelmed us (*gavar*):** There is a difference between *ko'ach* and *g'vurah*. *Koach* relates to power, the readiness to militate aggressively in order to be victorious. *G'vurah* is the attribute of forbearance, the ability to hold back, contract, and with quiet, kindly strength, prevail.

הַלְלוּיָהּ - **Hallelujah:** A mixture of three words: *hallel*, to praise; *laila*, night; *Yah*, the Name of God.

At night, when feeling forlorn, we offer endless praise of the Lord for being with us – even then.

Hallelu - הַלְלוּ

Praise the name of the Lord, all nations;
Extol Him all peoples.
Since His kindness has overwhelmed us
And the truth of the Lord is forever.
Hallelujah! (Psalm 117)

Hodu L'Adonai Ki Tov - הוֹדוּ

Thank the Lord, for He is good,   His lovingkindness is forever.
Let Israel now say,   "His lovingkindness is forever."
Let the House of Aaron now say,   "His lovingkindness is forever."
Let those that fear the Lord now say,   "His lovingkindness is forever."

(Psalms 118:1-4)

Hodu L'Adonai Ki Tov

הוֹדוּ לַה' כִּי־טוֹב כִּי לְעוֹלָם חַסְדּוֹ - **Thank the Lord for He is good, His lovingkindness is forever:** A general headline followed by detailing in an all-encompassing way those who offer praise to God.

יֹאמַר נָא יִשְׂרָאֵל כִּי לְעוֹלָם חַסְדּוֹ - **Let Israel now say, His lovingkindness is forever:** More than a nation, we're the house of Israel, a family; and the test of family is not how we love when we agree but how we love when we disagree.

יֹאמְרוּ נָא בֵית אַהֲרֹן כִּי לְעוֹלָם חַסְדּוֹ - **Let the House of Aaron now say, His lovingkindness is forever:** Aaron learned well from God as he emerges in the Bible as the quiet, soft defender of the Jewish people, attempting to calm them when the Golden Calf was built and later on during the Korach rebellion.

יֹאמְרוּ נָא יִרְאֵי ה' כִּי לְעוֹלָם חַסְדּוֹ - **Let those that fear the Lord now say, His lovingkindness is forever:** Rashi claims that this line refers to converts. In this way, the progression moves up in holiness – from the Israelite grassroots, to Aaron the high priest, to the convert. Not coincidentally, from Ruth, the convert par excellence, the Messiah will one day come, teaching that while born Jews may be holy, the convert is the holy of holies.

מִן-הַמֵּצַר קָרָאתִי יָּהּ, עָנָנִי בַמֶּרְחָב יָהּ.
יהוה לִי, לֹא אִירָא – מַה-יַּעֲשֶׂה לִי אָדָם.
יהוה לִי בְּעֹזְרָי וַאֲנִי אֶרְאֶה בְשֹׂנְאָי.

טוֹב לַחֲסוֹת בַּיהוה מִבְּטֹחַ בָּאָדָם.
טוֹב לַחֲסוֹת בַּיי מִבְּטֹחַ בִּנְדִיבִים.

כָּל-גּוֹיִם סְבָבוּנִי, בְּשֵׁם יהוה כִּי אֲמִילַם.
סַבּוּנִי גַם-סְבָבוּנִי, בְּשֵׁם יהוה כִּי אֲמִילַם.
סַבּוּנִי כִדְבֹרִים, דֹּעֲכוּ כְּאֵשׁ קוֹצִים, בְּשֵׁם יהוה כִּי אֲמִילַם.

דָּחֹה דְחִיתַנִי לִנְפֹּל, וַיהוה עֲזָרָנִי.
עָזִּי וְזִמְרָת יָהּ וַיְהִי-לִי לִישׁוּעָה.

Min Hameitzar

מִן הַמֵּצַר - From the straits (*meitzar*) I have called, Lord; He answered me from the wide expanse: After the Yom Kippur War, a rabbi visited wounded Israeli soldiers, singing and trying to offer meaning to Rav Nachman's words, "The whole world is a narrow bridge, but the main thing to recall is to have no fear at all." A seriously injured soldier thanked the rabbi for his interpretations, adding that Rav Nachman's words related to his personal war experience.

I was part of the brigade that "threw" pontoon bridges over the Suez Canal, just days after we suffered catastrophic losses. Our leader, General Ariel Sharon, told us: Defend this bridge with every ounce of your

Min Hameitzar

From the straits I have called, Lord; He answered me from the wide expanse. The Lord is with me, I will not fear, what can anyone do to me? The Lord is with me, He helps me, seeing to it that my enemies are destroyed.

It is better to take refuge with the Lord than to trust in any person. It is better to take refuge with the Lord than to trust in nobles.

All the nations surrounded me, but in the name of the Lord, I will defeat them. They surrounded me, they also encircled me - in the name of the Lord, I will defeat them. They surrounded me like bees, they were extinguished like a fire of thorns - in the name of the Lord, as I will defeat them.

You (the enemy) have pushed me over and over to fall, but the Lord helped me. My boldness and song is the Lord, and He has become my salvation.

strength – it is our lifeline, Israel's lifeline for survival. That night, the whole world, for me, was that narrow bridge.

כָּל גּוֹיִם סְבָבוּנִי - **All the nations surrounded me:** This phrase resonates today, as Israel is surrounded by terrorist organizations and nations bent on its destruction. And yet, Israel with God's help prevails, not only defending itself and Jews around the world, but serving as the frontline against the spread of terror everywhere.

וְזִמְרָת - **And song:** *Zimrat*, normally translated "song," may also come from the word *zomer* (prune), a process that abets and prepares trees for greater growth. So, too, when approaching God – as Rabbi Yosef Dov Soloveitchik said, "there is no holiness without preparation."

קוֹל רִנָּה וִישׁוּעָה בְּאָהֳלֵי צַדִּיקִים,
יְמִין יהוה עֹשָׂה חָיִל.

יְמִין יהוה רוֹמֵמָה,
יְמִין יהוה עֹשָׂה חָיִל.

לֹא אָמוּת כִּי־אֶחְיֶה, וַאֲסַפֵּר מַעֲשֵׂי יָהּ.
יַסֹּר יִסְּרַנִּי יָּהּ, וְלַמָּוֶת לֹא נְתָנָנִי.

פִּתְחוּ לִי שַׁעֲרֵי־צֶדֶק, אָבֹא־בָם, אוֹדֶה יָהּ.
זֶה־הַשַּׁעַר לַיהוה, צַדִּיקִים יָבֹאוּ בוֹ.

חָיִל... חָיִל - Acts powerfully…is doing good deeds: *Chayil* can have two meanings. On the one hand, it has military connotations like the Hebrew *chayal*, soldier. Hence, the first translation "acts powerfully." On the other hand, *chayil* can be spiritual in nature. The Lubavitcher Rebbe called those doing acts of kindness as being part of *Tzivos Hashem* – God's army of do-gooders, as our translation indicates "is doing good deeds."

לֹא אָמוּת כִּי אֶחְיֶה - I will not die, but rather I will live: This phrase underscores the importance of choosing life, enhancing, contributing to the wellbeing of our people and the world. This has been the mission of so many Holocaust survivors, as Solomon the King wrote in the Song of Songs, "Place me as a seal upon your heart, for love overpowers death." The response to death is to love, to marry, to bring more life into the world.

פִּתְחוּ לִי שַׁעֲרֵי צֶדֶק - Open up for me the gates of righteousness: A call to make our synagogues, JCCs,

The sound of happy song and salvation is in the tents of the righteous,
the right hand of the Lord acts powerfully.

The Lord's right hand is lifted high.
The Lord's right hand is doing good deeds.

I will not die, but rather I will live and tell over the acts of the Lord.
The Lord has surely chastised me, but He has not given me over to death.

Open up for me the gates of righteousness;
I will enter them, and thank the Lord.
This is the gate of the Lord, the righteous will enter it. (Psalms 118:5-20)

schools, accessible so all can enter. A photograph in my office says it all. A man sits in his wheelchair at the bottom of a flight of steps that leads to the entrance of the synagogue. Over its door is emblazoned the sentence "Open the gates of righteousness for me, I will enter through them." The man sits with his back to the doors, unable to enter. As a Jewish community, we have too often failed him. Our task is to ensure that he can face the door and be welcomed as he enters, to make *Am Yisrael* complete.

צַדִּיקִים יָבֹאוּ בוֹ - **The righteous will enter it:** But who decides who is righteous? Only God. His assessment may be very different from ours. A personal anecdote: At a rabbinic conference many years ago, a senior colleague turned to me and said, "Avi, you're so non-judgmental that for you there is no such thing as a righteous or wicked person." Respectfully, I responded, "I'm sure there is. But I'll let God decide who falls into which category."

אוֹדְךָ כִּי עֲנִיתָנִי וַתְּהִי-לִי לִישׁוּעָה.
אוֹדְךָ כִּי עֲנִיתָנִי וַתְּהִי-לִי לִישׁוּעָה.

אֶבֶן מָאֲסוּ הַבּוֹנִים הָיְתָה לְרֹאשׁ פִּנָּה.
אֶבֶן מָאֲסוּ הַבּוֹנִים הָיְתָה לְרֹאשׁ פִּנָּה.

מֵאֵת יהוה הָיְתָה זֹּאת הִיא נִפְלָאת בְּעֵינֵינוּ.
מֵאֵת יהוה הָיְתָה זֹּאת הִיא נִפְלָאת בְּעֵינֵינוּ.

זֶה-הַיּוֹם עָשָׂה יהוה. נָגִילָה וְנִשְׂמְחָה בוֹ.
זֶה-הַיּוֹם עָשָׂה יהוה. נָגִילָה וְנִשְׂמְחָה בוֹ.

Od'cha Ki Anitani

אוֹדְךָ כִּי עֲנִיתָנִי - **I will thank You, since You answered me (*anitani*):** *Anitani* can also mean "affliction" (*inuy*). Even then, even in affliction, You answered me.

Even Ma'asu Habonim

אֶבֶן מָאֲסוּ הַבּוֹנִים הָיְתָה לְרֹאשׁ פִּנָּה - **The stone rejected by the builders has become the main cornerstone:** Sometimes it's the individual we think is least likely to succeed who reaches the highest levels of success. In high school, I shared a double desk with a friend who often doodled, and so I thought he would have difficulty moving ahead in life. As it turns out, he founded a major Jewish publishing company, making one of the greatest contributions to Jewish learning in recent history. You never know.

Me'et Adonai

מֵאֵת ה' הָיְתָה זֹּאת - **From the Lord was this:** Sometimes, even when denying our request – God saves us. In this spirit, the great singer Garth Brooks wrote in his song "Unanswered Prayers":

Od'cha

I will thank You, since You answered me and You have become my salvation.

The stone rejected by the builders has become the main cornerstone.

From the Lord was this, it is wondrous in our eyes.

This is the day of the Lord, let us exult and rejoice upon it. (Psalms 118:21-24)

> Sometimes I thank God for unanswered prayers
> Remember when you're talkin' to the Man upstairs
> That just because He doesn't answer doesn't mean He don't care.
> Some of God's greatest gifts are unanswered prayers.

Zeh Hayom

זֶה הַיּוֹם - **This is the day:** Often we are so mired in the past, so concerned about the future, that we fail to live in the present. Here, the Psalmist stresses *hayom* – being mindful of the moment as a gift from God.

This is the message of Thornton Wilder's famous play *Our Town*, about a woman who dies at a young age. After her death, the woman, named Emily, is given the opportunity to revisit any day of her life. In one magnificent scene, she is allowed to view her twelfth birthday. The dead Emily calls out to her living family but cannot be heard. She is anguished as she observes her family going about the day perfunctorily. The poignant narrative reads:

> I can't. I can't go on. It goes so fast. We don't have time to look at one another. (*She breaks down sobbing.*) I didn't realize. So all

אָנָּא יהוה, הוֹשִׁיעָה נָּא.

אָנָּא יהוה, הוֹשִׁיעָה נָּא.

אָנָּא יהוה, הַצְלִיחָה נָּא.

אָנָּא יהוה, הַצְלִיחָה נָּא.

בָּרוּךְ הַבָּא בְּשֵׁם יהוה, בֵּרַכְנוּכֶם מִבֵּית יהוה.

בָּרוּךְ הַבָּא בְּשֵׁם יהוה, בֵּרַכְנוּכֶם מִבֵּית יהוה.

אֵל יהוה וַיָּאֶר לָנוּ. אִסְרוּ חַג בַּעֲבֹתִים עַד קַרְנוֹת הַמִּזְבֵּחַ.

אֵל יהוה וַיָּאֶר לָנוּ. אִסְרוּ־חַג בַּעֲבֹתִים עַד־קַרְנוֹת הַמִּזְבֵּחַ.

אֵלִי אַתָּה וְאוֹדֶךָּ, אֱלֹהַי – אֲרוֹמְמֶךָּ.

אֵלִי אַתָּה וְאוֹדֶךָּ, אֱלֹהַי – אֲרוֹמְמֶךָּ.

הוֹדוּ לַיהוה כִּי־טוֹב, כִּי לְעוֹלָם חַסְדּוֹ.

הוֹדוּ לַיהוה כִּי־טוֹב, כִּי לְעוֹלָם חַסְדּוֹ. (תהלים קיח)

that was going on and we never noticed. Take me back – up the hill – to my grave.

But first: wait! One more look. Good-by, Good-by, world. Good-by, Grover's Corners… Mama and Papa. Good-by to clocks ticking… and Mama's sunflowers. And food and coffee. And new-ironed dresses and hot baths… and sleeping and waking up. Oh, earth you're too wonderful for anybody to realize you. Do any human beings ever realize life while they live it? – every, every minute?

Two thousand years earlier, the Talmud (Tamid 32a) makes this very point when Alexander the Great asked the Sages of Israel the secret to life. They responded, let every person imagine that each moment is his or her last – not to live in fear, but to be inspired to live fully, conscious of every moment as it unfolds.

As the popular adage goes, "Yesterday is history; tomorrow is a mystery; today is God's gift; that's why it's called the present."

Ana Adonai Hoshiya Na

Please, Lord, save us now;
Please, Lord, save us now;

Please, Lord, give us success now!
Please, Lord, give us success now! (Psalms 118:25)

Baruch Haba

Blessed be the one who comes in the name of the Lord, we have blessed you from the house of the Lord.

God is the Lord, He has given us light; tie up the festival offering with ropes until it reaches the corners of the altar.

You are my God and I will Thank You; my God and I will exalt You.

Thank the Lord, for He is good, His lovingkindness is forever. (Psalms 118:26-29)

Ana Adonai

אָנָּא ה', הוֹשִׁיעָה נָא. אָנָּא ה', הַצְלִיחָה נָא - **Please, Lord, save us now** (*hoshia*); **Please, Lord, give us success now** (*hatzlicha*): *Hatzlicha* (*hatzalah*) involves being unilaterally saved by another. *Hoshia* (*yeshua*) involves being part of the process. Only then do we achieve success.

Baruch Haba

בָּרוּךְ הַבָּא בְּשֵׁם ה' - **Blessed be the one who comes in the name of the Lord**: A blessing recited at ceremonies of birth – a *brit*, a *zeved habat*, not only welcoming the infant but praying that, as the child grows, all will be joyful when she or he enters a room.

אֵל ה' וַיָּאֶר לָנוּ - **God is the Lord, He has given us light**: The Psalmist writes: "In your light, there is light - *be'ohrcha nir'eh ohr* (Psalms 36:10)." This is the light of God; this is the light of Torah (*ohr Torah*); this is the new light shining upon Israel and Tzion ("*ohr chadash al Tzion ta'ir*") this is the light of the world (*ohr lagoyim*). Note the juxtaposition of the two blessings said every morning before Shema: *Blessed are You, O Lord, creator of the lights; With great love have I loved you.* This is the light of love (*ohr ahavah*).

אלי אתה...אלהי ארוממך – **You are**

יְהַלְלוּךָ יהוה אֱלֹהֵינוּ כָּל מַעֲשֶׂיךָ, וַחֲסִידֶיךָ צַדִּיקִים עוֹשֵׂי רְצוֹנֶךָ, וְכָל עַמְּךָ בֵּית יִשְׂרָאֵל בְּרִנָּה יוֹדוּ וִיבָרְכוּ, וִישַׁבְּחוּ וִיפָאֲרוּ, וִירוֹמְמוּ וְיַעֲרִיצוּ, וְיַקְדִּישׁוּ וְיַמְלִיכוּ, אֶת שִׁמְךָ, מַלְכֵּנוּ. כִּי לְךָ טוֹב לְהוֹדוֹת וּלְשִׁמְךָ נָאֶה לְזַמֵּר, כִּי מֵעוֹלָם וְעַד עוֹלָם אַתָּה אֵל.

יש נוהגים לברך ולשתות עוד כוס כאן לגאולת ישראל

my God… my God and I will exalt You (*aromemekah***):** On the one hand, "You are my God" refers to one's personal relationship with Hashem. On the other hand, *aromemekah*, from the word *rum*, meaning "above," refers to God who is sometimes beyond our personal reach.

So, too, did Israel, after being saved at the sea, declare: "This is my God (*zeh Eli*) and I will glorify Him (*ve'anvehu*); the God of my father (*Elohei avi*) and I will exalt him (*va'aromemenhu*)."

One approach to God is found in the first part of the sentence. Here the Jews proclaimed, "This is *my* God (*zeh Eli*)," the God with whom I have a very personal relationship. Hence, the modifying term *ve'anvehu* (and I will glorify Him) appears here. *Anvehu* is a compound of *ani veHu* (I and Him). This points to one who feels a connection to God and believes independently, having been closely touched by the Almighty.

A second approach to God is that of "*Elohei avi*" (the God of my father): to believe simply because of my inherited history, to believe because my parents believe. Hence, the text states *va'aromemenhu*, also from the root *rum*. In other words, although God is above me and I have little understanding of Him, nonetheless, I accept God because my parents accepted Him; doing so is part of my family DNA.

Which approach is more meaningful? Since both are mentioned, each has validity. Indeed, when reciting the Amidah (the central prayer of the thrice-daily prayer service), we refer to both "our God (*Eloheinu*)" and "the God of our patriarchs (*Elohei avoteinu*)." Note the inclusion of both personal relationships and a belief in God because He was the God of our ancestors. The sequence of these terms in both the biblical text and in the Amidah shows us which approach

Yehalelucha - יְהַלְלוּךָ

All of Your works shall praise You, Lord our God, and Your pious ones, the righteous ones who do Your will; and all of Your people, the House of Israel will thank and bless You joyously: and extol and glorify, and exalt and acclaim, and sanctify and coronate Your name, our Ruler. It is good to thank You, and pleasant to sing Your praises, since always and forever are you God.

Some bless and drink an additional cup of wine celebrating the hope for our future national redemption.

has the most significance. In both instances, God is first described as a personal God. Similarly, in the Hallel, "You are my God" comes first.

An important lesson emerges from this principle: It is not enough for parents to expect their children to believe simply because they themselves believe. Transmission of belief in God is not automatic. What is most necessary is an atmosphere wherein a child comes to experience belief through personal strivings and actions. Such children are in the best position to maintain their belief and to transmit it to their children and they to their children until the end of time.

הוֹדוּ לַה' כִּי טוֹב - **Thank the Lord for He is good:** After every stage of creation, God sees and says, "It is good." Our task in life is to do the same. Note the sentence in Ecclesiastes, "More good [*tov*] is the day of death than the day of birth" (Ecclesiastes 7:1). The text does not say the day of death is happier than the day of birth – it is not. Rather, it is "more good." Hence, in the Genesis creation story, goodness [*ki tov*] is not mentioned after Adam is created as the term can only be used *after* one has lived a meaningful life.

Yehalelucha

יְהַלְלוּךָ ה' אֱלֹהֵינוּ כָּל מַעֲשֶׂיךָ - **All of Your works shall praise You, Lord our God:** There is a praise that is loud, all joining in, voices raised, shouting with glee to the Lord. And then, there is a praise that is so deep it transcends words, song, even melody. It is the praise of silence, what Rav Kook calls the holiness of silence, *kedushat hadumiya*. It is that instant when all existence, human, animal, vegetation, even the inanimate, is silent, with a silence that is pregnant with meaning – calling out in praise of

הלל הגדול

הוֹדוּ לַיהוה כִּי־טוֹב כִּי לְעוֹלָם חַסְדּוֹ.
הוֹדוּ לֵאלֹהֵי הָאֱלֹהִים כִּי לְעוֹלָם חַסְדּוֹ.
הוֹדוּ לַאֲדֹנֵי הָאֲדֹנִים כִּי לְעוֹלָם חַסְדּוֹ.
לְעֹשֵׂה נִפְלָאוֹת גְּדֹלוֹת לְבַדּוֹ כִּי לְעוֹלָם חַסְדּוֹ.
לְעֹשֵׂה הַשָּׁמַיִם בִּתְבוּנָה כִּי לְעוֹלָם חַסְדּוֹ.
לְרוֹקַע הָאָרֶץ עַל־הַמָּיִם כִּי לְעוֹלָם חַסְדּוֹ.
לְעֹשֵׂה אוֹרִים גְּדֹלִים כִּי לְעוֹלָם חַסְדּוֹ.
אֶת־הַשֶּׁמֶשׁ לְמֶמְשֶׁלֶת בַּיּוֹם כִּי לְעוֹלָם חַסְדּוֹ.
אֶת־הַיָּרֵחַ וְכוֹכָבִים לְמֶמְשְׁלוֹת בַּלַּיְלָה כִּי לְעוֹלָם חַסְדּוֹ.

the Lord.

Universal Redemption

Having completed the Hallel Hamitzri, the particularistic Hallel focusing on our hope for national redemption, we transition to the Hallel Hagadol, the Great Hallel, focusing on universal redemption.

Hodu L'Adonai Ki Tov

הוֹדוּ לַה' כִּי טוֹב כִּי לְעוֹלָם חַסְדּוֹ -
Thank the Lord for He is good; His kindness is forever (*le'olam*): For Jews, the messianic era is not a narrow time, exclusively benefitting the Jewish people, but a time when the world at large will be suffused with the messianic spirit of peace.

Ki Le'Olam Chasdo: From National to Universal Redemption

Thank the Lord for He is good,	His lovingkindness is forever.
Thank the Power of powers	His lovingkindness is universal.
To the Master of masters,	His lovingkindness is forever.
To the One who alone does wondrously great deeds	His lovingkindness is universal.
To the one who made the Heavens with discernment,	His lovingkindness is forever.
To the One who spread the earth over the waters,	His lovingkindness is universal.
To the One who made great lights,	His lovingkindness is forever.
The sun to rule in the day,	His lovingkindness is universal.
The moon and the stars to rule in the night,	His lovingkindness is forever.

This is the deeper meaning of the refrain *ki le'olam chasdo*. *Le'olam* is not only time centered, i.e. God's kindness is eternal, but space centered; that is, a praising of the Lord for His kindness extends universally – to the whole world.

- הוֹדוּ לַה' כִּי טוֹב כִּי לְעוֹלָם חַסְדּוֹ
Thank the Lord for He is good; His kindness is forever: The first nine lines of the Great Hallel are universal in nature: God creating the heavens and the earth, the sun, moon and stars. As the narrative in Genesis spells out, God then chooses humankind over all other life, gifting humans with the *tzelem Elohim*, the image of God. As God is one, so, too, is every human being unique. As God is infinite, so, too, is every human of infinite worth. And the image of God "placed" in Adam from whom we all come reflects the inherent equality of value of all people.

לְמַכֵּה מִצְרַיִם בִּבְכוֹרֵיהֶם כִּי לְעוֹלָם חַסְדּוֹ.
וַיּוֹצֵא יִשְׂרָאֵל מִתּוֹכָם כִּי לְעוֹלָם חַסְדּוֹ.
בְּיָד חֲזָקָה וּבִזְרוֹעַ נְטוּיָה כִּי לְעוֹלָם חַסְדּוֹ.
לְגֹזֵר יַם-סוּף לִגְזָרִים כִּי לְעוֹלָם חַסְדּוֹ.
וְהֶעֱבִיר יִשְׂרָאֵל בְּתוֹכוֹ כִּי לְעוֹלָם חַסְדּוֹ.
וְנִעֵר פַּרְעֹה וְחֵילוֹ בְיַם-סוּף כִּי לְעוֹלָם חַסְדּוֹ.
לְמוֹלִיךְ עַמּוֹ בַּמִּדְבָּר כִּי לְעוֹלָם חַסְדּוֹ.
לְמַכֵּה מְלָכִים גְּדֹלִים כִּי לְעוֹלָם חַסְדּוֹ.
וַיַּהֲרֹג מְלָכִים אַדִּירִים כִּי לְעוֹלָם חַסְדּוֹ.
לְסִיחוֹן מֶלֶךְ הָאֱמֹרִי כִּי לְעוֹלָם חַסְדּוֹ.
וּלְעוֹג מֶלֶךְ הַבָּשָׁן כִּי לְעוֹלָם חַסְדּוֹ.
וְנָתַן אַרְצָם לְנַחֲלָה כִּי לְעוֹלָם חַסְדּוֹ.
נַחֲלָה לְיִשְׂרָאֵל עַבְדּוֹ כִּי לְעוֹלָם חַסְדּוֹ.

שֶׁבְּשִׁפְלֵנוּ זָכַר לָנוּ כִּי לְעוֹלָם חַסְדּוֹ.
וַיִּפְרְקֵנוּ מִצָּרֵינוּ כִּי לְעוֹלָם חַסְדּוֹ.
נֹתֵן לֶחֶם לְכָל-בָּשָׂר כִּי לְעוֹלָם חַסְדּוֹ.
הוֹדוּ לְאֵל הַשָּׁמָיִם כִּי לְעוֹלָם חַסְדּוֹ. (תהלים קלו)

וַיּוֹצֵא יִשְׂרָאֵל מִתּוֹכָם - And brought Israel forth from among them (the Egyptians): But humankind did not fulfill the chosen role assigned to it by God. And so – after Adam and Eve are banished from the Garden of Eden, after Cain is exiled for killing Abel, after the world is destroyed by the flood, after humankind is dispersed for building a tower to challenge God – Abraham and Sarah enter the biblical story.

Our psalm, in its middle part, summarizes the beginning of the history of their descendants, the Jewish people; freedom from Egyptian enslavement, receiving the Torah, settling in Israel – a coalescing of the three pillars of nationhood: people, ideology, land. Here, the focus is on our nationalistic responsibilities.

נֹתֵן לֶחֶם לְכָל בָּשָׂר - He gives

To the One who struck Egypt through their firstborn,	His lovingkindness is universal.
And brought Israel forth from among them,	His lovingkindness is forever.
With a mighty hand and an outstretched arm,	His lovingkindness is universal.
To the One who cut up the Reed Sea into strips,	His lovingkindness is forever.
And He made Israel to pass through it,	His lovingkindness is universal.
And He jolted Pharaoh and his troop in the Reed Sea,	His lovingkindness is forever.
To the One who led his people in the wilderness,	His lovingkindness is universal.
To the One who smote great kings,	His lovingkindness is forever.
And he killed mighty kings,	His lovingkindness is universal.
Sichon, king of the Amorite,	His lovingkindness is forever.
And Og, king of the Bashan,	His lovingkindness is universal.
And he gave their land as an inheritance,	His lovingkindness is forever.
An inheritance for Israel, His servant,	His lovingkindness is universal.
That in our lowliness, He remembered us,	His lovingkindness is forever.
And he delivered us from our adversaries,	His lovingkindness is universal.
He gives food to all,	His lovingkindness is forever.
Offer gratitude to the God of heaven,	His lovingkindness is forever.

(Psalms 136)

food to all: Counterintuitively, our nationalistic agenda is not to be insular but to be a blessing for the entire world. We are meant to do our share to redeem the Jewish people and all humankind. Hence, the last four lines of our psalm underscore our responsibility to be there for the vulnerable, provide for all humankind. Thus, the movement of the psalm: from universal, to national, to universal.

This, in sum, is the trajectory of our history. Israel emerged as a people post-facto, as God originally chose all of humankind. When that experiment failed, we were "chosen" not to be privileged but to bear responsibility — *le'taken olam be'malchut Sha-ddai* – to [help] repair the world under the reign of the Almighty.

נִשְׁמַת כָּל חַי תְּבָרֵךְ אֶת שִׁמְךָ, יהוה אֱלֹהֵינוּ, וְרוּחַ כָּל בָּשָׂר תְּפָאֵר וּתְרוֹמֵם זִכְרְךָ, מַלְכֵּנוּ, תָּמִיד. מִן הָעוֹלָם וְעַד הָעוֹלָם אַתָּה אֵל, וּמִבַּלְעָדֶיךָ אֵין לָנוּ מֶלֶךְ גּוֹאֵל וּמוֹשִׁיעַ, פּוֹדֶה וּמַצִּיל וּמְפַרְנֵס וּמְרַחֵם בְּכָל עֵת צָרָה וְצוּקָה. אֵין לָנוּ מֶלֶךְ אֶלָּא אָתָּה.

אֱלֹהֵי הָרִאשׁוֹנִים וְהָאַחֲרוֹנִים, אֱלוֹהַּ כָּל בְּרִיּוֹת, אֲדוֹן כָּל תּוֹלָדוֹת, הַמְהֻלָּל בְּרֹב הַתִּשְׁבָּחוֹת, הַמְנַהֵג עוֹלָמוֹ בְּחֶסֶד וּבְרִיּוֹתָיו בְּרַחֲמִים. וַיהוה לֹא יָנוּם וְלֹא יִישָׁן – הַמְעוֹרֵר יְשֵׁנִים וְהַמֵּקִיץ נִרְדָּמִים, וְהַמֵּשִׂיחַ אִלְּמִים וְהַמַּתִּיר אֲסוּרִים וְהַסּוֹמֵךְ נוֹפְלִים וְהַזּוֹקֵף כְּפוּפִים. לְךָ לְבַדְּךָ אֲנַחְנוּ מוֹדִים.

The Haggadah now cites prayers from the Shabbat morning service (Shacharit), taking us to new highs in its description of universal redemption.

Nishmat Kol Chai

נִשְׁמַת כָּל חַי - **The breath of all life will bless Your Name, Lord our God:** At creation, the Lord God breathed into Adam the breath of life – what the Torah also calls the image of God. This contrasts with Michelangelo's painting extraordinaire of God's finger touching Adam, bringing him to life, limiting the creation process to the physical realm.

Breathing into another is an intimate portrayal of God's love for all of humankind. In fact, on Rosh Hashana, when we celebrate the universal creation of woman and man, what we are really celebrating is the creation of breath.

Our task is to breathe out the breath God breathed into us. This may be the deeper meaning of blowing the shofar, whose sound comes forth from the deepest inner breath. Only when all humans engage

Nishmat - נִשְׁמַת

נִשְׁמַת כָּל חַי - The breath of all life will bless Your Name, Lord our God; the spirit of all flesh will glorify and exalt Your remembrance always, our Ruler. From eternity to eternity, You are God, and other than You we have no ruler, redeemer, or savior, restorer, rescuer, provider, and merciful one in every time of distress and anguish; we have no ruler, besides You!

אֱלֹהֵי הָרִאשׁוֹנִים וְהָאַחֲרוֹנִים - God of the first ones and the last ones, God of all creatures, Master of all generations, Who is praised through a multitude of praises, Who guides His world with lovingkindness and His creatures with mercy. The Lord neither slumbers nor sleeps. He who rouses the sleepers and awakens the dozers; He who makes the mute speak, and frees the captives, and supports the falling, and straightens the bent. We thank You alone.

in this holy process, only when the breath of all life extolls God and His characteristics of kindness, goodness, and mercy will redemption come.

אֱלֹהֵי הָרִאשׁוֹנִים וְהָאַחֲרוֹנִים - **God of the first ones and the last ones:** On its face, "first" and "last" posit that God is eternal. That is, God precedes all and will follow all. Homiletically, however, the "first" and "last" may relate to the more and less important beings, or perhaps even elements, of creation. God's presence and concern is not reserved for those considered important.

In philosophy, the term "*yesh me'ayin*," creatio ex nihilo, refers to the first creation. From nothing (*ayin*) God created the first something (*yesh*) from which all of existence emanates.

Mystically, *yesh* refers to everything in the world – the inanimate, the vegetative, animal and human life. Every "*yesh*," everything that is, is suffused with the "*ayin*," short for *Ein Sof*, God who is endless. Recognizing that God is everywhere as God is in everything may help us treat the other with respect, ushering in the peaceful redemptive messianic era.

אִלּוּ פִינוּ מָלֵא שִׁירָה כַּיָּם, וּלְשׁוֹנֵנוּ רִנָּה כַּהֲמוֹן גַּלָּיו, וְשִׂפְתוֹתֵינוּ שֶׁבַח כְּמֶרְחֲבֵי רָקִיעַ, וְעֵינֵינוּ מְאִירוֹת כַּשֶּׁמֶשׁ וְכַיָּרֵחַ, וְיָדֵינוּ פְרוּשׂוֹת כְּנִשְׁרֵי שָׁמַיִם, וְרַגְלֵינוּ קַלּוֹת כָּאַיָּלוֹת – אֵין אֲנַחְנוּ מַסְפִּיקִים לְהוֹדוֹת לְךָ, יהוה אֱלֹהֵינוּ וֵאלֹהֵי אֲבוֹתֵינוּ, וּלְבָרֵךְ אֶת שְׁמֶךָ עַל אַחַת מֵאֶלֶף, אַלְפֵי אֲלָפִים וְרִבֵּי רְבָבוֹת פְּעָמִים הַטּוֹבוֹת שֶׁעָשִׂיתָ עִם אֲבוֹתֵינוּ וְעִמָּנוּ.

מִמִּצְרַיִם גְּאַלְתָּנוּ, יהוה אֱלֹהֵינוּ, וּמִבֵּית עֲבָדִים פְּדִיתָנוּ, בְּרָעָב זַנְתָּנוּ וּבְשָׂבָע כִּלְכַּלְתָּנוּ, מֵחֶרֶב הִצַּלְתָּנוּ וּמִדֶּבֶר מִלַּטְתָּנוּ, וּמֵחֳלָיִם רָעִים וְנֶאֱמָנִים דִּלִּיתָנוּ. עַד הֵנָּה עֲזָרוּנוּ רַחֲמֶיךָ וְלֹא עֲזָבוּנוּ חֲסָדֶיךָ, וְאַל תִּטְּשֵׁנוּ, יהוה אֱלֹהֵינוּ, לָנֶצַח.

אִלּוּ פִינוּ מָלֵא שִׁירָה כַּיָּם - Were our mouth as full of song as the sea… we still could not thank you sufficiently: No matter how articulate we are, there is no way to properly express our gratitude to God for all that He has done on our behalf. Sometimes we are swept away with appreciation for another; we find it impossible to express our emotions. Similarly, love can be so deep, so overwhelming, we are at a loss for words. This is a love that transcends all – it is the love of just being with the other.

Here, when reciting these words, may be an opportunity for Seder participants to share what they feel is an experience that is beyond description.

מִמִּצְרַיִם גְּאַלְתָּנוּ - From Egypt… You redeemed us: And yet, expressing gratitude, expressing love to the extent we can, is the right thing to do.

A good formula to begin this process is to intellectually list events that have touched our lives. Here, in the Nishmat, we do so by beginning with particularistic events and shifting into a universal thank you expressed by all to God for delivering us from sickness, poverty, and much more.

אִלּוּ פִינוּ מָלֵא שִׁירָה כַיָּם - Were our mouths as full of song as the sea, and our tongues as full of joyous song as its multitude of waves, and our lips as full of praise as the breadth of the heavens, and our eyes as sparkling as the sun and the moon, and our hands as outspread as the eagles of the sky and our feet as swift as deer - we still could not thank You sufficiently, Lord our God and God of our ancestors, and to bless Your Name for one thousandth of the thousands of thousands of thousands, and myriad myriads, of goodnesses that You performed for our ancestors and for us.

מִמִּצְרַיִם גְּאַלְתָּנוּ - From Egypt, Lord our God, You redeemed us and from the house of slaves You restored us. In famine You nourished us, and in plenty You sustained us. From the sword You saved us, and from plague You spared us; and from severe and enduring diseases You delivered us. Until now Your mercy has helped us, and Your kindness has not forsaken us; and do not abandon us, Lord our God, forever.

עַל כֵּן אֵבָרִים שֶׁפִּלַּגְתָּ בָּנוּ וְרוּחַ וּנְשָׁמָה שֶׁנָּפַחְתָּ בְּאַפֵּינוּ וְלָשׁוֹן אֲשֶׁר שַׂמְתָּ בְּפִינוּ – הֵן הֵם יוֹדוּ וִיבָרְכוּ וִישַׁבְּחוּ וִיפָאֲרוּ וִירוֹמְמוּ וְיַעֲרִיצוּ וְיַקְדִּישׁוּ וְיַמְלִיכוּ אֶת שִׁמְךָ מַלְכֵּנוּ. כִּי כָל פֶּה לְךָ יוֹדֶה, וְכָל לָשׁוֹן לְךָ תִשָּׁבַע, וְכָל בֶּרֶךְ לְךָ תִכְרַע, וְכָל קוֹמָה לְפָנֶיךָ תִשְׁתַּחֲוֶה, וְכָל לְבָבוֹת יִירָאוּךָ, וְכָל קֶרֶב וּכְלָיוֹת יְזַמְּרוּ לִשְׁמֶךָ. כַּדָּבָר שֶׁכָּתוּב, כָּל עַצְמוֹתַי תֹּאמַרְנָה, יְהוָה מִי כָמוֹךָ מַצִּיל עָנִי מֵחָזָק מִמֶּנּוּ, וְעָנִי וְאֶבְיוֹן מִגֹּזְלוֹ (תהלים לה:י).

מִי יִדְמֶה לָּךְ וּמִי יִשְׁוֶה לָּךְ וּמִי יַעֲרָךְ לָךְ הָאֵל הַגָּדוֹל, הַגִּבּוֹר וְהַנּוֹרָא, אֵל עֶלְיוֹן, קֹנֵה שָׁמַיִם וָאָרֶץ. נְהַלֶּלְךָ וּנְשַׁבֵּחֲךָ וּנְפָאֶרְךָ וּנְבָרֵךְ אֶת שֵׁם קָדְשֶׁךָ, כָּאָמוּר (תהלים קג:א): לְדָוִד, בָּרְכִי נַפְשִׁי אֶת־יְהוָה וְכָל־קְרָבַי אֶת שֵׁם קָדְשׁוֹ. הָאֵל בְּתַעֲצֻמוֹת עֻזֶּךָ, הַגָּדוֹל בִּכְבוֹד שְׁמֶךָ, הַגִּבּוֹר לָנֶצַח וְהַנּוֹרָא בְּנוֹרְאוֹתֶיךָ, הַמֶּלֶךְ הַיּוֹשֵׁב עַל כִּסֵּא רָם וְנִשָּׂא.

Therefore, עַל כֵּן אֵבָרִים שֶׁפִּלַּגְתָּ בָּנוּ the limbs you gave us… will thank and bless You… for every mouth shall offer thanks to you: Thank-yous to God can be expressed in many ways. How I remember waiting to receive a COVID inoculation in the Montefiore clinical trials. As doctors and nurses gathered around, I asked for an opportunity to offer a prayer. Reciting the words "Blessed are You, O God, who heals and does wonderous things," I explained that the wonder may not be God's direct input but the miracle of God granting humans the capacity to bring healing to the world. This was a humble example of expressing, as best we can with all of our limitations, gratitude to God and His healing partners.

Once again, a new ritual at the Seder would be for all of us to share to the degree we can, our personal thank-yous to God and others for all they have done for us.

עַל כֵּן אֵבָרִים שֶׁפִּלַּגְתָּ בָּנוּ - Therefore, the limbs You gave us and the spirit and soul that You breathed into our nostrils, and the tongue that You placed in our mouth - verily, they will thank and bless You and praise and glorify, and exalt and revere, and sanctify and coronate Your name, our Ruler. For every mouth shall offer thanks to You; and every tongue shall swear allegiance to You; and every knee shall bend to You; and every upright one shall prostrate himself before You; every heart will be in awe of You; and all innermost feelings and thoughts will sing praises to Your name, as it is written (Psalms 35:10), "All my bones shall say, 'Lord, who is like You? You save the poor person from one who is stronger, the poor and destitute from the one who would steal from him or her.'"

מִי יִדְמֶה לָּךְ - Who is similar to You? And who is equal to You? And who can be compared to You? O great, mighty and awesome Power, God above, Creator of the heavens and the earth. We shall praise and extol and glorify and bless Your holy name, as it is stated (Psalms 103:1), "A Psalm of David. Bless the Lord, O my soul; and all that is within me, His holy name." God, in Your powerful boldness; the Great One, in the glory of Your name; the Mighty One forever; the Ruler who sits on His high and elevated throne.

מִי יִדְמֶה לָּךְ - **Who is similar to You? ... O great, mighty and awesome Power:** As powerful as God may be, there are, of course, moments when He has disappointed us. It may be wise to step back and view our lives and our experiences from a distance, in an exercise some call "go to the balcony." This teaching goes something like this.

You're on a dance floor, and someone asks how it's going. One may respond that it's rather crowded, and people are stepping on each other's toes. Now go to the balcony and view the same scene. When asked the same question, one may respond that, from here, the floor looks rather sparse, and people are quite graceful. Viewing life from a distance may help us appreciate God's manifold gifts we too often take for granted.

שׁוֹכֵן עַד מָרוֹם וְקָדוֹשׁ שְׁמוֹ. וְכָתוּב (תהלים לג:א): רַנְּנוּ צַדִּיקִים בַּיהוה, לַיְשָׁרִים נָאוָה תְהִלָּה.

בְּפִי יְשָׁרִים תִּתְהַלָּל,
וּבְדִבְרֵי צַדִּיקִים תִּתְבָּרַךְ,
וּבִלְשׁוֹן חֲסִידִים תִּתְרוֹמָם,
וּבְקֶרֶב קְדוֹשִׁים תִּתְקַדָּשׁ.

Shochen Ad

שׁוֹכֵן עַד - **He who dwells always (shochen ad, spelled ayin daled):** The verb *shochen* interfaces with the feminine noun *Shechinah*, a divine term expressing God's Omnipresence. Here, we offer praise in the spirit of the two-letter word that follows – *ad*, made up of an *ayin* and *daled*.

The letters *ayin-daled* can be read *eid*, which means "to bear witness" to the Omnipresence of God.

Alternatively, the letters *ayin-daled* can be read *ad*, which means "until." In other words, no matter one's belief in God, it can never be perfect, never absolutely absolute. One can come near to the Lord but never quite reach Him.

Finally, the letters *ayin-daled* can be read *od*, meaning "still." This perhaps accentuates that, against all odds, Jews throughout history in the darkest of times still declared belief in God. This is similar to the use of the word *od* when Joseph reveals himself to his brothers, asking, "*Ha'od avi chai?*" (Is my father still alive?). In amazement, Joseph rhetorically asks, *Having endured so much, is my father still alive?*

One of the best-known sentences in the Torah is, "*Shema Yisrael, Hashem Eloheinu, Hashem Echad*" ("Hear O Israel, the Lord our God, the Lord is One"). Interestingly, the *ayin*, the last letter of the Hebrew word "hear," is written large in the Torah scroll, as is the *daled*, the last letter of the Hebrew word for "one." Our different readings of these combined two letters may reveal why this is so.

Shochen Ad - שׁוֹכֵן עַד

שׁוֹכֵן עַד - He who dwells always; lofty and holy is His name. As it is written (Psalms 33:10), "Sing joyfully to the Lord, righteous ones, praise is beautiful from the upright."

By the mouth of the upright You shall be praised;

By the sounds of the righteous You shall be blessed;

By the words of the pious You shall be exalted;

In the midst of the holy You shall be sanctified.

בְּפִי יְשָׁרִים תִּתְהַלָּל - By the mouth of the upright You shall be praised: These four phrases have three words each: A verb which describes how God will be praised; a noun that describes who will praise God; and a word that explains the means by which that praise will come. Note how each subsequent phrase shows an increase in intensity for each word.

Mouth	Upright	Praised	תִּתְהַלָּל	יְשָׁרִים	בְּפִי
Sounds	Righteous	Blessed	תִּתְבָּרַךְ	צַדִּיקִים	וּבְדִבְרֵי
Words	Pious	Exalted	תִּתְרוֹמָם	חֲסִידִים	וּבִלְשׁוֹן
Midst	Holy	Sanctified	תִּתְקַדָּשׁ	קְדוֹשִׁים	וּבְקֶרֶב

The ways of praise: mouth (*pi*), sounds (*divrei*), words (*leshon*), in the midst (*kerev*)

From the mouth comes sounds which make up words that enter into the souls of listeners.

The nouns of praise: upright, righteous, pious, holy

The upright live ethical lives; the righteous follow ritual as well; the pious do so beyond the letter of the law; resulting in holy living.

The verbs of praise: You will be praised, blessed, exalted, sanctified

Praise – being lauded — leads to being blessed, as one is recognized as an exalted role model who sanctifies life.

וּבְמַקְהֲלוֹת רִבְבוֹת עַמְּךָ בֵּית יִשְׂרָאֵל בְּרִנָּה יִתְפָּאֵר שִׁמְךָ, מַלְכֵּנוּ, בְּכָל דּוֹר וָדוֹר, שֶׁכֵּן חוֹבַת כָּל הַיְצוּרִים לְפָנֶיךָ, יהוה אֱלֹהֵינוּ וֵאלֹהֵי אֲבוֹתֵינוּ, לְהוֹדוֹת לְהַלֵּל לְשַׁבֵּחַ, לְפָאֵר לְרוֹמֵם לְהַדֵּר לְבָרֵךְ, לְעַלֵּה וּלְקַלֵּס עַל כָּל דִּבְרֵי שִׁירוֹת וְתִשְׁבְּחוֹת דָּוִד בֶּן יִשַׁי עַבְדְּךָ מְשִׁיחֶךָ.

Uvmak'halot

וּבְמַקְהֲלוֹת - And in the assemblies of the myriads of Your people: The previous paragraph emphasized the nobility (the "upright"/"righteous"/"pious"/"holy"), who recognize and acknowledge God. This paragraph is more encompassing, including the myriads, the multitudes of Israel and all of humankind – all having the capacity to join in thanksgiving to God.

שֶׁכֵּן חוֹבַת כָּל הַיְצוּרִים - This is the obligation of all creatures: Although it is an obligation to thank, praise, exalt, bless, adore, and extol God, we should do so as if it is voluntary, an emotional flow from the deepest recesses of the heart.

We see a similar combination of obligation and emotion in Judaism's unique approach to charity. The Hebrew word *tzedakah*, often translated as "charity," comes from the word *tzedek* and literally means "justice."

There is an important difference between the English translation and Hebrew meaning: The word charity has its roots in French and Latin words denoting mercy and affection, voluntary connections. *Tzedakah* as justice is based upon responsibility.

Uvmak'halot - וּבְמַקְהֵלוֹת

וּבְמַקְהֵלוֹת - And in the assemblies of the myriads of Your people, the House of Israel, in joyous song will Your name be glorified, our Ruler, in each and every generation; this is the obligation of all creatures, before You, Lord our God, and God of our ancestors, to thank, to praise, to extol, to glorify, to exalt, to lavish, to bless, to raise high and to acclaim - beyond the words of the songs and praises of David, the son of Yishai, Your servant, Your anointed one.

Giving, in Judaism, is not only the charitable thing to do but the *just* thing to do.

Our challenge is to weave the two approaches together. While giving is our responsibility, we ought to give as if our contribution is an optional choice, relecting an abundance of love.

We should do the same when offering gratitude to God.

עַל כָּל דִּבְרֵי שִׁירוֹת וְתִשְׁבָּחוֹת דָּוִד בֶּן יִשַׁי - **Beyond the words of the songs and praises of David, the son of Yishai, Your servant, Your anointed one:** You never know. Sometimes, the prayer of a plain person may be deeper and higher than David's magical psalms. A famous story makes this point. At the conclusion of Yom Kippur, a humble shepherd approached the ark and whistled. Congregants were aghast and tried to chase him away, only to be stopped by their rebbe, who later explained: I sensed our prayers were empty. The heavens were closed. But this shepherd's whistle was so deep, so sincere, it pierced the heavens; it was the highest of prayers, allowing our supplications to flow through, ascending to the heavenly throne.

יִשְׁתַּבַּח שִׁמְךָ לָעַד מַלְכֵּנוּ, הָאֵל הַמֶּלֶךְ הַגָּדוֹל וְהַקָּדוֹשׁ בַּשָּׁמַיִם וּבָאָרֶץ, כִּי לְךָ נָאֶה, יהוה אֱלֹהֵינוּ וֵאלֹהֵי אֲבוֹתֵינוּ, שִׁיר וּשְׁבָחָה, הַלֵּל וְזִמְרָה, עֹז וּמֶמְשָׁלָה, נֶצַח, גְּדֻלָּה וּגְבוּרָה, תְּהִלָּה וְתִפְאֶרֶת, קְדֻשָּׁה וּמַלְכוּת, בְּרָכוֹת וְהוֹדָאוֹת מֵעַתָּה וְעַד עוֹלָם.

בָּרוּךְ אַתָּה יהוה, אֵל מֶלֶךְ גָּדוֹל בַּתִּשְׁבָּחוֹת, אֵל הַהוֹדָאוֹת, אֲדוֹן הַנִּפְלָאוֹת, הַבּוֹחֵר בְּשִׁירֵי זִמְרָה, מֶלֶךְ אֵל חֵי הָעוֹלָמִים.

Yishtabach

יִשְׁתַּבַּח שִׁמְךָ לָעַד - **Praise be Your Name everywhere (la'ad)… Blessings and thanskgivings from now and forever (ve'ad olam):** The term *la'ad* as it first appears in this paragraph may be understood as spatial, that is, people everywhere will praise the Lord. As it appears a few sentences later (*ve'ad olam*) it is time-centered – lasting forever. Thus, the section of the Haggadah expressing the universal hope for peace ends as it started – *ki le'olam chasdo* – "God's kindness being everywhere (*le'olam*) and lasting forever (*le'olam*)."

בָּרוּךְ אַתָּה - **Blessed are You, Lord…the life of the world:** This blessing summarizes the essence of this Haggadah section – God being accepted for all time by all humans. As noted, the entire section is lifted from the Shabbat morning prayer service. By integrating the inner message of Shabbat into the Haggadah, we may all be drawn closer to achieving the ideal era of messianic peace, the time when "the Merciful One [will] let us inherit 'the day' when 'every day' will be Shabbat."

Yishtabach - יִשְׁתַּבַּח

יִשְׁתַּבַּח - Praised be Your name everywhere, our Ruler, the Great, holy God - in the heavens and in the earth. Since for You it is pleasant — O Lord our God and God of our ancestors — song and lauding, praise and hymn, boldness and dominion, triumph, greatness and strength, psalm and splendor, holiness and kingship, blessings and thanksgivings, from now and forever.

Blessed are You Lord, God, Ruler – exalted through praises, God of thanksgivings, Master of wonders, who delights in hymns of song – Ruler, God, the life of the world.

כוס רביעית

מברכים ושותים כוס רביעית בהסבה שמאלה.

בָּרוּךְ אַתָּה יהוה, אֱלֹהֵינוּ מֶלֶךְ הָעוֹלָם, בּוֹרֵא פְּרִי הַגָּפֶן.

בָּרוּךְ אַתָּה יהוה, אֱלֹהֵינוּ מֶלֶךְ הָעוֹלָם, עַל הַגֶּפֶן וְעַל פְּרִי הַגֶּפֶן, עַל תְּנוּבַת הַשָּׂדֶה וְעַל אֶרֶץ חֶמְדָּה טוֹבָה וּרְחָבָה שֶׁרָצִיתָ וְהִנְחַלְתָּ לַאֲבוֹתֵינוּ לֶאֱכוֹל מִפִּרְיָהּ וְלִשְׂבֹּעַ מִטּוּבָהּ.

רַחֶם נָא יהוה אֱלֹהֵינוּ עַל יִשְׂרָאֵל עַמֶּךָ וְעַל יְרוּשָׁלַיִם עִירֶךָ וְעַל צִיּוֹן מִשְׁכַּן כְּבוֹדֶךָ וְעַל מִזְבְּחֶךָ וְעַל הֵיכָלֶךָ וּבְנֵה יְרוּשָׁלַיִם עִיר הַקֹּדֶשׁ בִּמְהֵרָה בְיָמֵינוּ וְהַעֲלֵנוּ לְתוֹכָהּ וְשַׂמְּחֵנוּ בְּבִנְיָנָהּ וְנֹאכַל מִפִּרְיָהּ וְנִשְׂבַּע מִטּוּבָהּ וּנְבָרֶכְךָ עָלֶיהָ בִּקְדֻשָּׁה וּבְטָהֳרָה (בשבת: וּרְצֵה וְהַחֲלִיצֵנוּ בְּיוֹם הַשַּׁבָּת הַזֶּה) וְשַׂמְּחֵנוּ בְּיוֹם חַג הַמַּצּוֹת הַזֶּה,

כִּי אַתָּה יהוה טוֹב וּמֵטִיב לַכֹּל, וְנוֹדֶה לְךָ עַל הָאָרֶץ וְעַל פְּרִי הַגָּפֶן.

בָּרוּךְ אַתָּה יהוה, עַל הָאָרֶץ וְעַל פְּרִי הַגָּפֶן.

Boreh P'ri Hagafen

בּוֹרֵא פְּרִי הַגָּפֶן - **Who creates the fruit of the vine:** Appropriately, we drink the last cup celebrating our fervent dream, that just as we were redeemed from Egypt, so may we soon experience the ultimate redemption for us and the world.

Here, as noted in the introductory Passover Ritual Symbols section, may lie the simple reason that we drink four cups at the Seder. The first for kiddush and the third after the Grace After Meals follow the normative pattern of drinking wine at a festival meal. The second cup celebrates the past redemption, and the fourth honors the hope for future redemption. Alternatively, the fourth celebrates national redemption, the fifth universal redemption.

Fourth Cup of Wine

We recite the blessing and drink the fourth cup while reclining to the left

בּוֹרֵא פְּרִי הַגֶּפֶן - Blessed are You, Lord our God, Ruler of the universe, who creates the fruit of the vine.

After drinking we recite:

עַל הַגֶּפֶן וְעַל פְּרִי הַגֶּפֶן - Blessed are You, Lord our God, Ruler of the universe, for the vine and for the fruit of the vine; and for the bounty of the field;

And for a desirable, good and broad land, which You wanted to give to our ancestors, to eat from its fruit and to be satiated from its goodness.

Please have mercy, Lord our God upon Israel Your people. And upon Jerusalem, Your city: and upon Zion, the dwelling place of Your glory; and upon Your altar; and upon Your sanctuary; and build Jerusalem Your holy city quickly in our days, and bring us up into it and gladden us in its building; and we shall eat from its fruit, and be satiated from its goodness, and bless You in holiness and purity. [On Shabbat: And may You be pleased to embolden us on this Shabbat day] and gladden us on this day of the Festival of Matzot.

Since You, Lord, are good and do good to all, we thank You for the land and for the fruit of the vine.

Blessed are You, Lord, for the land and for the fruit of the vine.

Al HaGefen

עַל הַגֶּפֶן וְעַל פְּרִי הַגֶּפֶן - **For the vine and for the fruit of the vine:** This paragraph, said after drinking wine, is a microcosm of the larger Grace After Meals. It moves from thanksgiving for food (vine), to words related to Israel, Jerusalem and *tov umeitiv* (good and beneficial) as explicated in our Barech analysis.

More generally, *tov* may relate to God's goodness, echoing His refrain when creating the world: "And God saw that it was good." *Meitiv* (who inspires goodness) may focus on humans being empowered by God to join in partnership to bring about the future redemption as stressed in this latter half of the Seder.

BIDDING FAREWELL

Nirtzah

After a powerful experience, it's difficult to abruptly say goodbye. One lingers, one takes in all that occurred, sometimes reminiscing about its key moments. So too at the Seder. Although officially over, the Seder's teachings overflow in the Nirtzah which literally means "favorable." In context, this is a hope that the Seder was favorably received.

The Nirtzah begins with our declaration that we've completed the Seder "according to its laws and statutes" emotionally bursting forth with the hope of לשנה הבאה בירושלים" – Next Year in Jerusalem." We remain at the Seder, unable to move on, dreaming of the hope for ultimate redemption as we sing melodies in this order:

- A melody of hope – And It Happened at Midnight (*Vayhi bachatzi halaila*); It is the Pesach sacrifice (*Va'amartem zevach Pesach*)
- A melody of gratitude – For to Him Praise is Proper (*Ki lo na'eh*)
- A melody of the dream of Jerusalem spiritually rebuilt – Mighty is He (*Adir Hu*)
- A melody of people living life with foundational principles of faith – Who Knows One (*Echad Mi Yode'a*)
- And a final intriguing melody – One Kid (*Chad Gadya*) – speaking to the absurdity of Jewish existence – how against all odds we have prevailed. Stronger empires that once were are no longer, but *Am Yisrael Chai*.

נִרְצָה

חסל סדור פסח

חֲסַל סִדּוּר פֶּסַח כְּהִלְכָתוֹ, כְּכָל מִשְׁפָּטוֹ וְחֻקָּתוֹ.
כַּאֲשֶׁר זָכִינוּ לְסַדֵּר אוֹתוֹ כֵּן נִזְכֶּה לַעֲשׂוֹתוֹ.
זָךְ שׁוֹכֵן מְעוֹנָה, קוֹמֵם קְהַל עֲדַת מִי מָנָה.
בְּקָרוֹב נַהֵל נִטְעֵי כַנָּה פְּדוּיִם לְצִיּוֹן בְּרִנָּה.

לשנה הבאה

לְשָׁנָה הַבָּאָה בִּירוּשָׁלַיִם הַבְּנוּיָה.

Chasal

חֲסַל סִדּוּר פֶּסַח - Completed is the Pesach Seder: With this, the formal Seder ends. The final paragraph offers a summary as we declare that we properly performed the Passover ritual of remembering and reenacting the exodus from Egypt. It concludes with "Pure One… uplift [Israel]… speedily lead Your redeemed people… to Zion in joyous song."

L'Shana HaBa'ah B'Yerushalayim

לְשָׁנָה הַבָּאָה בִּירוּשָׁלַיִם - Next Year in Jerusalem: In our daily prayers, at weddings, at houses of mourning, when we conclude the Yom Kippur service, and as we close the Seder, we dream Jerusalem, a dream that for centuries was virtually unreachable but today is firmly within our grasp.

Our task is not only to rebuild Jerusalem terrestrially but celestially, bringing the heavenly Jerusalem down to earth, assuring that the dream of Jerusalem, a city of godly peace, will always be.

Natan Sharansky expressed this human responsibility for

NIRTZAH

Chasal Siddur Pesach - חֲסַל סִדּוּר פֶּסַח

חֲסַל סִדּוּר פֶּסַח - Completed is the Pesach Seder
According to its laws and statutes.
Just as we have merited to observe it,
So too, may we merit to celebrate it again.
Pure One who dwells in His habitation,
Uplift the many, many in Your congregation,
Speedily lead Your redeemed people,
Redeemed, to Zion in joyous song.

L'Shana HaBa'ah B'Yerushalayim! - לְשָׁנָה הַבָּאָה בִּירוּשָׁלָיִם

Next year in Jerusalem [this year in Jerusalem]!

Yerushalayim beautifully. Standing beside his wife Avital in Jerusalem at the wedding of their children Rachel and Micha, Natan suggested that the challenge of the dream of Jerusalem, symbolized by the breaking the glass, was greater for them today than under his and Avital's *chuppah* in the Soviet Union many years earlier, not long before he was sentenced to the Gulag.

Our aim was so simple and so clear. We had to win the [physical] battle [to return to Jerusalem] and nothing could deter us. Today, on the one hand you have to be builders and guardians of [the physical] Jerusalem, and at the same time guardians of the idea of Jerusalem…. The power of unity and connection to the generations of our people is in heavenly Jerusalem, in *Yerushalayim shel ma'ala*.

Whether the earthly Jerusalem reflects the values of the heavenly Jerusalem becoming the holy Jerusalem is up to us.

ויהי בחצי הלילה

בליל ראשון אומרים:

וּבְכֵן וַיְהִי בַּחֲצִי הַלַּיְלָה.

אָז רוֹב נִסִּים הִפְלֵאתָ בַּלַּיְלָה, בְּרֹאשׁ אַשְׁמוֹרֶת זֶה הַלַּיְלָה.

גֵּר צֶדֶק נִצַּחְתּוֹ כְּנֶחֱלַק לוֹ לַיְלָה, וַיְהִי בַּחֲצִי הַלַּיְלָה.

דַּנְתָּ מֶלֶךְ גְּרָר בַּחֲלוֹם הַלַּיְלָה,

הִפְחַדְתָּ אֲרַמִּי בְּאֶמֶשׁ לַיְלָה.

וַיָּשַׂר יִשְׂרָאֵל לְמַלְאָךְ וַיּוּכַל לוֹ לַיְלָה, וַיְהִי בַּחֲצִי הַלַּיְלָה.

Vayhi Bachatzi Halaila: Hope

וַיְהִי בַּחֲצִי הַלַּיְלָה - **And it was in the middle (chatzi) of the night:** Night in the Torah symbolizes suffering and exile. The word *chatzi* takes this interpretation a step further. That time is not only night, but it is the night of the night – midnight, the time of the deepest suffering and exile, when the voice of God seems silent.

The first time midnight is found in the Torah is when Moses says God will slay the first born, *ka-chatzot halaila* (literally, "like midnight"). The prefix *ka*, like, adds an important dimension: As we were saved from Egypt, and all the historically dangerous midnights as listed in this hymn, so will we in the future survive other midnights, other times of pain and despair.

In our times, this prediction has

Vayhi Bachatzi Halaila - ויהי בחצי הלילה

On the first night we say:

וַיְהִי בַּחֲצִי הַלַּיְלָה - And it was in the middle of the night.

It was then, that You wondrously performed miracles at night.
At the first of the watches this night.
    (The night is divided into three or four "watches")
You helped the righteous convert to victory
    when the night was divided for him at night
    (referring to Abraham in his war against the four kings – Genesis 14:15.)

    And it was in the middle of the night.

You sentenced the King of Gerrar in a dream of night.
    (Referring to Avimelech who forcefully abducted Sarah
    after Abraham told him "she is my sister" – Genesis 20:3.)
You frightened an Aramean in the dark of the night;
    (Referring to God's warning to Laban not to harm Jacob – Genesis 31:29.)
And Israel dominated an angel and was able to withstand Him at night
    (Referring to Jacob's wrestling with a mysterious being
    just before he encounters Esau - Genesis 32:25-30.)

    And it was in the middle of the night.

become reality. In 1976, terrorists hijacked an Air France plane flying its passengers to Entebbe, Uganda. All seemed lost when Israeli paratroopers heroically descended on the scene, freeing virtually all of the hostages. It didn't take long for this moment to become legendary in Israeli history, with documentary movies describing the event in detail. Soon, too, a popular melody was composed and sung everywhere. Not surprisingly, its first words are *"bachatzi halaila,"* at midnight, a description not only of when the paratroopers arrived but of how ominous the situation was.

What is true about the nation of Israel is similarly true about individual lives. Often, God intervenes precisely when one thinks there is no hope. Thus, the message of this hymn is that the darkest moments, *chatzi halaila*, contain sparks of hope.

זֶרַע בְּכוֹרֵי פַתְרוֹס מָחַצְתָּ בַּחֲצִי הַלַּיְלָה,
חֵילָם לֹא מָצְאוּ בְּקוּמָם בַּלַּיְלָה,
טִיסַת נְגִיד חֲרֹשֶׁת סִלִּיתָ בְּכוֹכְבֵי לַיְלָה,
וַיְהִי בַּחֲצִי הַלַּיְלָה.

יָעַץ מְחָרֵף לְנוֹפֵף אִוּוּי, הוֹבַשְׁתָּ פְגָרָיו בַּלַּיְלָה,
כָּרַע בֵּל וּמַצָּבוֹ בְּאִישׁוֹן לַיְלָה,
לְאִישׁ חֲמוּדוֹת נִגְלָה רָז חֲזוֹת לַיְלָה,
וַיְהִי בַּחֲצִי הַלַּיְלָה.

חֵילָם **- Their wealth they did not find when they rose**: Aside from referring to their first born children, wealth may refer to the wealth of Egypt which the Torah tells us was given by the Egyptians to the Israelites after the Israelites requested it from them. God, the Torah tells us, helped the Israelites find favor in the eyes of the Egyptians and they gave them their gold and silver as they were getting ready to leave Egypt. Finally, it may refer to the wealth of Egypt that drifted onto the shores of the Red Sea after they were drowned in the water by the hand of God.

You crushed the firstborn of Patros in the middle of the night,
  (Referring to the first born of Pharaoh, as per Ezekiel 30:14.)

Their wealth they did not find when they rose at night;
  (Wealth refers to their first born children.)

You swept away Charoshet by the stars of the night
  (Sisera, the Canaanite general who was defeated by Deborah and Barak, lived in Charoshet Goyim – Judges 5:20.)

      And it was in the middle of the night.

You dried the corpses of the blasphemer
  who tried to ravage Your chosen space at night
  (The blasphemer refers to Sancheriv King of Assyria who tried to demoralize the inhabitants of Jerusalem by blaspheming God – II Kings 19:35.)

Bel and his pedestal were thrown down in the darkness of night
  (Bel was a major deity of the Babylonians, also known by the name Marduk. The idol of Bel appeared in Nebuchadnezzar's dream – Daniel 2.)

To the man of delight was revealed the secret visions at night,
  (The man of delight refers to Daniel, to whom was revealed the interpretation of Nebuchadnezzar's dream – Daniel 2:19)

      And it was in the middle of the night.

מִשְׁתַּכֵּר בִּכְלֵי קֹדֶשׁ נֶהֱרַג בּוֹ	בַּלַּיְלָה,
נוֹשַׁע מִבּוֹר אֲרָיוֹת פּוֹתֵר בִּעֲתוּתֵי	לַיְלָה,
שִׂנְאָה נָטַר אֲגָגִי וְכָתַב סְפָרִים	בַּלַּיְלָה,
	וַיְהִי בַּחֲצִי הַלַּיְלָה.
עוֹרַרְתָּ נִצְחֲךָ עָלָיו בְּנֶדֶד שְׁנַת	לַיְלָה.
פּוּרָה תִדְרוֹךְ לְשׁוֹמֵר מַה	מִלַּיְלָה,
צָרַח כַּשּׁוֹמֵר וְשָׂח אָתָא בֹקֶר וְגַם	לַיְלָה,
	וַיְהִי בַּחֲצִי הַלַּיְלָה.
קָרֵב יוֹם אֲשֶׁר הוּא לֹא יוֹם וְלֹא	לַיְלָה,
רָם הוֹדַע כִּי לְךָ הַיּוֹם אַף לְךָ	הַלַּיְלָה,
שׁוֹמְרִים הַפְקֵד לְעִירְךָ כָּל הַיּוֹם וְכָל	הַלַּיְלָה,
תָּאִיר כְּאוֹר יוֹם חֶשְׁכַּת	לַיְלָה,
	וַיְהִי בַּחֲצִי הַלַּיְלָה.

קָרֵב יוֹם אֲשֶׁר הוּא לֹא יוֹם וְלֹא לַיְלָה - The day will come when it is no longer day or night: There is a mystical theory that people reflect the physical settings within which they live. In Israel, for example, the time between sunset and darkness seems relatively short. In other words, it is either day, or night. Most Israelis, I believe, think accordingly — in absolutes. You're either right or wrong; you're either with me or against me. Yes, it's either day or night.

On a very personal level, I know this phenomenon well. As a younger activist, I took positions wherein I could not see any truth aside from my own. But as I grew older, I came to recognize that Israel will not make it with the right alone or the left alone. Concerning Israel and the well-being of the Jewish community, each side has much to contribute.

And so, in our Seder song, we sing out *karev yom asher hu lo yom v'lo laila*, the day will come when it is no longer day nor night. This is the dream of "twilight expanded," wherein opposites not only coexist but, for the sake of the greater good, contract (*tzimtzum*) to make space for the other, thus thriving and flourishing in dialectic.

The one who got drunk from the holy vessels was killed   that night
   (Referring to Balshatzar, who during a great feast got drunk when drinking from the vessels plundered from the Temple – Daniel 5:30.)

The one saved from the pit of lions
   interpreted the scary visions   of the night;
   (Referring to Daniel – Daniel 6:21-22, 7:2.)

Hatred was preserved by the Agagite who wrote books   at night,
   (The Agagite is Haman, who sent letters to Achashverosh's kingdom ordering the destruction of the Jews – Esther 3:12-15.)

                 And it was in the middle of the night.

You aroused your victory upon him by disturbing the sleep   of night
   (Referring to Achashverosh's inability to sleep, leading to the fall of Haman – Esther 6:1.)

You will stomp the wine press for the One
   who guards Israel against its enemies   at night
   (Israel calls out to God for protection from Edom – Isaiah 21:11, the stomping refers to Isaiah 63:2-4.)

He called out like a guard and spoke,
   "the morning has come and also   the night,"
   (Referring to the day of victory – when "morning" will come for Israel and "night" for the enemy – Isaiah 21:12.)

                 And it was in the middle of the night.

The day will come when it is no longer day or   night
   (Referring to the end of days – Zechariah 14:7.)

High One, make known that Yours is the day and also Yours is   the night

Appoint guards for Your city all the day and all   the night,
   (Referring to Isaiah 62:6.)

Illuminate like the light of the day, the darkness   of the night,

                 And it was in the middle of the night.

זבח פסח

בליל שני בחו״ל:

וּבְכֵן וַאֲמַרְתֶּם זֶבַח פֶּסַח (שמות יב:כז).

אֹמֶץ גְּבוּרוֹתֶיךָ הִפְלֵאתָ בַּפֶּסַח,
בְּרֹאשׁ כָּל מוֹעֲדוֹת נִשֵּׂאתָ פֶּסַח.
גִּלִּיתָ לְאֶזְרָחִי חֲצוֹת לֵיל פֶּסַח,
וַאֲמַרְתֶּם זֶבַח פֶּסַח.

Va'Amartem Zevach Pesach: Hope

וּבְכֵן וַאֲמַרְתֶּם זֶבַח פֶּסַח - And you shall say, "It is the Pesach sacrifice": This refrain is the biblical response to children who ask "What is the meaning of the Passover rituals?" including the offering of the Passover lamb. "You shall say," the Torah commands, "it is the sacrifice of the Passover," commemorating God passing over Jewish homes as he struck the Egyptian firstborns. Here, the theme is similar to *bachatzi halaila* as it, too, deals with the many times in history when – against all probability, on Passover night no less – the Jewish People was saved.

While the laws of the Passover sacrifice are intricate, they include many spiritual messages. In my Thematic Commentary on the Torah, *Torat Ahavah - Loving Torah*, we present fourteen such teachings, suggesting they be reviewed one a day during the days of Nissan leading up to the Passover holiday. Here we record some of these teachings:

Stay humble: By noon on the day before Passover, when the sacrifice can first be offered, no *chametz* (leaven) can be in the house. The sacrifice is a celebration of the great victory over Egypt, but when one is victorious, one can become "bloated" with self-pride. And so, *chametz*, puffed-up dough, identified in the Talmud and in later Chassidic

Zevach Pesach - זבח פסח

This hymn is recited at the second diaspora Seder. When there were no calendars, that night may have been the first night of Passover, a time when the Passover sacrifice was offered.

"And you shall say, 'it is the Pesach sacrifice'" (Exodus 12:27).

The boldness of Your mighty deeds did you wondrously show at Pesach;
At the head of all the holidays did You raise Pesach;
(Often Passover is mentioned first in the Biblical listing of the holidays.)
You revealed to the Ezrachite, at the midnight of Pesach.
(The Ezrachite is Abraham, who came from the East [*mizrach*] and was, if you will, a citizen [*ezrach*] of Israel. The revealed event was the Covenant of the Pieces – Genesis 15.)

"And you shall say, 'it is the Pesach sacrifice.'"

literature as being symbolic of hubris and self-absorption, cannot be in one's possession by the time the Passover sacrifice is offered, reminding us to remain humble even when most successful.

Make space: The twice-daily *korban tamid* (standard sacrifice) is the first offered in the morning and last to be offered in the late afternoon. There is one exception: The paschal lamb is offered after the afternoon *tamid*. Although, because of its constancy, the *tamid* has the right to maintain its position as first and last always, it makes way for the paschal lamb, teaching the importance of stepping back and making space for others when necessary.

Empathize: The paschal sacrifice must be brought in a state of spiritual purity and is not offered by individuals who, for various reasons (such as contact with a dead body), are impure at the time of the offering. (These individuals do get a second chance a month after Passover.) If the majority of the community is impure, however, the paschal lamb is still offered by everyone based on the principle that impurity is waived for the sake of community. Interestingly, even those who are pure offer their sacrifices as if they are in an impure state. In this way, we do not split the community. In other words, no

דְּלָתָיו דָּפַקְתָּ כְּחֹם הַיּוֹם בַּפֶּסַח,	
הִסְעִיד נוֹצְצִים עֻגּוֹת מַצּוֹת בַּפֶּסַח,	
וְאֶל הַבָּקָר רָץ זֵכֶר לְשׁוֹר עֵרֶךְ פֶּסַח,	
וַאֲמַרְתֶּם זֶבַח פֶּסַח.	

זוֹעֲמוּ סְדוֹמִים וְלֹהֲטוּ בָּאֵשׁ בַּפֶּסַח,
חֻלַּץ לוֹט מֵהֶם וּמַצּוֹת אָפָה בְּקֵץ פֶּסַח,
טִאטֵאתָ אַדְמַת מוֹף וְנֹף בְּעָבְרְךָ בַּפֶּסַח.
וַאֲמַרְתֶּם זֶבַח פֶּסַח.

יָהּ רֹאשׁ כָּל הוֹן מָחַצְתָּ בְּלֵיל שִׁמּוּר פֶּסַח,
כַּבִּיר, עַל בֵּן בְּכוֹר פָּסַחְתָּ בְּדַם פֶּסַח,
לְבִלְתִּי תֵּת מַשְׁחִית לָבֹא בִּפְתָחַי בַּפֶּסַח,
וַאֲמַרְתֶּם זֶבַח פֶּסַח.

matter my purity, if the majority is impure, I too am impure, reflecting my required empathy with *am'cha* (one's people).

Make a difference: And suppose, the Talmud asks, half the people are pure, and half are not – what then? The Talmud weaves a discussion about what to do in such circumstances (Pesachim 79b). Why debate such an unlikely event? Here, the law may inspire us to consider the observation made by Maimonides that we should view our deeds and the world as evenly balanced (Maimonides, *Mishneh Torah*, Laws of Repentance 3:4). The next good deed we perform could make all the difference.

See good in others: The skewer used to roast the sacrifice

Upon his doors did You knock at the heat of the day   on Pesach;
He sustained shining ones [angels] with cakes of matza   on Pesach;
And to the cattle he ran,
    in commemoration of the ox that was set up   for Pesach.
    (This paragraph refers to Abraham and Sarah welcoming the three guests which, according to rabbinic tradition, occurred on Pesach. The ox in the last line refers to the calf that Abraham brought for the guests that day – Genesis 18. It may also refer to the Pesach reading from the Torah about an ox – Leviticus 22:27.)

                                           "And you shall say, 'it is the Pesach sacrifice.'"

The Sodomites felt Your indignation and were set on fire   on Pesach;
Lot was rescued from them and baked matzot at the end   of Pesach;
    (Sodom is destroyed; while Lot and his family were saved – Genesis 19.)
You swept the land of Mof and Nof   on Pesach.
    (Mof and Nof are cities in Egypt. This line begins the description of the slaying of the firstborn, continuing through the next stanza – Exodus 12:29-30.)

                                           "And you shall say, 'it is the Pesach sacrifice.'"

The head of every firstborn You did crush on the watchful night of Pesach;
Powerful One, over the firstborn son
    did You pass over with the blood   on Pesach;
Not allowing the destroyer to come in my doors   on Pesach.
    (Exodus 12:23)

                                           "And you shall say, 'it is the Pesach sacrifice.'"

is pomegranate wood. The pomegranate reminds us of the rabbinic teaching that even the greatest sinners – seemingly like the pomegranate's outer shell, which is disposed of as useless – contain endless inner pure seeds, giving them the capacity to return. This concept is reflected in the story told by Dr. Yaffa Eliach, of blessed memory, of a Kapo named Schneeweiss, who turned on his own people and worked under the Nazis at the Janowska concentration camp in what is now Ukraine. One Yom Kippur, however, he refused to submit to Nazi demands that he force Jews in the camp to eat. He was shot dead on the spot. The saintly Bluzhever Rebbe, who told this story

מִסְגֶּרֶת סֻגְּרָה בְּעִתּוֹתֵי   פֶּסַח,
נִשְׁמְדָה מִדְיָן בִּצְלִיל שְׂעוֹרֵי עֹמֶר   פֶּסַח,
שׂוֹרְפוּ מִשְׁמַנֵּי פּוּל וְלוּד בִּיקַד יְקוֹד   פֶּסַח,
וַאֲמַרְתֶּם זֶבַח פֶּסַח.

עוֹד הַיּוֹם בְּנֹב לַעֲמוֹד עַד גָּעָה עוֹנַת   פֶּסַח,
פַּס יַד כָּתְבָה לְקַעֲקֵעַ צוּל בַּ   פֶּסַח,
צָפֹה הַצָּפִית עָרוֹךְ הַשֻּׁלְחָן   בַּפֶּסַח,
וַאֲמַרְתֶּם זֶבַח פֶּסַח.

קָהָל כִּנְּסָה הֲדַסָּה לְשַׁלֵּשׁ צוֹם   בַּפֶּסַח,
רֹאשׁ מִבֵּית רָשָׁע מָחַצְתָּ בְּעֵץ חֲמִשִּׁים   בַּפֶּסַח,
שְׁתֵּי אֵלֶּה רֶגַע תָּבִיא לְעוּצִית   בַּפֶּסַח,
תָּעֹז יָדְךָ תָּרוּם יְמִינְךָ כְּלֵיל הִתְקַדֵּשׁ   חַג פֶּסַח,
וַאֲמַרְתֶּם זֶבַח פֶּסַח.

to Dr. Eliach, commented that this was the moment when he understood the Talmudic dictum that "Even the transgressors in Israel are as full of good deeds as a pomegranate is filled with seeds." (Berachot 57a).

There are second chances: If one is too far from the Temple to arrive for the paschal sacrifice, one has another opportunity to offer the sacrifice thirty days later, on Pesach Sheni. How far is too far away? One position insists it is even one step outside of the Temple area (Pesachim 93b). Truth be told, one can be far but close, just as one can be close and yet far. And so Pesach Sheni could be a second chance for one who is physically close but spiritually distant. Such individuals are warmly welcomed.

The walls of Jericho fell in the season of Pesach;
>(Referring to Joshua's defeat of Jericho – Joshua 6.)

Midian was destroyed with a portion of the omer-barley on Pesach
>(Gideon's victory over Midian was foretold by a Midianite who saw a loaf of barley overthrowing a large tent; so Israel, a small nation, would defeat the powerful Midianites – Judges 7:13-14.)

The Assyrian tribes of Pul and Lud
>were burned in a mighty fire on Pesach.
>(Pul was king of Assyria – II Kings 15:19; Pul and Lud are names of foreign nations – Isaiah 66:19)

"And you shall say, 'it is the Pesach sacrifice'"

This very day, he [Sancheriv] will go no further than Nov,
>crying at the time of Pesach;
>(Sancheriv was defeated in Nov, near Jerusalem, on Pesach – Isaiah 10:32.)

A palm of the hand wrote to rip up the deep one on Pesach
>(This refers to the handwriting on the wall explained by Daniel to denote the upcoming destruction of Babylonia - Daniel 5:1-30).

"Light the watch," "set the table" on Pesach.
>(Referring to Babylonian overconfidence. In the end, they were defeated – Isaiah 21:5.)

"And you shall say, 'it is the Pesach sacrifice'"

Hadassah [Esther] asked the people to fast for three days on Pesach;
The head of the house of evil [Haman]
>did you hang on a tree of fifty cubits on Pesach;
>(The above two lines refer to the defeat of Haman led by Esther and Mordechai – Esther 4:15; 7:10.)

These two [plagues] You will bring in an instant
>against the Utzi [Esav] on Pesach;
>(Utz is Edom, or Rome – Lamentations 4:21.)

Embolden Your hand, raise Your right hand,
>as on the night You were sanctified on the festival of Pesach.
>(As God redeemed us from Egypt on Passover, so it will occur, God-willing, in the future – Psalms 89:14.)

"And you shall say, 'it is the Pesach sacrifice'"

כי לו נאה

כִּי לוֹ נָאֶה, כִּי לוֹ יָאֶה.

אַדִיר בִּמְלוּכָה, בָּחוּר כַּהֲלָכָה, גְּדוּדָיו יֹאמְרוּ לוֹ: לְךָ וּלְךָ, לְךָ כִּי לְךָ, לְךָ אַף לְךָ, לְךָ יהוה הַמַּמְלָכָה, כִּי לוֹ נָאֶה, כִּי לוֹ יָאֶה.

דָּגוּל בִּמְלוּכָה, הָדוּר כַּהֲלָכָה, וָתִיקָיו יֹאמְרוּ לוֹ: לְךָ וּלְךָ, לְךָ כִּי לְךָ, לְךָ אַף לְךָ, לְךָ יהוה הַמַּמְלָכָה, כִּי לוֹ נָאֶה, כִּי לוֹ יָאֶה.

זַכַּאי בִּמְלוּכָה, חָסִין כַּהֲלָכָה טַפְסְרָיו יֹאמְרוּ לוֹ: לְךָ וּלְךָ, לְךָ כִּי לְךָ, לְךָ אַף לְךָ, לְךָ יהוה הַמַּמְלָכָה, כִּי לוֹ נָאֶה, כִּי לוֹ יָאֶה.

Ki Lo Na'eh: Gratitude

כִּי לוֹ נָאֶה, כִּי לוֹ יָאֶה - **For to Him praise is proper, for to Him praise is due:** Each paragraph of this song contains two descriptions of God's greatness, followed by a third phrase recording a group (i.e. senior advisors, intellectuals, ethicists, the grassroots) that declares allegiance to God alone. Cumulatively, the phrases in the paragraphs are in *alef-bet* acrostic.

One wonders, however, what of those who do not believe. After all, belief is a feeling, and, as I first heard at a Marriage Encounter seminar, "Feelings are neither right nor wrong; they just are." Here, the great Rashi provides a formula through which one can come to believe.

The formula is first mentioned when Moses meets God at the *s'neh* (burning bush). There, God tells Moses that His name is *Ehyeh asher Ehyeh*, literally "I will be that which I will be." Through this name, Rashi insists, God teaches how the Jews can come to believe in Him. Tell them, God says, "I will be with you in this time of distress, even as I will be

Ki Lo Na'eh - כי לו נאה

כִּי לוֹ נָאֶה, כִּי לוֹ יָאֶה - For to Him praise is proper, for to Him praise is due.

Mighty in rulership, properly chosen, His legions shall say to Him,
> "Yours and Yours, Yours since it is Yours, Yours and even Yours,
> Yours, Lord is the kingdom;
> For to Him praise is proper, for to Him praise is due."

Noted in rulership, properly splendid, His faithful ones will say to Him,
> "Yours and Yours, Yours since it is Yours, Yours and even Yours,
> Yours, Lord is the kingdom;
> For to Him praise is proper, for to Him praise is due."

Meritorious in rulership, properly faithful, His scribes shall say to him,
> "Yours and Yours, Yours since it is Yours, Yours and even Yours,
> Yours, Lord is the kingdom;
> For to Him praise is proper, for to Him praise is due."

you in other times of distress."

Rashi similarly explains God's first words at Sinai, "I am the Lord Your God who took you out of Egypt" as "I, the God who took you out of the Egyptian exile, now continue the redemption process by giving you the Torah." Here again, God says, the Jews will come to know Him through these experiences. In this sense, belief in God is similar to knowing you are in love. Just as you cannot prove you're in love – it can only be experienced – so too belief in God is an experiential reality.

A powerful understanding of God emerges when assessing how we as a people have endured. After all, as some historians have noted, a rational assessment of the forces of history would conclude that Judaism today should be a fossil. We would respond that Jewish history is not logical or rational; the improbability and vast breadth of Jewish history points to the existence of God.

Jewish ritual can be seen as a reenactment of Jewish history. As noted earlier in our Haggadah commentary, on Passover we do not

יָחִיד בִּמְלוּכָה, כַּבִּיר כַּהֲלָכָה לִמּוּדָיו יֹאמְרוּ לוֹ: לְךָ וּלְךָ, לְךָ כִּי לְךָ, לְךָ אַף לְךָ, לְךָ יהוה הַמַּמְלָכָה, כִּי לוֹ נָאֶה, כִּי לוֹ יָאֶה.

מוֹשֵׁל בִּמְלוּכָה, נוֹרָא כַּהֲלָכָה סְבִיבָיו יֹאמְרוּ לוֹ: לְךָ וּלְךָ, לְךָ כִּי לְךָ, לְךָ אַף לְךָ, לְךָ יהוה הַמַּמְלָכָה, כִּי לוֹ נָאֶה, כִּי לוֹ יָאֶה.

עָנָיו בִּמְלוּכָה, פּוֹדֶה כַּהֲלָכָה, צַדִּיקָיו יֹאמְרוּ לוֹ: לְךָ וּלְךָ, לְךָ כִּי לְךָ, לְךָ אַף לְךָ, לְךָ יהוה הַמַּמְלָכָה, כִּי לוֹ נָאֶה, כִּי לוֹ יָאֶה.

קָדוֹשׁ בִּמְלוּכָה, רַחוּם כַּהֲלָכָה שִׁנְאַנָּיו יֹאמְרוּ לוֹ: לְךָ וּלְךָ, לְךָ כִּי לְךָ, לְךָ אַף לְךָ, לְךָ יהוה הַמַּמְלָכָה, כִּי לוֹ נָאֶה, כִּי לוֹ יָאֶה.

תַּקִּיף בִּמְלוּכָה, תּוֹמֵךְ כַּהֲלָכָה תְּמִימָיו יֹאמְרוּ לוֹ: לְךָ וּלְךָ, לְךָ כִּי לְךָ, לְךָ אַף לְךָ, לְךָ יהוה הַמַּמְלָכָה, כִּי לוֹ נָאֶה, כִּי לוֹ יָאֶה.

only *recall* the exodus; we simulate and *reenact* the event. The truth is, as I first heard formulated by Rabbi Shlomo Riskin, the mitzvah may not be the result of one's belief but rather the means to come to believe. So too, Jewish history can be a vehicle that inspires belief in God, "the Lord who took us out of Egypt."

And so, after journeying through the Haggadah with this emphasis on recalling God as the God of encounter, the God of experience, we sing out, for to Him, praise is proper, for to Him, praise is due. And, we add, almost as if we are in a romantic dance, extolling our Beloved, "Yours and Yours, Yours but Yours, Yours only Yours, Yours O Lord is the world's sovereignty."

Unique in rulership, properly powerful, His wise ones say to Him,

> "Yours and Yours, Yours since it is Yours, Yours and even Yours, Yours, Lord is the kingdom;
> For to Him praise is proper, for to Him praise is due."

Reigning in rulership, properly awesome, His allies say to Him,

> "Yours and Yours, Yours since it is Yours, Yours and even Yours, Yours, Lord is the kingdom;
> For to Him praise is proper, for to Him praise is due."

Humble in rulership, properly restoring, His righteous ones say to Him,

> "Yours and Yours, Yours since it is Yours, Yours and even Yours, Yours, Lord is the kingdom;
> For to Him praise is proper, for to Him praise is due."

Holy in rulership, properly merciful, His angels say to Him,

> "Yours and Yours, Yours since it is Yours, Yours and even Yours, Yours, Lord is the kingdom;
> For to Him praise is proper, for to Him praise is due."

Dynamic in rulership, properly supportive, His perfect ones say to Him,

> "Yours and Yours, Yours since it is Yours, Yours and even Yours, Yours, Lord is the kingdom;
> For to Him praise is proper, for to Him praise is due."

אדיר הוא

אַדִּיר הוּא יִבְנֶה בֵיתוֹ בְּקָרוֹב. בִּמְהֵרָה, בִּמְהֵרָה, בְּיָמֵינוּ בְּקָרוֹב. אֵל בְּנֵה, אֵל בְּנֵה, בְּנֵה בֵיתְךָ בְּקָרוֹב.

בָּחוּר הוּא, גָּדוֹל הוּא, דָּגוּל הוּא יִבְנֶה בֵיתוֹ בְּקָרוֹב. בִּמְהֵרָה, בִּמְהֵרָה, בְּיָמֵינוּ בְּקָרוֹב. אֵל בְּנֵה, אֵל בְּנֵה, בְּנֵה בֵיתְךָ בְּקָרוֹב.

הָדוּר הוּא, וָתִיק הוּא, זַכַּאי הוּא יִבְנֶה בֵיתוֹ בְּקָרוֹב. בִּמְהֵרָה, בִּמְהֵרָה, בְּיָמֵינוּ בְּקָרוֹב. אֵל בְּנֵה, אֵל בְּנֵה, בְּנֵה בֵיתְךָ בְּקָרוֹב.

חָסִיד הוּא, טָהוֹר הוּא, יָחִיד הוּא יִבְנֶה בֵיתוֹ בְּקָרוֹב. בִּמְהֵרָה, בִּמְהֵרָה, בְּיָמֵינוּ בְּקָרוֹב. אֵל בְּנֵה, אֵל בְּנֵה, בְּנֵה בֵיתְךָ בְּקָרוֹב.

Adir Hu: Jerusalem Rebuilt

אַדִיר הוּא - **Mighty is He…God, build:** In an *alef-bet* acrostic, using accolades similar to those found in the previous hymn, we express our hope that God soon rebuild the Temple. But why is a Temple necessary? Here, it is important to recognize the immense obstacles preventing a finite, limited human being from dialoguing with the infinite, unlimited God. The chasm is too great. As a consequence, the Temple was necessary as a medium through which the people could experience the divine.

While people need a place to feel God's presence, is it possible for God to be contained in any particular space? King Solomon makes this point when he dedicates the Holy Temple. He declares "Behold, heaven and the heaven of

Adir Hu

אַדִיר הוּא - Mighty is He, may He build His house soon.
    Speedily, speedily, in our days, soon.
    God build, God build, build Your house soon.

Chosen is He, great is He, noted is He.
    Speedily, speedily, in our days, soon.
    God build, God build, build Your house soon.

Splendid is He, distinguished is He, meritorious is He.
    Speedily, speedily, in our days, soon.
    God build, God build, build Your house soon.

Pious is He, pure is He, unique is He.
    Speedily, speedily, in our days, soon.
    God build, God build, build Your house soon.

heavens cannot contain You; nor can this house that I have built".

To answer this question, we must distinguish between sign and symbol. A sign is a self-contained entity. Outside its parameters, it has no meaning. In contrast, a symbol represents something beyond itself. It points in a direction beyond its own limits. The symbol catapults us to experience a message that transcends its immediacy.

The Holy Temple and, for that matter, contemporary synagogues are symbols of God, not God Himself. While God cannot be contained in a space, a space can become a symbol of God. Whether the symbol inspires us to integrate its teaching into our lives depends upon us. While the symbol can help catapult us to a higher plane, the journey requires intense human effort.

כַּבִּיר הוּא, לָמוּד הוּא, מֶלֶךְ הוּא יִבְנֶה בֵיתוֹ בְּקָרוֹב. בִּמְהֵרָה, בִּמְהֵרָה, בְּיָמֵינוּ בְּקָרוֹב. אֵל בְּנֵה, אֵל בְּנֵה, בְּנֵה בֵיתְךָ בְּקָרוֹב.

נוֹרָא הוּא, סַגִּיב הוּא, עִזּוּז הוּא יִבְנֶה בֵיתוֹ בְּקָרוֹב. בִּמְהֵרָה, בִּמְהֵרָה, בְּיָמֵינוּ בְּקָרוֹב. אֵל בְּנֵה, אֵל בְּנֵה, בְּנֵה בֵיתְךָ בְּקָרוֹב.

פּוֹדֶה הוּא, צַדִּיק הוּא, קָדוֹשׁ הוּא יִבְנֶה בֵיתוֹ בְּקָרוֹב. בִּמְהֵרָה, בִּמְהֵרָה, בְּיָמֵינוּ בְּקָרוֹב. אֵל בְּנֵה, אֵל בְּנֵה, בְּנֵה בֵיתְךָ בְּקָרוֹב.

רַחוּם הוּא, שַׁדַּי הוּא, תַּקִּיף הוּא יִבְנֶה בֵיתוֹ בְּקָרוֹב. בִּמְהֵרָה, בִּמְהֵרָה, בְּיָמֵינוּ בְּקָרוֹב. אֵל בְּנֵה, אֵל בְּנֵה, בְּנֵה בֵיתְךָ בְּקָרוֹב.

One sentence in the Torah advances this rationale: "And let them make Me a sanctuary, that I may dwell among them" (Exodus 25:8). One wonders: Why does the phrasing include *b'tocham* (among them) and not *b'tocho* (within it)? The answer is that *b'tocho* would imply that God could be contained within the Tabernacle whereas *b'tocham* emphasizes that, through the Tabernacle, God has the potential to dwell among the people — if we are willing to receive Him.

Powerful is He, learned is He, Ruler is He.
> Speedily, speedily, in our days, soon.
> God build, God build, build Your house soon.

Awesome is He, exalted is He, heroic is He.
> Speedily, speedily, in our days, soon.
> God build, God build, build Your house soon.

A redeemer is He, righteous is He, holy is He.
> Speedily, speedily, in our days, soon.
> God build, God build, build Your house soon.

Merciful is He, the Omnipotent is He, dynamic is He.
> Speedily, speedily, in our days, soon.
> God build, God build, build Your house soon.

ספירת העומר

ספירת העומר בחוץ לארץ, בליל שני של פסח.

בָּרוּךְ אַתָּה יהוה, אֱלֹהֵינוּ מֶלֶךְ הָעוֹלָם, אֲשֶׁר קִדְּשָׁנוּ בְּמִצְוֹתָיו וְצִוָּנוּ עַל סְפִירַת הָעֹמֶר.

הַיּוֹם יוֹם אֶחָד בָּעֹמֶר.

Sefirat HaOmer

The fifty days between Passover and Shavuot are commonly known as Sefirat Ha'omer (Leviticus 23:15, 16). From a biblical perspective, these days relate to the barley offering brought on the second day of Passover and the wheat offering brought on the festival of Shavuot. These are days of hope that the produce from the ground grow fruitfully and plentifully.

Not coincidentally, the Hebrew for fifty is *chamishim*, which recalls the word *chamsin*, the hot, often destructive wind prevalent during that time of year. We pray that it not harm the successful reaping of the crop.

In addition, this period of time relates to the counting of time from Passover, the holiday marking our physical exodus from Egypt, to Shavuot, the holiday commemorating the giving of the Torah. For this reason, we count up and not down from Pesach to Shavuot, spiritually ascending as we approach that moment in history when the Torah was given.

It is fitting that we count up to forty-nine. This is because the number seven in Judaism symbolizes completion, wholeness, and spirituality – the number of Shabbat. Forty-nine is seven sets

Sefirat HaOmer - ספירת העומר

One the second night we begin counting the Omer:

> Blessed are You, Lord our God, Ruler of the Universe, who has sanctified us with His commandments and has commanded us on the counting of the omer.
>
> Today is day one of the omer.

of seven; therefore the *omer* period is the ultimate completion of the completion, the holiest of the holiest.

As Jewish history progressed, though, these joyous days became sad ones. Between Passover and Shavuot, the students of Rabbi Akiva died. According to tradition, this occurred because these learned men were involved in endless dispute (Yevamot 62b).

And so, the days of the *omer*, which were originally joyous, became days of mourning. In fact, the *Aruch Hashulchan* notes that the most intense attacks against the Jewish People during the Crusades occurred during Sefirat Ha'omer (Orach Chayim 493:1). Indeed, Dr. Yaffa Eliach implored children of survivors to be especially kind to their parents between Pesach and Shavuot, as the Nazis – aware of the importance of these holidays to Jews – were particularly brutal during this time of year.

Today, we see a slow reversal, as Yom Ha'atzmaut (Israel's Independence Day) and Yom Yerushalayim (commemorating the liberation of Jerusalem) are joyously celebrated during Sefirat Ha'omer. May the day soon come when God wipes away tears from all faces (Isaiah 25:8), and all days of "mourning turn into dancing" (Psalms 30:12).

אחד מי יודע

אֶחָד מִי יוֹדֵעַ? אֶחָד אֲנִי יוֹדֵעַ: אֶחָד אֱלֹהֵינוּ שֶׁבַּשָּׁמַיִם וּבָאָרֶץ.

שְׁנַיִם מִי יוֹדֵעַ? שְׁנַיִם אֲנִי יוֹדֵעַ: שְׁנֵי לֻחוֹת הַבְּרִית. אֶחָד אֱלֹהֵינוּ שֶׁבַּשָּׁמַיִם וּבָאָרֶץ.

שְׁלֹשָׁה מִי יוֹדֵעַ? שְׁלֹשָׁה אֲנִי יוֹדֵעַ: שְׁלֹשָׁה אָבוֹת, שְׁנֵי לֻחוֹת הַבְּרִית, אֶחָד אֱלֹהֵינוּ שֶׁבַּשָּׁמַיִם וּבָאָרֶץ.

Echad Mi Yode'a: Principles of Faith

The Seder's penultimate song echoes its beginning. It started with questions and here, in *Echad Mi Yode'a*, we ask questions and offer answers. The Seder that begans in a child-friendly fashion ends the same way.

אֶחָד מִי יוֹדֵעַ - Who Knows One? In Temple times, Judaism was uni-centered: All roads pointed to Jerusalem, to the *Mikdash*. Its destruction was devastating and yet, as in all negatives, there was a sliver of light. That positive expressed itself in the development of a Judaism that was multi-centered with Jewish communities growing worldwide. The centerpiece of many of these communities were Torah learning centers, all based on fundamental principles of faith. Some of these principles are highlighted in the popular song *Echad Mi Yode'a*.

Sung late at night with many Seder participants struggling to stay awake, it's purposely written in a folksy, playful manner to keep everyone's attention. Accordingly, while it climbs the ladder of numbers, each representing a foundational Jewish concept, each can also be interpreted anecdotally and spiritually, hopefully inspiring purposeful discussion.

אֶחָד אֱלֹהֵינוּ - One is our God: My paternal grandparents were blessed with ten children, three of whom perished with their entire families during the Shoah. The other seven made their way to the United States, raising families there; at last count, over 1100 individuals descended from my Bubby Sarah and Zaidy Dovid. Recently, I heard my grandfather's voice for the first time on a scratchy recording of a Saturday night Melaveh Malkah he celebrated

Who Knows One - Echad Mi Yode'a

Who knows one? I know one:

> One is our God in the heavens and the earth.

Who knows two? I know two:

> two are the tablets of the covenant, One is our God in the heavens and the earth.

Who knows three? I know three:

> three are the fathers, two are the tablets of the covenant, One is our God in the heavens and the earth.

in May of 1948 with his surviving children. He spoke about belief in God, how everything – all we do – is only with God's help. The gathering was held just three years after the Shoah. I was astounded by the depth of his belief; after all that my Zaidy and his family and our people had endured, God was still ever-present in his life.

As I listened, I thought of the many, many who left that horror of horrors without belief, rejecting God. I was reminded of the incisive thought of Rabbi Dr. Eliezer Berkovits. For Dr. Berkovits, all who were victimized by the Nazis were holy. Those who went to their death or survived praising God were holy believers; and those who went to their death or survived cursing God were no less holy – they were holy disbelievers.

שְׁנֵי לֻחוֹת הַבְּרִית - **Two are the tablets:** The two tablets relate to the different columns of the Ten Declarations. Homiletically, it can also refer to the two sets that were given – the first that were shattered, and the second that served as its replacement. The rabbis wonder where the broken pieces were placed. In the Ark alongside the second whole tablets, they responded, teaching an important lesson: Even as one moves forward to experience a new day, we ought to learn from our mistakes. Yes, we learn from the shattered pieces, lifting us to even higher heights.

שְׁלֹשָׁה אָבוֹת - **Three are the fathers:** Each of our patriarchs was a devout believer in God, and yet they connected to the divine in their own ways. Thus, in our Amidah, we say, "the God of Abraham, the God of Isaac, the God of Jacob." There is, of course, only one God; still, Abraham's

אַרְבַּע מִי יוֹדֵעַ? אַרְבַּע אֲנִי יוֹדֵעַ: אַרְבַּע אִמָּהוֹת, שְׁלֹשָׁה אָבוֹת, שְׁנֵי לֻחוֹת הַבְּרִית, אֶחָד אֱלֹהֵינוּ שֶׁבַּשָּׁמַיִם וּבָאָרֶץ. חֲמִשָּׁה מִי יוֹדֵעַ?

חֲמִשָּׁה אֲנִי יוֹדֵעַ: חֲמִשָּׁה חוּמְשֵׁי תוֹרָה, אַרְבַּע אִמָּהוֹת, שְׁלֹשָׁה אָבוֹת, שְׁנֵי לֻחוֹת הַבְּרִית, אֶחָד אֱלֹהֵינוּ שֶׁבַּשָּׁמַיִם וּבָאָרֶץ.

approach to God differed from Isaac's, which differed from Jacob's. Everyone finds their own path to belief, singing their own melody, dancing their own dance.

Indeed, it has been suggested that the unique characteristics of each of the three avot (patriarchs) inspired them, as the Talmud suggests, to pray at different times (Berachot 26b):

Abraham, who introduced a new faith commitment to the world, prayed at dawn, the beginning of the new day. He is thus considered the progenitor of Shacharit, the morning prayer service.

Isaac, the mediator who evaluated and then transmitted Abraham's novel ideas, was passive, content to follow in his father's footsteps. He was taken to Moriah to be offered as a sacrifice, had a wife chosen for him, and reopened the wells that his father had previously discovered. He contemplated rather than initiated. Therefore, he prayed in the afternoon, as the sun set, an especially suitable time for contemplative thought. He is thus considered the progenitor of Minchah, the afternoon prayer service.

Jacob was the loneliest of the patriarchs. Hated by his brother Esau, he was separated from his parents for twenty-two years. His beloved wife, Rachel, died young. His favorite son, Joseph, disappeared and was believed to be dead. Appropriately, Jacob prayed at night, a time when one is often overcome by fear and loneliness. He is thus considered the progenitor of Maariv, the evening prayer service.

אַרְבַּע אִמָּהוֹת - **Four are the mothers:** Each of the matriarchs made crucial independent contributions to our nationhood.

Sarah: Sarah urged Abraham to have a child with Hagar, and so, on some level, was connected to Yishmael. And yet, when Yishmael vied to be the second patriarch, Sarah

Who knows four? I know four:

> four are the mothers, three are the fathers, two are the tablets of the covenant, One is our God in the heavens and the earth.

Who knows five? I know five:

> five are the books of the Torah, four are the mothers, three are the fathers, two are the tablets of the covenant, One is our God in the heavens and the earth.

stood her ground. In disagreement with her husband, she insisted, with God's approval, that Isaac be the covenantal heir.

Rebecca: Rebecca was perhaps the smartest person in the Torah. While her husband Isaac, according to Malbim, believed that the third patriarchal position should be shared – with Esau, their hunting eldest caring for the nation of Israel's physical needs and Jacob, their Torah immersed youngest, its spiritual strivings – Rebecca understood that we are not disembodied souls; rather, body and soul are in tandem, each influencing the other. In the end, Jacob incorporates Esau's strength, wrestling with a mysterious being and standing up to Esau. He synthesizes "the voice of Jacob and the hands of Esau." This foundational idea in Judaism was the credo of Rabbi Kook, who envisioned an Israeli soldier who would fight with a gun in one hand and a Torah in the other.

Rachel: Rachel, buried in Bethlehem, "refuses to be comforted." The Midrash tells us that as the Judeans passed by her grave after the destruction of the Temple, she cried out that they be permitted to return. In the same breath, she insisted that the descendants of her children, making up the leadership of the exiled ten tribes, be forever reunited with the southern kingdom of Judah.

Leah: Leah, although less loved by Jacob, loyally partnered with him in birthing and raising Judah, from whom the Messiah will one day come.

חֲמִשָּׁה חוּמְשֵׁי תוֹרָה - **Five are the books of the Torah:** In my thematic commentary on the Torah, *Torat Ahavah – Loving Torah*, different appellative titles are suggested for each of the five books, reflective of their central themes.

• **Bereishit:** The Book of Genesis can be called *Ahavat Mishpacha*, Family Love. Although the book is laden with the endless travails of

שִׁשָּׁה מִי יוֹדֵעַ? שִׁשָּׁה אֲנִי יוֹדֵעַ: שִׁשָּׁה סִדְרֵי מִשְׁנָה, חֲמִשָּׁה חוּמְשֵׁי תוֹרָה, אַרְבַּע אִמָּהוֹת, שְׁלֹשָׁה אָבוֹת, שְׁנֵי לֻחוֹת הַבְּרִית, אֶחָד אֱלֹהֵינוּ שֶׁבַּשָּׁמַיִם וּבָאָרֶץ.

fractured families, there is magic in its finale, a reconciliation occurs, the family is reunited. All of Jacob's sons are blessed. It is only then, when the family is whole at last, that Bereishit ends and Shemot, the Book of Exodus, which centers on the birth of the nation, begins. This teaches that the best model of nation is family.

✦ **Shemot:** The Book of Exodus can be called *Brit Am*, a Covenant of Peoplehood between God and Israel. The covenant begins with the exodus story. The redemptive process, however, is not limited to freedom from oppression. If that were the case, Judaism would only be reactive, and nothing solely reactive will endure. The struggle against oppression becomes significant only if the resulting freedom is used to pursue a greater mission. And so, soon after leaving Egypt, the covenant gathers momentum as the Jews receive the Torah at Sinai, and then build the Tabernacle, which some call a "Walking Sinai." The Sinaitic *mitzvot* become an integral part of a goal-oriented, proactive Judaism that is certain to endure.

✦ **Vayikra:** The Book of Leviticus can be called *Torat Kedushah*, the Laws of Holiness. Whereas the early portions engage in the specifics of the sacrificial service within the Tabernacle, the latter portions serve as guidelines for a holy life to be led outside of the Tabernacle. With the Kohen and Levi as our exemplars, we are asked to walk in their footsteps and usher the holiness of the Temple into our everyday lives.

✦ **Bamidbar:** The Book of Numbers can be called *Hitgadlut Yisrael*, the Maturation of Israel. And so it is, that whereas the first three books introduced laws which were initiated by God, this book includes laws initiated by the people. The book is divided by the incident of the spies scouting the land, and the decree that only the second generation would enter Israel, forty years later. Herein lies a testament to the gradual maturation of the Jewish people, which can be gauged by how setbacks are handled. Only when a nation succeeds in learning from its mistakes can it grow.

Who knows six? I know six:

> six are the orders of the Mishnah, five are the books of the Torah, four are the mothers, three are the fathers, two are the tablets of the covenant, One is our God in the heavens and the earth.

♦ **Devarim:** The Book of Deuteronomy can be called *Sichat He'Atid*, a Conversation about Times to Come. It deals with Moses' address to the Israelites, reminding them of past misdeeds, but also significantly looks forward. New laws applicable upon entering the Land of Israel are included. Faith, however, is foremost – belief in God is the premise upon which all else is based.

שִׁשָּׁה סִדְרֵי מִשְׁנָה **- Six are the orders of the Mishnah:** The Pentateuch empowers rabbis and leaders of ensuing generations to comment on, interpret and expand the meaning of the Torah through the development of the Oral Law represented here by the six sections of the Mishnah. Jewish law is a covenantal partnership between God and humans. God purposefully gave the Torah cryptically, leaving it to spiritual leaders in every generation to apply it properly, taking into account varying situations and new conditions. That process continues to this day, challenging decisors of law in our generation to fix the inequities that still exist in Jewish Law (including questions about gender, sexuality, and *agunot*).

Commenting on the interplay of the Written Law and Oral Law, the Zohar claims, the former is the "harsh law" while the latter is the "soft law." For example, the biblical dictum "eye for an eye" seems literal. And yet, the oral tradition insists that the penalty is monetary. Why doesn't the Torah articulate this interpretation clearly? In the spirit of the Zohar, it can be suggested that the Written Law sets the tone, gives the direction, and presents the teaching. As the Torah is read, the listener hears the words "eye for an eye" and concludes that removing the eye of another is a crime so heinous that it is deserving of my eye being removed. In the words of *Haktav v'Hakabbalah*, "The Torah mentions here only what punishment the perpetrator of bodily injuries deserves."

The Oral Law, however, which interprets the Torah, explains how these rules are actually practiced. While one who removes the eye of another may deserve physical punishment, in practical terms he

שִׁבְעָה מִי יוֹדֵעַ? שִׁבְעָה אֲנִי יוֹדֵעַ: שִׁבְעָה יְמֵי שַׁבַּתָּא, שִׁשָּׁה סִדְרֵי מִשְׁנָה, חֲמִשָּׁה חוּמְשֵׁי תוֹרָה, אַרְבַּע אִמָּהוֹת, שְׁלֹשָׁה אָבוֹת, שְׁנֵי לֻחוֹת הַבְּרִית, אֶחָד אֱלֹהֵינוּ שֶׁבַּשָּׁמַיִם וּבָאָרֶץ.

שְׁמוֹנָה מִי יוֹדֵעַ? שְׁמוֹנָה אֲנִי יוֹדֵעַ: שְׁמוֹנָה יְמֵי מִילָה, שִׁבְעָה יְמֵי שַׁבַּתָּא, שִׁשָּׁה סִדְרֵי מִשְׁנָה, חֲמִשָּׁה חוּמְשֵׁי תוֹרָה, אַרְבַּע אִמָּהוֹת, שְׁלֹשָׁה אָבוֹת, שְׁנֵי לֻחוֹת הַבְּרִית, אֶחָד אֱלֹהֵינוּ שֶׁבַּשָּׁמַיִם וּבָאָרֶץ.

receives a monetary penalty.

In the end, the two combine and weave a beautiful tapestry, as the Written Law cannot be understood without the Oral Law. Together they form one unit. As the Psalmist proclaims, *"Torat Hashem temimah"* (Psalms 19:8) – the Torah of the Lord is whole… holy… holistic.

שִׁבְעָה יְמֵי שַׁבַּתָּא - **Seven are the days of the week:** Not long ago, a blogger developed the idea of "Disconnect." With millions addicted to their phones – emails, social media, streaming – for one day a year, this young man thought, why not disconnect, step back, freeing oneself of these devices? The idea so resonated, he went on to suggest that the disconnect be observed one day monthly. And then, he thought, one day weekly. As noted in our commentary on the kiddush, this concept, in broad strokes, is what Shabbat is all about. For six days we're engaged in how we can get ahead. Shabbat is an island in time when we ask the deeper questions: Why? For what purpose?

Yet another understanding of the Shabbat speaks to the idea that the world is Theocentric, not anthropocentric. When God unleashed His unlimited power to create the world, He did so incompletely. And so, the last word of the creation story is *la'asot* (to do). Here, God asks that we complete creation and, in partnership with Him, redeem the world.

Over the millennia, human beings have by and large successfully fulfilled the *la'asot* mandate. In fact, humans have been so successful that we are in danger of forgetting that God is the source of our creativity. Hence the laws of Shabbat would have us refrain from activities that indicate

Who knows seven? I know seven:

> seven are the days of the week, six are the orders of the Mishnah, five are the books of the Torah, four are the mothers, three are the fathers, two are the tablets of the covenant, One is our God in the heavens and the earth.

Who knows eight? I know eight:

> eight are the days of circumcision, seven are the days of the week, six are the orders of the Mishnah, five are the books of the Torah, four are the mothers, three are the fathers, two are the tablets of the covenant, One is our God in the heavens and the earth.

our mastery over the world. In this way, we assert the centrality of God (Dayan Grunfeld, *The Sabbath*). Thus, as creative as humans can be, God is the source of all creation.

שְׁמוֹנָה יְמֵי מִילָה - **Eight are the days of circumcision:** Six is the number of physicality, as the world was created in six stages; seven is the number of spirituality – Shabbat; eight takes us to a meta-spiritual level. In music, it is the same note as the first, but an octave higher. It's on the eighth day that the Temple was dedicated, that the Chanukah lights reach their crescendo, and that males enter covenantal circumcision.

Moreover, circumcision can be seen as the ritual symbol of the plight of Am Yisrael. In the ritual, an innocent child has blood drawn from its organ of propagation, representing the suffering of the Jewish People as innocent servants of God throughout the ages. It is no coincidence that, before biblical redemptive events (e.g., the first time Moses demanded of Pharaoh "Let my people go"; the exodus from Egypt; the entry into Israel), there is always circumcision, teaching that built into redemption is sacrifice.

Never will I forget seeing Yosef Tobi at a conference a few years after he lost his grandson, Yuval, in battle. His nametag read, "Yuval Yosef Tobi." "Don't you have only one name, Yosef?" I asked. To which he responded, "I have formally decided to add the name of my grandson, and so I am, for however long I am given life — Yuval Yosef." It shouldn't be this way. Grandchildren are named after grandparents, not the reverse. Surveys indicate that Israel is one of the happiest countries in the world, and yet, too often, suffering is built into redemption.

תִּשְׁעָה מִי יוֹדֵעַ? תִּשְׁעָה אֲנִי יוֹדֵעַ: תִּשְׁעָה יַרְחֵי לֵדָה, שְׁמוֹנָה יְמֵי מִילָה, שִׁבְעָה יְמֵי שַׁבַּתָּא, שִׁשָּׁה סִדְרֵי מִשְׁנָה, חֲמִשָּׁה חוּמְשֵׁי תוֹרָה, אַרְבַּע אִמָּהוֹת, שְׁלֹשָׁה אָבוֹת, שְׁנֵי לֻחוֹת הַבְּרִית, אֶחָד אֱלֹהֵינוּ שֶׁבַּשָּׁמַיִם וּבָאָרֶץ.

עֲשָׂרָה מִי יוֹדֵעַ? עֲשָׂרָה אֲנִי יוֹדֵעַ: עֲשָׂרָה דִבְּרַיָּא, תִּשְׁעָה יַרְחֵי לֵדָה, שְׁמוֹנָה יְמֵי מִילָה, שִׁבְעָה יְמֵי שַׁבַּתָּא, שִׁשָּׁה סִדְרֵי מִשְׁנָה, חֲמִשָּׁה חוּמְשֵׁי תוֹרָה, אַרְבַּע אִמָּהוֹת, שְׁלֹשָׁה אָבוֹת, שְׁנֵי לֻחוֹת הַבְּרִית, אֶחָד אֱלֹהֵינוּ שֶׁבַּשָּׁמַיִם וּבָאָרֶץ.

תִּשְׁעָה יַרְחֵי לֵדָה - **Nine are the months of birth:** My dear friend Rabbi Yitz Greenberg has called his magnum opus book on theology "The Triumph of Life." To bring life into the world is the greatest mitzvah, made possible by the holiness of the nine month gestation period.

Indeed, survivors of the Shoah who had every right to give up on the world, performed the greatest of mitzvot. In the wake of experiencing all-consuming death, they brought life into the world. As King Solomon declared, *ki aza ka'mavet ahavah*, love will overpower death.

And yet, as noted earlier, there are countless people struggling with infertility. As we sing the miracle of pregnancy, we think of those couples struggling to have children, or those who have lost children, and resolve to help them. We resolve, as well, to help those who are not married who yearn to have children, to do so as single parents.

עֲשָׂרָה דִבְּרַיָּא - **Ten are the Declarations:** Note that they are not called commandments. Belief in God may not be a mitzvah – if so, only nine are left (Rashi). Others maintain all of the 613 commandments are

Who knows nine? I know nine:

> nine are the months of birth, eight are the days of circumcision, seven are the days of the week, six are the orders of the Mishnah, five are the books of the Torah, four are the mothers, three are the fathers, two are the tablets of the covenant, One is our God in the heavens and the earth.

Who knows ten? I know ten:

> ten are the declarations, nine are the months of birth, eight are the days of circumcision, seven are the days of the week, six are the orders of the Mishnah, five are the books of the Torah, four are the mothers, three are the fathers, two are the tablets of the covenant, One is our God in the heavens and the earth.

in the ten. Hence, the better term is Ten Declarations. Note as well, they can be split horizontally – with each intersecting with another. As an example, "I am the Lord your God" sits opposite the prohibition of "Thou shalt not murder." Taking the life of an other means that the image of God, as manifested in the victim, has been diminished – thus, there is less of God in the world.

In this sense, our interpersonal responsibilities intersect with laws governing our relationship with God. Conversely, Jewish ritual, commonly associated with our relationship to God, connects us to other humans. For example, Shabbat, the day we acknowledge the centrality of God, reminds us that all humans are of equal value, all rest on the Sabbath day as the Bible says: "Six days you shall do your work, but on the seventh day you shall rest… the son of your handmaid and the stranger shall be refreshed." Thus, the human-to-God and human-to-human laws do not stand independently, but rather intersect, complementing and ennobling each other.

אַחַד עָשָׂר מִי יוֹדֵעַ? אַחַד עָשָׂר אֲנִי יוֹדֵעַ: אַחַד עָשָׂר כּוֹכְבַיָּא, עֲשָׂרָה דִבְּרַיָּא, תִּשְׁעָה יַרְחֵי לֵדָה, שְׁמוֹנָה יְמֵי מִילָה, שִׁבְעָה יְמֵי שַׁבְּתָא, שִׁשָּׁה סִדְרֵי מִשְׁנָה, חֲמִשָּׁה חוּמְשֵׁי תוֹרָה, אַרְבַּע אִמָּהוֹת, שְׁלֹשָׁה אָבוֹת, שְׁנֵי לוּחוֹת הַבְּרִית, אֶחָד אֱלֹהֵינוּ שֶׁבַּשָּׁמַיִם וּבָאָרֶץ.

שְׁנֵים עָשָׂר מִי יוֹדֵעַ? שְׁנֵים עָשָׂר אֲנִי יוֹדֵעַ: שְׁנֵים עָשָׂר שִׁבְטַיָּא, אַחַד עָשָׂר כּוֹכְבַיָּא, עֲשָׂרָה דִבְּרַיָּא, תִּשְׁעָה יַרְחֵי לֵדָה, שְׁמוֹנָה יְמֵי מִילָה, שִׁבְעָה יְמֵי שַׁבְּתָא, שִׁשָּׁה סִדְרֵי מִשְׁנָה, חֲמִשָּׁה חוּמְשֵׁי תוֹרָה, אַרְבַּע אִמָּהוֹת, שְׁלֹשָׁה אָבוֹת, שְׁנֵי לוּחוֹת הַבְּרִית, אֶחָד אֱלֹהֵינוּ שֶׁבַּשָּׁמַיִם וּבָאָרֶץ.

אַחַד עָשָׂר כּוֹכְבַיָּא - **Eleven are the Stars [in Joseph's dream]**: God tells Abraham he'll be as numerous as the earthly dust and heavenly stars. There's a difference between the two. We walk on sand. We reach for the stars. It is virtually impossible to isolate one speck of dust; they are all connected. By contrast, each star is distinct, speaking to the uniqueness of every human being. The stars we see are lights that began their journeys light years ago; so, too, one's potential legacy can continue years, decades, centuries after physically leaving this world.

It has also been suggested that Joseph, the dreamer of eleven stars, could be described as visualizing, yearning for a new world order. A new economy: and so he dreamed of sheaves; that is a society of farmers rather than shepherds. A new social order: and so he dreamed of stars, the sun and the moon – much like the religious Zionists of the early twentieth century. As Rabbi Yosef Dov Soloveitchik said: "The Joseph of 5662 (1902) unconsciously sensed… that great changes were about to occur in Jewish life… they dreamed the advent of a new era when… the State of Israel, not Brisk or Vilna, would become the core center of Torah, of Jewish life." A new era we are blessed to experience every day.

שְׁנֵים עָשָׂר שִׁבְטַיָּא - **Twelve are the tribes [of Israel]**: The Southern Kingdom of Judea separated from the Northern Kingdom of Israel (the

Who knows eleven? I know eleven:

> eleven are the stars [in Joseph's dream], ten are the declarations, nine are the months of birth, eight are the days of circumcision, seven are the days of the week, six are the orders of the Mishnah, five are the books of the Torah, four are the mothers, three are the fathers, two are the tablets of the covenant, One is our God in the heavens and the earth.

Who knows twelve? I know twelve:

> twelve are the tribes [of Israel], eleven are the stars, ten are the declarations, nine are the months of birth, eight are the days of circumcision, seven are the days of the week, six are the orders of the Mishnah, five are the books of the Torah, four are the mothers, three are the fathers, two are the tablets of the covenant, One is our God in the heavens and the earth.

Ten Tribes). Redemption will come when they reunite. As the prophet Ezekiel (37:16-17) proclaims, "And you, son of man, take one stick, and write upon it, 'For Judah, and for the children of Israel his companions.' Then take another stick and write upon it, 'For Joseph, the stick of Efraim, and for all the house of Israel his companions,' and join them one to the other to make one stick; and they shall become one in your hand." As already noted at the outset of our commentary, and deserving mention because of its importance as we draw to a close: unity is not uniformity. Uniformity is when we become one by eradicating the ideas of those with whom we differ. Unity is the blending of differences, listening to each other, recognizing we have much to learn from one another.

An important anecdote. Most recently, I heard a moving talk from a former hostage, Sapir Cohen, who spent 51 horrific days in Gaza. She emotionally shared that at times, terrorists demanded she watch news of the mass protests in Tel Aviv, demanding freedom for the hostages. Turning to her, her captors remarked, *you see, now Israel is together, they cannot be defeated. But soon, they will be divided, fighting with each other. Then, they will be vulnerable. Then, we will succeed.* The charge: it's up to us. No matter our differences, to always remember we are one family, forever *Am Yisrael Chai*.

שְׁלֹשָׁה עָשָׂר מִי יוֹדֵעַ? שְׁלֹשָׁה עָשָׂר אֲנִי יוֹדֵעַ: שְׁלֹשָׁה עָשָׂר מִדַּיָּא, שְׁנֵים עָשָׂר שִׁבְטַיָּא, אַחַד עָשָׂר כּוֹכְבַיָּא, עֲשָׂרָה דִבְּרַיָּא, תִּשְׁעָה יַרְחֵי לֵדָה, שְׁמוֹנָה יְמֵי מִילָה, שִׁבְעָה יְמֵי שַׁבְּתָא, שִׁשָּׁה סִדְרֵי מִשְׁנָה, חֲמִשָּׁה חוּמְשֵׁי תוֹרָה, אַרְבַּע אִמָּהוֹת, שְׁלֹשָׁה אָבוֹת, שְׁנֵי לֻחוֹת הַבְּרִית, אֶחָד אֱלֹהֵינוּ שֶׁבַּשָּׁמַיִם וּבָאָרֶץ.

שְׁלֹשָׁה עָשָׂר מִדַּיָּא - Thirteen are the Attributes [of the Lord]: More than ever, we need a Judaism of love, a Judaism of compassion, a Judaism of emulating God's thirteen attributes. At its foundation, my theology is based on love, love of Israel, *ahavat Yisrael*; love of humankind, *ahavat hab'riyot*. The law, the halacha, that shapes our lives, in my mind, reflects the thirteen loving attributes of God: "The Lord, the Lord, God, merciful and gracious, slow to anger, and abounding in kindness and truth."

Who knows thirteen? I know thirteen:

> thirteen are the attributes [of the Lord], twelve are the tribes, eleven are the stars, ten are the declarations, nine are the months of birth, eight are the days of circumcision, seven are the days of the week, six are the orders of the Mishnah, five are the books of the Torah, four are the mothers, three are the fathers, two are the tablets of the covenant, One is our God in the heavens and the earth.

חד גדיא

חַד גַּדְיָא, חַד גַּדְיָא דְזַבִּין אַבָּא בִּתְרֵי זוּזֵי, חַד גַּדְיָא, חַד גַּדְיָא.

וְאָתָא שׁוּנְרָא וְאָכְלָה לְגַדְיָא, דְזַבִּין אַבָּא בִּתְרֵי זוּזֵי. חַד גַּדְיָא, חַד גַּדְיָא.

וְאָתָא כַלְבָּא וְנָשַׁךְ לְשׁוּנְרָא, דְאָכְלָה לְגַדְיָא, דְזַבִּין אַבָּא בִּתְרֵי זוּזֵי. חַד גַּדְיָא, חַד גַּדְיָא.

וְאָתָא חוּטְרָא וְהִכָּה לְכַלְבָּא, דְנָשַׁךְ לְשׁוּנְרָא, דְאָכְלָה לְגַדְיָא, דְזַבִּין אַבָּא בִּתְרֵי זוּזֵי. חַד גַּדְיָא, חַד גַּדְיָא.

Chad Gadya: Against All Odds

The Seder closes with the delightful *Chad Gadya*. Some see it as representing different eras of Jewish exile, with God prevailing in the end, when Israel and the world will be redeemed.

At our Seder, participants having enjoyed each other's company for hours, "kick off their shoes" and, in novel ways, attempt to connect to each of the *Chad Gadya* stanzas, beginning with imitating the sound of each paragraph's subject – the cat's meow, the dog's bark.

Attendees can also share personal stories or sweet Torah thoughts related to what they or others have done to make a difference, contributing to the repair of our people and the world. We do so using the *Chad Gadya*'s subjects as a starting point. From this perspective, *Chad Gadya* may not only mean one kid, but one story. Indeed, "*Chad*" means one, *echad*. *Gadya* sounds like *lehagid* – the telling of a story. For the larger world, the tale may be worth a mere two *zuzim*, but to the storyteller it is priceless. Here are some personal examples.

One **kid**: The goat represents deception, referring to the goat's skin worn by Jacob as he fooled his father when taking the blessings from his brother; additionally, it could refer to the brothers deceiving their father Jacob as they dipped Joseph's coat of many colors into goat's blood. We all wear masks. There are times when my dear wife Toby lovingly tells me to take off my rabbi mask as we converse with each other.

Chad Gadya - One Kid

חַד גַּדְיָא - One kid, one kid that my father bought for two zuzim, one kid, one kid.

Then came a cat and ate the kid that my father bought for two zuzim, one kid, one kid.

Then came a dog and bit the cat, that ate the kid that my father bought for two zuzim, one kid, one kid.

Then came a stick and hit the dog, that bit the cat, that ate the kid that my father bought for two zuzim, one kid, one kid.

The **cat** reminds me of Jerusalem, as there, as in few other places, cats are everywhere. Anecdotally, the face of a cat looks something like the little fuzzies I used to give out to the youngsters when I was serving as rabbi of the Bayit. Attached to the fuzzy was a small note which read, "Rav Avi thinks I'm great." That was my way of sharing with each of these children that they have the capacity to make a real contribution to better the world. The idea came from my brother, Mordechai, a master rabbi-educator who gave these fuzzies out to students in the school he led for decades. I wasn't sure I should do the same, as it seemed a bit corny. Right about then, however, I visited IDF troops during the Second Lebanon War in 2005. I met the head of a tank corps, and we began talking. Introducing ourselves, he was flabbergasted. He had been a student in my brother's school. With deep emotion he said to me, "And you know what got me through this war?" Putting his hand into his pocket, he pulled out a tarred fuzzy. "That's how I made it. Rabbi Mordechai's fuzzy gave me the confidence that I could succeed." That moment inspired me to give out fuzzies by the hundreds in the hope that maybe, for one child, it would make a difference and inspire them to reach for the impossible.

The **dog** reminds me of one of the first questions I received in my rabbinate. Serving in St. Louis, a congregant called, frantic. Her dog had died, and she wanted the rabbi — me — to preside over his funeral and burial, insisting the *kaddish* be said. To me, it was not only strange

וְאָתָא נוּרָא וְשָׂרַף לְחוּטְרָא, דְּהִכָּה לְכַלְבָּא, דְּנָשַׁךְ לְשׁוּנְרָא, דְּאָכְלָה לְגַדְיָא, דְּזַבִּין אַבָּא בִּתְרֵי זוּזֵי. חַד גַּדְיָא, חַד גַּדְיָא.

וְאָתָא מַיָּא וְכָבָה לְנוּרָא, דְּשָׂרַף לְחוּטְרָא, דְּהִכָּה לְכַלְבָּא, דְּנָשַׁךְ לְשׁוּנְרָא, דְּאָכְלָה לְגַדְיָא, דְּזַבִּין אַבָּא בִּתְרֵי זוּזֵי. חַד גַּדְיָא, חַד גַּדְיָא.

וְאָתָא תּוֹרָא וְשָׁתָה לְמַיָּא, דְּכָבָה לְנוּרָא, דְּשָׂרַף לְחוּטְרָא, דְּהִכָּה לְכַלְבָּא, דְּנָשַׁךְ לְשׁוּנְרָא, דְּאָכְלָה לְגַדְיָא, דְּזַבִּין אַבָּא בִּתְרֵי זוּזֵי. חַד גַּדְיָא, חַד גַּדְיָא.

but absurd, as I grew up fearful of dogs, perhaps because of stories I heard from my parents of how dogs were used by the Nazis during the Shoah to attack Jews. Looking back, I now appreciate the congregant's question. A dog displays great loyalty, as its Hebrew name, *kelev*, "like my heart," suggests. In the exodus story too, dogs played a critical role, not barking to tip off the Egyptians as the Jews hurried out of Egypt. Thus, they remained true to the Jewish escapees to the end.

The **stick** reminds me of Mr. Frankel, my father's shul *shames*. As a youngster no more than eight or nine years old, I would often walk with Mr. Frankel, who made his way, with a stick in each hand. Over and over he'd say, "these sticks, they keep me straight, they allow me to walk, *un mit mein shteken vell ich mekabel zein der Mashiach* (and with my sticks I will walk to greet the Messiah)." Indeed, in the Torah, Moses used a stick to part the sea and hit the rock, highs and lows in his career. The stick is neutral; how it's used makes all the difference. In Mr. Frankel's case, his stick gave him the feet to walk steadily; and one day, who knows, to receive the Messiah.

The **fire** is the Torah scroll, made up of black fire on white fire. Black fire are the letters that impart deep intellectual messages. The white fire are the spaces between the letters, the story, the song – together they merge, a flame intensifying, rising, giving direction on how to make our world a better world. The Midrash compares the black letters to a half-brick resting on a whole brick, the white spaces between and surrounding the letters. Thus, the white fire, often seen as secondary, is primary. On its shoulders all rests. For me, the

Then came fire and burnt the stick, that hit the dog, that bit the cat, that ate the kid that my father bought for two zuzim, one kid, one kid.

Then came water and extinguished the fire, that burnt the stick, that hit the dog, that bit the cat, that ate the kid that my father bought for two zuzim, one kid, one kid.

Then came an ox and drank the water, that extinguished the fire, that burnt the stick, that hit the dog, that bit the cat, that ate the kid that my father bought for two zuzim, one kid, one kid.

personality who synthesized the black fire and white fire was Rabbi Ahron Soloveichik. How I remember the first time I met him. I was all of eighteen, and foolishly believed I could learn on my own and had no need for a rebbe. When placed in the class of Rabbi Soloveichik, I purposely sat in the back of the room. After all, I thought, what could he teach me? And then, Rav Ahron, as he was affectionately called, walked in. Bent over, with total humility, he slowly made his way to his desk. Something about the way he carried himself profoundly touched me. I felt Rav Ahron was reflecting the white fire, foundational to his brilliant black fire. The next day, and for months afterward, I sat front and center before Rav Ahron. I still consider Rav Ahron *mori v'rabbi*, my dear teacher.

Water: Unlike fire, which leaps upwards, water flows towards the lowest level, as it is basic to life. Without it, one cannot live. Holocaust survivors have told me that when liberated from the camps, they walked half-dead through the fields. When seeing a stranger, they called out, *am'cha* (my people)? If the response was *am'cha*, they knew they were safe. In their weakened state, they begged, *vasser* (water)? And if their newly found brother or sister shared with them a sip of water from a jug, both lifted their voices in song, singing *Lechaim! To Life!*

The **ox**: One of the most devastating moments in the Gaza war occurred when the IDF mistakenly killed hostage escapees, believing they were terrorists. Remarkably, the daf of that day records the following case, one I'll be thinking about when reading this paragraph of the Haggadah: If an ox intends to kill a Canaanite but kills a Jew,

וְאָתָא הַשּׁוֹחֵט וְשָׁחַט לְתוֹרָא, דְּשָׁתָה לְמַיָּא, דְּכָבָה לְנוּרָא, דְּשָׂרַף לְחוּטְרָא, דְּהִכָּה לְכַלְבָּא, דְּנָשַׁךְ לְשׁוּנְרָא, דְּאָכְלָה לְגַדְיָא, דְּזַבִּין אַבָּא בִּתְרֵי זוּזֵי. חַד גַּדְיָא, חַד גַּדְיָא.

וְאָתָא מַלְאַךְ הַמָּוֶת וְשָׁחַט לְשׁוֹחֵט, דְּשָׁחַט לְתוֹרָא, דְּשָׁתָה לְמַיָּא, דְּכָבָה לְנוּרָא, דְּשָׂרַף לְחוּטְרָא, דְּהִכָּה לְכַלְבָּא, דְּנָשַׁךְ לְשׁוּנְרָא, דְּאָכְלָה לְגַדְיָא, דְּזַבִּין אַבָּא בִּתְרֵי זוּזֵי. חַד גַּדְיָא, חַד גַּדְיָא.

the ox's owner, said Shmuel, is criminally exempt, but must pay *kofer* (atonement money). These two situations are not analogous (ox and human). Still, it reminded me of the touching words of Iris, mother of Yotam (one of the hostages killed in this incident), words in which she did not fault the soldiers, in fact, she invited them to the shiva. As she said, "at the first opportunity…you are welcomed to come to us, whoever wants to. And we want to see you with our own eyes and hug you and tell you that what you did – however hard it is to say this, and sad – it was apparently the right thing in that moment… and nobody is going to judge you or be angry… We love you very much. And that is all."

Her heartfelt message drew many civilians to make a condolence call. When arriving with others, we saw Iris sitting with four IDF soldiers (who we were told were present when the shooting occurred). They sat alone for an hour. When finished, Iris moved towards the many waiting for her. As the soldiers remained, a few of us made our way to them. Together we sat, in silence, in dialogue – some of the chayalim, strong, were in tears. I thought of the Talmudic Shmuel's comment, "exempt, but forever needing atonement."

The **slaughterer** (*shochet*) recalls for me the Sedarim we spent with the great Dr. Charles Kremer, a Nazi

Then came the slaughterer (shochet) and slaughtered the ox, that drank the water, that extinguished the fire, that burnt the stick, that hit the dog, that bit the cat, that ate the kid that my father bought for two zuzim, one kid, one kid.

Then came the angel of death and slaughtered the shochet, who slaughtered the ox, that drank the water, that extinguished the fire, that burnt the stick, that hit the dog, that bit the cat, that ate the kid that my father bought for two zuzim, one kid, one kid.

hunter who successfully pursued the Romanian Nazi Valerian Trifa, doing his share to fulfill the biblical mandate "Justice, justice you shall pursue." Trifa had become the Romanian Church's Archbishop of Detroit but, during World War II, served as the head of the Romanian Nazi Iron Guard – in one horrific event, hanging two hundred Jews from meat hooks in the central square of Bucharest. When, at our Seder, we came to the slaughterer of the *Chad Gadya*, Dr. Kremer blurted out, "Trifa, *mach shnell*." He meant, "*yemach shemo*," may his name be erased, but instead cried out, "*mach shnell*," which means, make it fast. Already in his 80s, Charlie feared he'd never see Trifa face justice. He did: Trifa was forced to leave the United States in 1984. Soon after, his mission complete, Charlie, of blessed memory, left this world.

The **Angel of Death:** Built into life is death; no one lives forever. Our role is to live life fully, passing our legacy to the next generation, and they to the next, slowly, slowly culminating in redemption. Still, the fear of dying can be overwhelming, reminding me of the deep conversations I had with my soul brother, Stewart Harris, in his last days, as he was struggling with terminal cancer. Together, we studied a Talmudic story of a dying rabbi who promises his students, broken by his imminent demise, that

וְאָתָא הַקָּדוֹשׁ בָּרוּךְ הוּא וְשָׁחַט לְמַלְאַךְ הַמָּוֶת, דְּשָׁחַט לְשׁוֹחֵט, דְּשָׁחַט לְתוֹרָא, דְּשָׁתָה לְמַיָּא, דְּכָבָה לְנוּרָא, דְּשָׂרַף לְחוּטְרָא, דְּהִכָּה לְכַלְבָּא, דְּנָשַׁךְ לְשׁוּנְרָא, דְּאָכְלָה לְגַדְיָא, דְּזַבִּין אַבָּא בִּתְרֵי זוּזֵי. חַד גַּדְיָא, חַד גַּדְיָא.

he'll come back in a dream to share with them how he's doing. He does just that, describing the beauty of the afterlife. One student brazenly asked: "Given your description, would you ever consider coming back to this world?" "Oh no," said the rabbi, "the fear of dying is too much to handle."

The **Holy One, Blessed be He**: Feeling God's presence is critical to personal, communal, national, and universal well-being. A sweet story: A rabbi was once informed that a crazed woman was in the *beit midrash* (the study hall, which is sometimes used as a prayer room). "She is standing in front of the Ark, the Ark is open, and she is babbling and gesturing wildly," he was told. "She seems to be mentally imbalanced. Perhaps you can go in

Then came the Holy One, blessed be He and slaughtered the angel of death, who slaughtered the shochet, who slaughtered the ox, that drank the water, that extinguished the fire, that burnt the stick, that hit the dog, that bit the cat, that ate the kid that my father bought for two zuzim, one kid, one kid.

and help her." The rabbi went in. As he sat quietly in the back, he could see that the woman was deeply immersed in *tefillah*. The rabbi overheard some of her words as she swayed and cried out: "Dear God, I know I was here just last week, but I am back because I need your help. My daughter is still not well. Please, please, in my hour of need, do not forsake me, do not leave me!" Understanding the privacy of her *tefillah*, the rabbi left the woman alone. Upon his return, he was asked, "So what did you do with the babbling crazy lady?" The rabbi responded, "This morning I got up, put on my prayer shawl, donned my *tefillin* and *davened*. But this woman wasn't *davening*, she was talking to God. That's a whole different world."

התקוה

כָּל עוֹד בַּלֵּבָב פְּנִימָה
נֶפֶשׁ יְהוּדִי הוֹמִיָּה
וּלְפַאֲתֵי מִזְרָח קָדִימָה
עַיִן לְצִיּוֹן צוֹפִיָּה

עוֹד לֹא אָבְדָה תִּקְוָתֵנוּ
הַתִּקְוָה בַּת שְׁנוֹת אַלְפַּיִם
לִהְיוֹת עַם חָפְשִׁי בְּאַרְצֵנוּ
אֶרֶץ צִיּוֹן וִירוּשָׁלַיִם

The Seder guided us on a journey from past to future redemption. And so, in our home, we conclude with Israel's national anthem as our way of declaring that the flowering of redemption is upon us. Our task is to do all we can to push that process along.

Hatikvah - התקוה

נֶפֶשׁ יְהוּדִי הוֹמִיָּה - **The Jewish soul is yearning [for Zion]:** Returning to Zion is the culmination of the connection between three ascending steps: our relationship with the land, our yearning for the land, and our settling in our Homeland, the Land of Israel.

When does one know love is real and will last? Loving when one has never been disappointed – when one doesn't see the imperfections in the other, when the love has never faltered, when one has never been let down – is untested love. But loving after being disappointed – after seeing the imperfections, after it has faltered, after being let down – is different. If I can love you then, if I have not given up on you, if I resolve to love you no matter what, that is a love that endures forever.

This concept has contemporary meaning, especially when considering the establishment of the modern State of Israel after two thousand years of exile. If the Jews, after being exiled, still believed in the land and

Hatikvah - התקוה

As long as the Jewish soul
is yearning deep in the heart
With eyes looking forward
to Zion

Then our hope, the two-thousand-year-old hope
is not lost
To be a free people in our land
the land of Zion and Jerusalem

returned, that love of the land, the holiness of the land, can never be shaken. To paraphrase Theodor Herzl, the great Zionist visionary: If you love it, it is no dream.

עַיִן לְצִיּוֹן צוֹפִיָּה - **With eyes looking forward to Zion:** Jeremiah the prophet proclaims (31:3), "From afar the Lord appeared to me, declaring, 'my love for you is everlasting.'"

There is, I believe, great beauty in this observation. When looking at each other, when looking closely at people we love most, even ourselves, we see warts and wrinkles, traits and habits we may not like. When stepping back, however, surveying the whole scene, the picture alters. The downside is overwhelmed by all the good we see in the other and in ourselves. The ugly spots are eclipsed by the wholeness of the beauty we behold.

In this spirit, looking toward Zion from afar may give us a greater appreciation of Israel. From a distance, we can better acknowledge the miracle of a fledgling state that, in its short lifetime, made possible what seemed impossible.

Here, in the spirit of the Haggadah's *Dayenu*, sung before the meal, is a list of some of Israel's accomplishments we too often take for granted, in the hope that Seder participants will add their own items.

+ If Israel had only increased in size from 600,000 Jews in 1948 to a country now of ten million with 7.7 million Jews, together making up about 50% of Jews worldwide – *dayenu*.

- If Hebrew, a language all but forgotten 150 years ago, would only have been reborn, with millions conversing in the holy tongue, agreeing, arguing, in business, in social settings, in love, in prayer – *dayenu*.
- If Israel had only absorbed almost 1.5 million Jews from the former Soviet Union; if it had only brought 150,000 of our Black Ethiopian sisters and brothers, not in the bowels of ships to slavery, but to freedom – *dayenu*.
- If Israel were only the place where more Torah is being studied by more people than at any time in all of history – *dayenu*.

It's not so common for people to realize their dreams, even parts of their dreams, in their lifetime. The dream of Israel has become reality. In the end, the greatest blessing is to know you're blessed.

עוֹד לֹא אָבְדָה תִּקְוָתֵנוּ - **Our hope… is not lost:** There are examples of the prophetic period falling short, leaving it up to us to do the repairing. Jeremiah, the prophet of the destruction of the First Temple, prophesized (7:34) "Then will I cause to cease from the cities of Judah, and from the streets of Jerusalem, the voice of mirth and the voice of gladness, the voice of the bridegroom and the voice of the bride". And yet under every *chuppah* we recite, "Soon there will be heard in the cities of Judah and in the streets of Jerusalem, the voice of mirth and the voice of gladness, the voice of the bridegroom and the voice of the bride." Here, bride and groom are challenged to fix the words of the prophets by bringing joy and gladness to Jerusalem and the larger world.

In a similar fashion, the experiment of kingship as recorded in the prophets ended in tragedy. With the establishment of the State of Israel, we are in a position to repair that failure. This idea is enunciated by Rabbi Kook, who writes that in the absence of the biblical king, the people vote. The leadership they elect then has the status of the biblical king.

The Hatikvah also includes words of hope. In fact, no other nation calls its national anthem "The Hope." One wonders, what is the pathway to feeling hope? The pathway is to talk hope, do hope, act with hope. From the action, hope will rise. Then, with God's help, we will turn Ezekiel's prophecy of the Valley of Dry Bones, "Our hope is lost – *av'da tikvateinu*" to the Hatikvah's "Our hope is not lost – *od lo av'da tikvateinu*." The hope of two thousand years, to be a free nation in our land, the Land of Israel, Jerusalem.

In Israel, the sounds of redemption sing out everywhere.

Go and Come in Peace

As we bid final, final farewell to the Seder, I think about one of the sweetest rituals in Judaism — the tradition of welcoming Shabbat with the singing of *Shalom Aleichem*. We sit around the Shabbat table greeting and blessing the Shabbat angels, even as we ask that they bless us. And then, something remarkable: We conclude by bidding the angels farewell (*tzetchem leshalom*). There was a time, when our children were younger, that they refused to sing the words of farewell. With the language of innocence, they argued, "We've just said hello to the angels, why now say goodbye?" Our children were not the only ones struggling with bidding farewell. It is told that the saintly Rabbi Abraham Isaac HaKohen Kook, one of the greatest rabbis of his time, would rise from his Shabbat table as he sang *tzetchem leshalom* – "go in peace." He would slowly walk to the door, escorting the angels out. Opening the door, he would look out as he longingly, silently, waved his hand in a farewell gesture.

After I shared Rabbi Kook's custom of waving goodbye to the angels on Friday night, Daniella Grunfeld, a wonderful congregant, told me that when her children were younger, she would accompany them to their school bus. As they boarded, she'd wave goodbye. But instead of doing so in the normal fashion, she reversed her fingers, motioning toward herself as if imploring her children to stay near. Even as she said goodbye, she was declaring: I love you, come closer, come closer.

As the Seder ends, we and God do the same – longing, yearning, searching for redemption. As Rabbi Yehuda HaLevi wrote,

I have sought Your nearness,	דְּרַשְׁתִּי קׇרְבָתְךָ
With all my heart have I called You,	בְּכָל לִבִּי קְרָאתִיךָ
And going out to meet You	וּבְצֵאתִי לִקְרָאתְךָ
I found You coming toward me.	לִקְרָאתִי מְצָאתִיךָ

About the Author

Over five decades in the rabbinate, Avraham (Avi) Weiss joined others in creating the Modern and Open Orthodox Hebrew Institute of Riverdale – the Bayit—serving as its founding rabbi. He was instrumental in the founding of two rabbinical schools, Yeshivat Chovevei Torah for men (YCT) in 1999 and then Yeshivat Maharat for women (YM) in 2009, as well as the International Rabbinic Fellowship (IRF), a Modern Orthodox rabbinic organization of over 300 rabbis. He considers his greatest professional blessing to be the success of the almost 300 ordained rabbis of YCT and YM, as well as former associate rabbis and interns at the Bayit who now serve in synagogues, Hillels, Modern Orthodox and pluralistic day schools, hospital chaplaincies and major Jewish organizations in America, Israel and beyond.

Avi was among the activist rabbis of the sixties to the nineties who did all they could to raise a voice to free Soviet Jewry. In the early nineties, he joined in founding the Coalition for Jewish Concerns, AMCHA, speaking out for Israel, Jewish causes, and human rights worldwide.

Avi served as the spiritual advisor of Garin Tzabar, a national program whose mission is to inspire young Americans to go on aliyah and serve in the IDF as lone soldiers. Amongst its participants is Edan Alexander, a lone soldier who at the time of this writing has been held hostage in Gaza for over 500 days.

For thirty years, Avi taught Judaic Studies at Yeshiva University's Stern College for Women, and for the last twenty eight years he has been teaching and mentoring rabbinic students at YCT and YM. He served on the faculty of the Wexner Institute and has led High Holiday Sermon Seminars for colleagues across the denominations around the country. The author of op-eds and scholarly essays as well as books on Jewish law, thought, and contemporary affairs, he is now working on a book, "Judaism: A Theology of Love," and a "Spiritual Madrich," outlining how deeper spiritual meaning can be soulfully integrated into lifecycle events.

Avi is married to Toby Hilsenrad Weiss. Together they are blessed with children, grandchildren, and great-grandchildren, the lights of their lives.

Also by Avi Weiss

Women at Prayer: A Halakhic Analysis of Women's Prayer Groups

Spiritual Activism: A Jewish Guide to Leadership and Repairing the World

Holistic Prayer: A Guide to Jewish Spirituality

Open Up the Iron Door: Memoirs of a Soviet Jewry Activist

Journey to Open Orthodoxy

Torat Ahavah – Loving Torah: A Thematic Commentary on the Torah

Haggadah for the Yom Hashoah Seder (Editor)

Defending Holocaust Memory (scheduled for publication this summer)